Nevertheless, Th

2017 opened with a new presidency in the United States sparking women's marches across the globe. One thing was clear: feminism and feminist causes are neither dead nor in decline in the United States. Needed then are studies that capture the complexity of U.S. feminism. *Nevertheless, They Persisted* is an edited collection of empirical studies of the U.S. women's movement, pushing the feminist dialogue beyond literary analysis and personal reflection by using sociological and historical data. This new collection features discussions of digital and social media, gender identity, the reinvigorated anti-rape climate, while focusing on issues of diversity, inclusion, and unacknowledged privilege in the movement.

Jo Reger is professor of sociology at Oakland University in Michigan. She is the author of *Everywhere and Nowhere: Contemporary Feminism in the United States* (2012), the editor of *Different Wavelengths: Studies of Contemporary Feminism in the United States* (2005) and a co-editor of *Identity Work in Social Movements* (2008). Her work on the U.S. women's movements has appeared in a variety of journals including *Gender & Society* and *Qualitative Sociology*.

Nevertheless, They Persisted

Feminisms and Continued Resistance in the U.S. Women's Movement

**Edited by
Jo Reger**

Routledge
Taylor & Francis Group

NEW YORK AND LONDON

First published 2019
by Routledge
52 Vanderbilt Avenue, New York, NY 10017

and by Routledge
2 Park Square, Milton Park, Abingdon, Oxon OX14 4RN

Routledge is an imprint of the Taylor & Francis Group, an informa business

© 2019 Taylor & Francis

Library of Congress Cataloging-in-Publication Data
Names: Reger, Jo, 1962- editor.
Title: Nevertheless they persisted : feminisms and continued resistance in
the U.S. women's movement / edited by Jo Reger.
Description: 1 Edition. | New York : Routledge, 2019. |
Includes bibliographical references and index. |
Identifiers: LCCN 2018034005 (print) | LCCN 2018036438 (ebook) |
ISBN 9780203728628 (Master Ebook) | ISBN 9781351394512
(Web pdf) | ISBN 9781351394505 (ePub) | ISBN 9781351394499
(Mobipocket) | ISBN 9781138306042 (hardback) |
ISBN 9781138306035 (pbk) | ISBN 9780203728628 (ebk)
Subjects: LCSH: Feminism--United States--History--21st century. |
Women's rights--United States--History–21st century. | Women--
Political activity--United States--History–21st century.
Classification: LCC HQ1426 (ebook) | LCC HQ1426 .N478 2019
(print) | DDC 305.420973/0905--dc23
LC record available at https://lccn.loc.gov/2018034005

ISBN: 978-1-138-30604-2 (hbk)
ISBN: 978-1-138-30603-5 (pbk)
ISBN: 978-0-203-72862-8 (ebk)

Typeset in Bembo
by Taylor & Francis Books

Contents

PART II
Issues 113

Images

Acknowledgements

No feminist scholar is an island (to borrow from John Donne) and I am grateful to many for making up the "continent" of this volume. Often when I begin a project, I am never exactly sure how it will turn out, what the final arguments, points and conclusions will be. I learned a long time ago in graduate school that writing is a form of discovery and that best describes how I work and conceptualize. This volume is no different and has been a journal of discovery. It started out in a conversation with Routledge editor Samantha Barbaro at the 2016 American Sociological Association annual meetings. At that meeting, I suggested that I update my 2005 anthology, *Different Wavelengths: Studies of the Contemporary Women's Movement,* with new chapters. For quite a while, I kept calling this volume *Different Wavelengths II* (or *DWII*), until I realized that this was not so much an update as a reconstruction. The first *DW* was published in a time when feminism was seen as languishing, or even worse, dead. The core argument of that volume was that feminism was plural, alive and lively even when it appeared not to be. Authors in that volume examined race, ethnicity, gender identity, relations to other feminist generations, and new places for activism (i.e., online, zines, performance) and new ways to conceptualize feminism.

Many of these aspects are addressed in this volume but instead of arguing feminism is alive, these chapters are set in a lively time of activism and protest. The question has changed from Is feminism gone for good? to Where did all this feminism come from? Each chapter offers its own take on answering this question. Most draw on a historical overview to put their arguments into context, creating a book that provides historical context, present assessments and future directions. The result of this creation is the need for a new name that conceptualizes how this volume is not just an update but a new take on U.S. feminisms and the women's movement. Colleague and friend Nancy Whittier helped name the book, suggesting "Nevertheless, She Persisted" and I tinkered with it to become "Nevertheless They Persisted" to address the diversity of the activists and the issues.

While this volume captures a chunk of the activism and activists in the current era, much is also left out which is the trap of trying to say big things in small spaces. I will leave the absences to be addressed by others. We continue to need more focused work on the way in which feminism as an ideology is wrapped around so many efforts at social change.

With this said, there are people to thank. Oakland University's Research Committee provided me with a small grant to hire a copy editor and an indexer and I thank them for this support. Nancy Whittier not only wrote an amazing chapter but also provided the idea that became the eventual title of this book. Verta Taylor was essential in helping me locate authors for chapters (and she continues to mentor some of the brightest new scholars working on social movements). Through Verta I have met new and emerging scholars (Alison, Heather, Lillian, and Fatima) and I am excited to see how their work continues. I also tapped on established scholars (with incredibly busy lives) who were gracious enough to contribute a chapter (Miriam, Kelsy, Kristen, and Deana) and made new connections and found colleagues I will continue to follow (Corrie, Allison and Jessi).

Jennifer Law–Sullivan and George Sanders make up my weekly writing group and because of them so much work got done in that icy room in the library where we meet. Their presence aided my persistence. Tara Henry copy edited every chapter, and created the index and I appreciate her work. (I am trying to get her to consider sociology for graduate school. We need more feminist scholars who have been bitten by the research bug.) The Young Feminist Council, started by Adams High School student Grace Haubert, invited me to come talk to their newly formed group and I was amazed by their excitement and dedication. I thank them for coming along and reminding me that this is a multi-generation and always generating movement. Finally, I thank my family, both biological and chosen, and my loves Angel and Faith for being in my life.

It is not always easy to be a feminist scholar and teacher, and as one of my colleagues likes to say "The struggle is real," and to that I would add "the blessings are many."

1   The Making of a March

Identity, Intersectionality and Diffusion of U.S. Feminism

Jo Reger

The day before Woodrow Wilson's inauguration in 1913, an "immense" parade of 5,000 to 8,000 women marched down Pennsylvania Avenue in support of women's suffrage (Papachristou 1976; Gibson 2011). Spurred by the lack of support for a federal amendment for women's suffrage, the organizers sought to gain the public's attention. Faced with large crowds gathered to celebrate the incoming president, "the parade became a riot as mobs of spectators disrupted the orderly march" (Papachristou 1976: 172) and troops were brought in to regain order (Gibson 2011). Moving forward 104 years, while the number of participants have grown, the protests that followed the inauguration of Donald Trump resonate with those at the Wilson inauguration. Both focused on the incoming president's policies. Suffragists saw Wilson's inauguration as an opportunity to move from the state-by-state work for suffrage to an all-encompassing federal amendment. In 2017, participants had a wider range of issues but core to many was a concern for the women's rights (Fisher, Dow and Ray 2017).

The 1913 march, while contested, was not much of a surprise to those who kept up on national politics. The suffrage movement had been mobilized for six decades and the organizers were visible and active leaders (one organizer was President Wilson's own niece). Moving ahead to 2017, the story changes. Societal pundits had declared that the U.S. women's movement was either dead or in a state of decline since the late 20th and early 21st centuries. Even the nomination and surprise defeat of Hilary Clinton as the Democratic candidate for president did not signal the coming demonstration with feminists divided on supporting her, and many white women voting for Donald Trump. While scholars debate the idea that the movement was dead (Hawkesworth 2004, Reger 2012), how do we explain the rise and global spread of Women's Marches in 2017 with a repeat emergence in 2018? Drawing on previous research and social movement theory, in this chapter I argue that the U.S. women's movement has transitioned from a state of "everywhere" (i.e. diffused into the culture and society) and "nowhere" (i.e. not visible on a mass mobilization or national level) in the 1990s and early 2000s, to a state of mobilization that moved local, grassroots feminism into mass protests. Those mass protests emerged in part because of three mechanisms: the formation of visible feminist collective identity, the importance of intersectionality in contemporary feminism, and the diffusion of feminism in contemporary society. Before I discuss those mechanisms, I begin by describing the Women's Marches of 2017.

The Women's Marches of 2017

On January 21, 2017, more than 4 million men, women and children gathered in 654 cities in the United States to protest the inauguration of Donald Trump and advocate for a range of social issues.[1] The United States was not the only site of protest. Globally, more than 300,000 people demonstrated from around the world with countries as far-flung as Ghana, Saudi Arabia, Mexico, Sweden, Portugal, Greece and New Zealand. There was even a small contingent protesting in Antarctica. The corner-stone of the marches was the Washington D.C. protest which brought as many as 500,000 to the streets. After some initial missteps in organizing and naming the march (which I discuss in more detail below), the national co-chairs for D.C. were a diverse group with a variety of grassroots, state and national level organizational as well as corporate and non-profit experience. The speakers included well-known activists (e.g., Angela Davis, Gloria Steinem, Michael Moore), directors of non-profits and ser-vice organizations (e.g., National Domestic Workers Alliance, Planned Parenthood, Council on American-Islamic Relations), celebrities (e.g., America Ferrera, Ashley Judd, Janet Mock, Scarlett Johansson) and the mothers of Trayvon Martin, Dontre Hamilton, Eric Garner and Jordan Davis, all victims of police violence.

While the inauguration of Donald Trump drew march participants, the issues covered a range of concerns as illustrated in the diversity of signs. A core sign and symbol in the march addressed Trump referring to women as "pussies," illustrated in signs such as "This Pussy Bites Back" and the wear-ing of knitted pink "pussy hats" complete with pointed kitty ears. While many of the protestors came in response to Trump's comments on women, others carried signs urging women's empowerment and organizing with slogans such as "Well Behaved Women Seldom Make History," "Glass Ceilings Are Meant to be Broken" and "Who Runs the World? Girls!" Many referred to the Hillary Clinton campaign with signs such as "I'm with her" with arrows pointing in all directions and "Nasty Women Make (her) Story." Others carried signs that called for activism during the Trump pre-sidency. For example, one sign was inscribed with a quote from civil rights legend and Congressman John Lewis: "We may not have chosen the time, but the time has chosen us." Marchers carried signs advocating for abortion and reproductive, transgender, LGBTQIA+ and immigrant rights, as well as valuing science, Black Lives Matter, men's activism for women, and the need to address climate change, xenophobia, sexual assault and the rape culture, equal pay and access to healthcare. These issues were often intertwined with each other as indicated by one common sign, captured in multiple sites on the Internet:

> Love is Love
> Black Lives Matter
> Climate Change is Real
> Immigrants Make America Great
> Women's Rights are Human Rights
> Remember Love

Also present at the Washington D.C. march were scholars working their way through the crowds of protestors to understand the why and who of the protests. A research team led by Professor Dana Fisher of the University of Maryland found that the protests drew in both experienced activists and those new to protest. Approximately one third of the protestors at the January 21 march had never protested before and most of them had no connection to the 400 plus sponsoring organizations. Although many of the protestors were new to this form of activism, the research team also found that many of them went on to participate in the March 4 Science and the People's Climate March, held later that year (Fisher 2017). While these researchers can tell us who the participants were and how experienced they were as activists, how was feminism a part of these protests? To answer that question, we need to look at the state of contemporary feminism in the United States.

Where Has Feminism Been?

Since the inception of feminism in the United States in the 1800s, the media has repeatedly declared feminism in decline or dead. Obituaries for feminism reoccur throughout the history of the movement. For example, after suffrage was obtained in 1920, the movement was declared dead by the 1950s (Rupp and Taylor 1987). Some fifty years later *Time Magazine's* cover story read, "Is Feminism Dead?" complete with pictures of Susan B. Anthony, Betty Friedan, Gloria Steinem and TV character Ally McBeal (Bellafante 1998). More contemporary coverage included headlines such as "Where to Pass the Torch?" (Winerip 2009) and "The End of the Women's Movement" (Martin 2009).

This death/not-death of feminism is what I call the "everywhere and nowhere" phenomenon of contemporary feminism (Reger 2012). In a society that has had an active feminist movement since the mid-1800s, feminism has diffused into the culture in ways that are often not easily discernible. Indeed, it is everywhere. It is in the co-ed baseball teams at the local high school, the body positive messages of Dove soap, the educational policies such as Title IX, and the push to get girls in STEM (science, technology, engineering and math) fields. In these examples, women's movement activism changed the society in profound ways that are often not credited to the movement. In addition, the 1990s and 2000s were times of only a few large national feminist protests and demonstrations. While the national picture of feminism may have looked defunct, an examination of communities provides a different picture. In a study of three different communities, I found that activists were entwined in a series of networks, informal groups and formal organizations focused on the local issues and concerns (Reger 2012). Although the focus of their activism was shaped by the community around them, all the communities articulated a feminist identity that was core to their activism. As Verta Taylor and Suzanne Staggenborg argue (2005), the movement has survived because of its diffusion into fields such as local communities.

In addition to creating local feminist communities, in the 1990s feminist activism moved to the Internet where a myriad of websites, blogs and Facebook pages developed and were devoted to aspects of feminism (Alfonso and Trigilio 1997; Crossley 2017; Daniels 2009; Reger 2012). As a result, when social pundits (or scholars) only examined the national scene for visible feminist organizations, they missed how feminism was embedded in new locales such as social media. Indeed, Alison Crossley notes that "While some people may wonder where the feminists have gone, it is clear that many feminists are online, fueling the feminist movement (2015: 265). This place of resistance and protest also has the potential to bring together generations of feminists (Everett 2004) addressing a range of issues. As such, for the last few decades, feminism has often been described as located in the digital world and focused on new technologies (Alfonso and Trigilio 1997). Crossley (2017: 5) argues that we need to understand how feminism is "enacted in everyday, interactional and intersectional ways, in unexpected locations, in online settings, and in organizations not solely concerned with gender inequality." (See Chapter 4 in this volume.) When feminists work in "unexpected" spaces on a myriad of issues, the movement can look like "nowhere" even when it is not.

In sum, although the U.S. women's movement has been declared dead repeatedly throughout its history, it has remained active on a variety of levels including the virtual world of the internet, and in grassroots community organizing where it has diffused into a range of ideas about human worth and marginalization, discrimination and subordination. This diffusion helps explain how locally-focused feminism was a foundation for the marches, but what sparked the mass protests in 2017?

How Do Mass Protests Emerge?

The factors that move people from concern to action are core questions of social movement scholars. Social movement scholars argue that three main factors contribute to the emergence of social movement activism: a plausible threat, pre-existing organizations and coalitions. First, people need to believe that there is a plausible threat to a right or an issue. (Meyer 1993; 2003). David Meyer argues "People pick the route they believe most likely to be effective after surveying their political resources and opportunities" (1993: 458). Those "routes to activism" can be spurred by threats to fundamental human rights, access to needed resources, opportunities and services or a concern for the future. As the signs and speakers at the various 2017 marches indicated, people saw the election of Donald Trump as posing a significant threat to issues important to them. For example, the Washington D.C. march speakers included mothers whose sons has been killed by the police. These women were not addressing hypothetical situations with the police but instead told the crowds the circumstances that resulted in the death of their sons. In sum, when issues of rights, opportunities or resources are threatened and people understand those threats as real, activism is the result. What is striking about the 2017 marches is that so many issues were framed as credible threats, from access to abortion to police brutality to obtaining equal pay to stopping climate change.

Second, once that credible threat has been identified and action to stop that threat seems possible, people often turn to pre-existing groups as a way to address the issues (Tilly 1978; Jenkins 1983). Pre-existing groups often have resources such as the ability to communicate with members and the greater public, funds for permits, and knowledge on how to organize. Some of the pre-existing women's rights groups that participated in the D.C. march include long-lived organizations such as EMILY's List, Planned Parenthood, National Abortion Rights Action League (NARAL) and National Organization for Women (NOW). While these pre-existing groups were not the primary organizers, they had the potential to provide resources such as membership lists, communication networks, meeting spaces, and funds for activists. Indeed, since 2017, the Women's March has grown into a national organization with grassroots outreach and national conventions. This group now serves as a pre-existing organization providing resources to activists who are continuing to organize their communities. For example, on the Women's March website, under the heading of "Power to the Polls," it reads:

> The national voter registration tour will target swing states to register new voters, engage impacted communities, harness our collective energy to empower grassroots leaders to advocate for policies and elect candidates that reflect the values we marched for on January 21, 2017.
> (http://www.powertothepolls.com)

Also on the page are places to volunteer to work on a California primary campaign and to register to vote.

Third and finally, large scale demonstrations need coalitions to link together disparate groups into a unified network (Ghaziani 2008; Tilly 1978; Jenkins 1983). The list of "partnering" organizations on the Women's

March website is in the hundreds and covers a range of issues (https://www.womensmarch.com/partner). While the long list of groups may seem hard to coordinate, the interests and affiliations of the four national co-chairs, Tamika Mallory, Bob Bland, Carmen Perez, Linda Sarsour, serve to link the groups together. Their activist resumes include work for civil rights, women rights, equality in health care, ending gun violence and mass incarceration, as well as promoting racial healing, community policing, intersectional movement building, domestic manufacturing, ethical supply chains and design entrepreneurship education (https://www.womensmarch.com/march-committee).

Pulling these three elements together (e.g., threat, pre-existing groups and coalitions) is the ability to draw on communication networks. In her analysis of women's movement activism in the 1970s, Jo Freeman (1973) argued, "Not just any communications network will do. It must be a network that is co-optable to the new ideas of the incipient movement. To be co-optable, it must be composed of like-minded people whose background, experiences, or location in the social structure make them receptive to the ideas of a specific new movement" (794). Communication networks of the 21st century are largely internet-based social media and are extremely co-optable and accessible. In the age of cell phones, laptops and ipads, feminism has found a home on the web and, as noted, the internet teems with feminist websites, blogs and virtual communities (see Chapter 4 in this volume). While some feminist scholars debate the efficacy and inclusiveness of digital feminist activism—often referred to as cyberfeminism (Daniels 2009)—some see internet-based activism as powerful in both transnational (Everett 2004; Langman 2005) and local contexts (Sassen 2002). Crossley (2017) notes that while online feminism is largely understudied, it is key to contemporary activism. She writes, "the accessibility of computers and the ease of blogging and using social media augment existing social movement organizations and allow participants to communicate their messages and create communities when other resources are unavailable" (p. 127).

The Women's Marches of 2017 drew on the same types of networks and communication pathways as the 2011 slutwalks that swept the globe (Reger 2014). On January 24, 2011, a Toronto police officer giving a safety-information session to students at York University reportedly told the audience: "I've been told I'm not supposed to say this; however, women should avoid dressing as sluts in order not to be victimized" (Rush 2011). After his statement was published in the campus newspaper, Sonya Barnett and Heather Jarvis posted their mutual outrage on Facebook and noted that perhaps they should hold a "slutwalk." With the help of three other local women, a Facebook page, SlutWalk Toronto, was created and resulted in an April march with an estimated crowd of 3,000–4,000 participating. SlutWalk Toronto attracted considerable media attention and the idea of a slut walk went viral, spreading around the world. Within six months, the Toronto organizers listed satellite groups planning marches in more than fifty cities and regions in Canada and the United States, as well as thirty-three cities around the world. By creating a web of Facebook pages dedicated to various slut walks with links to numerous feminist blogs and websites, activists quickly created a network of organizations around the globe.[2] (For more on the impact of the slutwalks on feminist activism, see Chapter 7 in this volume.)

The rise of the 2017 Women's Marches follow much the same pattern. The Women's March organizers drew upon methods of communication such as Instagram, Facebook and Twitter. Indeed, Facebook was the site of a multitude of pages devoted to spreading the information on particular marches and rallies planned for January 21, which then spread through websites, personal e-mails and listservs. Overall, the Women's Marches of 2017 follow a pattern set by previous activism in the women's movement. With the belief in a credible threat, the existence of groups already organized in society and the formation of coalition, individuals can find and align themselves with groups through communication networks like Twitter, Instagram and Facebook. Leaders emerge and work to frame the desired action and connect people to the event. These leaders faced criticism, made mistakes early in the organizing of the march, but went on to create a stable organization that continues to coordinate actions. In many ways, the 2017 Women's Marches resembled protests of the past, so what is *different* about these marches?

What Is Different About Women's Marches?

The Women's Marches of 2017 and the anniversary marches of 2018 brought a new period of mobilization to the U.S. women's movement, but why did the marches look the way they did? To answer this question, I turn to three mechanisms that drew on the elements that allow mass protests to emerge, yet added their own "twists" that created this specific configuration. Those mechanisms are: the construction of visible feminist collective identity, the importance of intersectionality in contemporary feminism, and the diffusion of feminist ideology, identities and tactics into other movements.

Creating a Visible Feminist Identity

Key to social movement organizing is the creation of an activist identity that can be shared by all the participants. This collective identity helps to bring the group together, fosters a common culture and distinguishes between those who are members of the movement and those who are not (Taylor and Whittier 1992). Collective identities are created when people interact with each other and share ideologies, goals and create a common culture. The formation of a boundary between who is a member of the identity group and who is not—that sense of "we" versus "them"—is critical in the construction of an activist identity. While the participants to the Women's

Marches came from a variety of social movements, organizations and networks, one solidifying and highly visible symbol of identity was created through the cultural object of the pink "pussyhat." When an audiotape of then-presidential candidate Donald Trump referring to women's "pussies" was made public, Krista Suh and Jayna Zweiman called upon knitters to start a "Pussyhat Project." They wrote:

> We love the clever wordplay of "pussyhat" and "pussycat," but yes, "pussy" is also a derogatory term for female genitalia. We chose this loaded word for our project because we want to reclaim the term as a means of empowerment. ... Women, whether transgender or cisgender, are mistreated in this society. In order to get fair treatment, the answer is not to take away our pussies, the answer is not to deny femaleness and femininity, the answer is to demand fair treatment. A women's body is her own. We are honoring this truth and standing up for our rights.
>
> (Pussyhatproject.com)

The call went viral and an estimated 100,000 hats were made and distributed (Walker 2017). The hats were a simple and easy way to broadcast an oppositional identity, and there was no shortage of knitters willing to make and distribute them. This is evident in photos of marches from around the world that show a sea of pink hats.

In addition to serving as markers of an oppositional feminist identity, the pussyhats were political in other ways. First, creating pussyhats can be seen as a form of "craftivism," which uses a traditional women's craft such as knitting to bring about "substantive, feminist social change" and to "push back against historical and contemporary stereotyping" (Black 2017: 698, 701). Beth Ann Pentney, in her study of fiber arts and feminism, quotes knitting "guru" Debbie Stoller as saying, "Valuing the craft of knitting is a feminist act in itself ... because the denigration of knitting correlates directly with the denigration of traditionally women-centred activity," (2008: 1). Indeed, the use of women's crafting as a form of political protest has a long history. Suffragists stitched banners to carry in marches. Feminist artist Judy Chicago created *The Dinner Party* in the 1970s, a multi-media exhibition using ceramics and embroidery to recapture women's history in a decidedly vulva-focused fashion. Contemporary feminists continue this tradition of reclaiming women's crafts in a political manner. In her study of 21st-century feminist knitting communities, Maura Kelly (2014; 2015) argues that they are a gendered form of activism that can shape alternative understandings of masculinity and femininity through adopting the feminized practice of knitting as well as through group interactions. Therefore, knitting pussyhats in community gatherings and distributing them to other marchers aligns with other contemporary feminist craftivism.

Second, the pussyhats drew on another tradition: the reclaiming of disparaged language and cultural symbols. This is particularly evident starting in

Image 1.1 A knitted pink pussyhat at one of the women's marches
Photo credit: Angella Abrams. Used with her permission.

the 1990s, when the performance piece *The Vagina Monologues* spread across North America. Conceptualized and written by Eve Ensler, *The Vagina Monologues* is a series of dramatized stories which celebrate and explore women's relationship to the word "vagina" through examining a range of experiences (Ensler 1998). The monologues include playing with the terms for the vagina (i.e., "coochie snorcher" and "down there"), and reclaiming of sexual language used against women (Reger and Story 2005). Also reclaiming language, feminist magazines such as *Bitch* and *Bust* began publishing in the 1990s. In addition, the 2011 slutwalks introduced the terms "sexual profiling" and "slut shaming" to a wider audience and reclaimed "slut" from being a pejorative for a sexually active woman (Reger 2014). Pussyhats followed in the same tradition and also reclaimed the color pink from being a symbol of "delicate" femininity to symbolizing feminist empowerment.

In sum, pussyhats drew on established forms of feminist resistance through craftivism and reclamation of femininity *and* came to symbolize an emergent oppositional identity. Social movement scholars argue that oppositional identities are created when participants can identify who does or does not belong in a group (Taylor and Whittier 1992). Although many were critical of the hats[3] (see Livingston 2017), they served to identify those who opposed the Trump presidency, separating them from those who did not. In the making and sharing of the hats, networks of protesters were creating, establishing a sense of "we," and in wearing them in public, the hats "transgressed space, raising public awareness" (Black 2017: 702).

Grappling With Intersectionality

In addition, to the identity of the "pussyhat feminist," another core identity of the march was that of the "intersectional feminist." While Fátima Suárez in Chapter 2 discusses the creation of this feminist identity and illustrates it through an analysis of Chicana feminism, I examine how the concept of intersectionality shaped these protests.

One of the biggest challenges that the U.S. women's movement has historically faced is how to deal with issues of both acknowledged and unacknowledged privilege leading to discrimination within feminist organizations and networks. This has troubled the movement since its inception and organizations have split over issues such as homophobia (Kreschmer 2019), racism (Roth 2002; Thompson 2002) and transphobia (see Chapter 3 this volume). In the 1980s and beyond, women of color began to articulate the concept of intersectionality (Combahee River Collective 1978; Collins 1991) with Kimberle Crenshaw credited with the concept in use today (1991). Intersectionality is "the consequence of the mutually reinforcing oppressions of gender, race/ethnicity, ... class, and ... sexual orientation" that has become the foundation for analyzing oppression and liberation (Roth 2017:131). In the late 20th century, the recognition of the intersectional nature of social identities became a core concern of both feminist activists and academics.

Intersectionality was evident in the number of issues addressed in the march. Fisher and her co-authors argue that "In many ways, we believe that the large turnout at the Women's March... is the direct result of the effective mobilization of various individuals and organizational constituencies that were motivated by intersectional issues" (2017: 5). Through their unique survey data, Fisher and her colleagues illustrate how individuals were often motivated by identity-related issues. For instance, they found the women were more likely to mention women's rights, men were more likely to mention Trump, Blacks more likely to mention racial justice and Hispanics more likely to mention immigration. Illustrating the intersectional nature of the march, they also found participants "reported being mobilized by reasons that extended beyond their social identities" (2017: 5). For example, they found that participants who identified women's rights as a primary reason for attending are also more likely to mention racial justice, immigration and social welfare as compelling issues. In sum, intersectionality propelled the adoption of multiple issues linked to individual identities.

The four co-organizers, Tamika Mallory, Bob Bland, Carmen Perez and Linda Sansour, played a key role in setting up this intersectional set of issues and identities (Fisher et al. 2017). In organizing social protest, leaders take what initially is sensed as a credible threat and coordinate and compose a response that meets the needs of the participants as well as focusing on making social change. Leadership in social movements can come in all forms from a single charismatic leader to the informal or unofficial "bridge" leaders (Robnett 1997) to teams (Reger and Staggenborg 2006). However, one aspect of the women's movement has been the criticism and scrutiny that leaders can face. In the women's movement, leaders have left after feeling like they were "trashed" by other participants. Jo Freeman, an activist and pioneering scholar of the women's movement in the 1960s and 1970s, recalled being forced out of radical feminist circles in Chicago after being accused of being "too male" and "an elitist" for taking on speaking engagements and interviews with the press (Freeman 1998:190). Her story is one of hurt and bewilderment about the treatment from her sister feminists. While earlier generations of feminists faced "trashing" for being seen as too eager to take credit or bask in the public's attention, contemporary feminist leaders are often accused of failing to put forth an intersectional perspective.

While Women's March organizers sought to include all women, as noted in the Unity Principles which specifically mentioned the rights of "Black women, Native women, poor women, immigrant women, disabled women, Muslim women, lesbian queer transwomen," (https://www.wom ensmarch.com/mission/), the initial title of the 2017 Women's March was "The Million Women March." This was the name of the 1997 march by women of color (http://millionwomanmarch20.com/) and by taking the same name, the march was seen as another example of white women not acknowledging the accomplishments or histories of women of color. After an outcry, mostly through social media, the leadership team was reconstituted and the protest was renamed the "Women's March."

The leadership team for the main Washington D.C. march, along with having previous experience in organizing large marches, running non-profits, coalition-building and interacting with the media, represented a variety of ethnic and racial identities. This diversity was key in convincing activists of the legitimacy of the march and its goal of addressing human rights across a range of identities and experiences. Yet despite the commitment to unity through diversity and the constitution of the leadership team, the organizers did not escape criticism. Tamika Mallory echoed some of the hurt articulated by Jo Freeman decades earlier in her speech at the October 2017 Women's Convention held in Detroit. Organized by the Women's March committee, the convention faced criticism as soon as it was announced as being too nationally focused and not inclusive (or knowledgeable) about Detroit issues and activism. Speaking in the opening plenary, Mallory noted that "Linda [Sansour], Carmen [Perez] and I have been through a lot of pain" (Detroit convention fieldnotes, 10/27/17). In response to the criticism the organizers faced when Bernie Sanders was announced as a speaker (see also Chapter 5 in this volume on this controversy), Mallory noted that she was not going to be pulled into a debate over whether or not Sanders should be at the convention and that she would rather focus on protecting the rights of her family and her son. When it came time for Sansour to speak, she noted that a "diverse movement" was present at the convention and it would never be a movement where all agreed with each other. Instead she stated "Unity is not uniformity." She continued that the convention and march were dogged by "critics without credentials"—"armchair activists" who need to "role up [their] sleeves and show up" (Detroit convention fieldnotes, 10/27/17). Their experiences resonated with past feminists and the co-organizers experienced intense pressure to create a diverse and inclusive protest, and were consequently criticized for their actions.

Pussyhats also came under fire around issues of diversity and intersectionality. As soon as they appeared on social media, the hats were seen by some as "cutesy," "diminutive" and "bourgeois," the kind of "positive" crafting associated with white, middle class women as opposed to those with a more critical and radical stance (Black 2017: 703.) The pussyhats were critiqued for being too essentialist with their focus on vaginas/ "pussies" and ignoring the struggles of transwomen for their bodily autonomy, as well as too pink in reference to skin color, leaving out women of color (Black 2017). These critiques surfaced again in 2018 at the anniversary marches with one blog eventually closing down comments after a debate raged on whether or not to wear the hats.[4]

The make up of the marches was also criticized for a lack of diversity. For some, the marches themselves "felt very white" with the goal creating an inclusive and diverse solidarity missing. CindiAnn and Rueben Rose-Redwoods write:

> While there was certainly more than a single 'story of white women' at the Women's March, the fact that many women of color perceived the solidarity of white feminism to be displayed in a 'very superficial way' speaks volumes to the challenges of coalition building and the ongoing need to reaffirm intersectional approaches to gender inequity that are equally sensitive to other forms of oppression and privilege.
>
> (2017: 648)

This sense that the march was mostly for and of white women was complicated by a CNN exit poll that found that more white women voted for Trump (52 percent) than for Clinton (43 percent) with Black men and women voting predominately in support of Clinton (80 percent, 93 percent respectively).[5] The racial gap was noted by marchers with signs that read,

"Don't Forget White Women Voted for Trump" and with those signs resurfacing at the 2018 anniversary marches.

Overall, intersectionality as a "mobilization tool" brought about the success of the marches with more people and more issues represented in "one of the largest protests ever observed in the United States" (Fisher et al. 2017: 1). The leaders of the marches purposively drew on an intersectional rhetoric that linked individual-focused issues with a broader scope of concerns. At the same time, the perceived presence (or absence) of an intersectional perspective was scrutinized at various points, from the critique of the pussyhats to the trashing of the organizers, the initial name of the march, and the overall diversity of the participants. These critiques were set in a movement that historically has been critiqued as being too white and too focused on the needs and issues of heterosexual, middle class, cisgender white women. This use of intersectionality as a framework for protest, combined with historical whiteness of the overall movement put in play the tensions that made this march unique. In other words, the 2017 Women's Marches centered intersectionality as essential to the protest and, as a result, the marches succeeded in drawing participants to a spectrum of interrelated issues; at the same time the protests were criticized for failing to achieve inclusivity and the acknowledgement of difference along a variety of fronts.

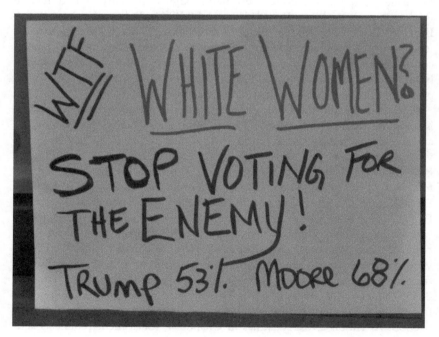

Image 1.2 A sign from an 2018 anniversary march with the same sentiment a year after the election.
Photo credit: Angella Abrams. Used with her permission.

While the marches may have grappled with intersectionality, there is no debating that there was a vast assortment of issues that drew marchers to protest.

The Diffusion of Feminism

Scholars note that social movements often influence and shape each other in a process of spillover (Meyer and Whittier 1994). While Heather Hurwitz documents that feminism has diffused into other social movements shaping organizations, tactics and issues (Chapter 6 in this volume), I argue that what we see in the Women's Marches is how issues spread and connect to each other in a society in which feminism has diffused.

The mixture of issues is evident in the signs and slogans at the march. A quick (and incomplete) sampling of photos from the D.C. Women's March make that clear. Democratic Clinton supporters ("Not My President" and "The Future is Nasty") mixed with advocates for reproductive choice ("Abortion is Healthcare" and "My Body, My Choice") with LGBTQ activists ("Black Trans Lives Matter" and "LGBT Rights are Human Rights) and those working for prison reform ("End Mass Incarceration"). Surveying the march attendees, Fisher and her colleagues (2017) collapse the issues into ten categories: Women's Rights, Equality, Reproductive Rights, Social Welfare, Racial Justice, LGBTQ, Politics/Voting, Police Brutality/Black Lives Matter, Peace and Religion. While these appear to be separate issues, most are centered on feminist ideologies around the right to control one's body and life, and eradicating domination of the less powerful by individuals (i.e., Trump) and institutions (i.e., the criminal justice system, prisons, health care, government in general, corporations, etc.).

Feminism was also the ideology shaping the rhetoric of some social change issues. One example is the use of ecofeminism and "Mother Earth" imagery and rhetoric to address climate change and climate justice (see Chapter 11 this volume). Feminism was also solidly at the core of issues. For example, the issue reported as the most motivating was Women's Rights (52.9 percent) followed by Equality (41.5 percent), Reproductive Rights (23.4 percent), Environment (22.5 percent) and Social Welfare (21.7 percent). "Women's Rights" issues were defined as marching for one's mothers, sisters, partners or women in general. The fact that approximately half the respondents were compelled by women's rights illustrates how core feminist issues were relevant to the protestors. One mechanism of that diffusion is in the digital world that contemporary feminists move in (Alfonso and Trigilio 1997; Crossley 2015; Daniels 2009; Everett 2004). The Internet is filled with contemporary feminist websites that serve as a foundation of feminist community and connection. As Alison Crossley argues in Chapter 4, social media connects activists to issues and helps forge the continuity of the movement.

Overall, I argue that this march happened within a national context in which feminist ideas have diffused into the culture. For the Women's

Marches, the "everywhere" of contemporary feminism helped facilitate the diffusion and connection of issues. Indeed, the second half of this volume illustrates how issues of sexual assault, reproductive rights, ecofeminism and climate justice, work and the labor market, as well as menstrual activism and anti-trafficking efforts are shaped by the diffusion of feminism into society.

Continuity and the U.S. Women's Movement

Returning to the scenario that opened this chapter, why is it important to consider the protest of 1913 in conjunction with the Women's Marches of 2017? There are some similarities, both are protests of incoming presidents shaped by women's activism, and resulting in unexpectedly large numbers of protests. But there are more than similarities to capture our attention. By looking to the past, we can come to understand the times that we live in. Social movements form in opposition to the status quo, and, through examining the past, we can understand the sources of movements and mass demonstrations. Through this we can see the issues that continue to trouble and the mechanisms that address them. I have argued that we can understand the present by looking at how activist identities are formed, applying an intersectional perspective and examining the diffusion of feminism into the larger society. These mechanisms are useful in also understanding the past.

The identity symbolized by the pussyhat-wearing feminist shares a connection to the purple, white and gold sashes of the suffragists. Those colors also had meaning symbolizing loyalty, purity and hope. Alison LaCroix writes:

> The power of the colors came from the unity and recognition that they afforded the members of the NWP [National Women's Party] and the broader public. No matter what the individual colors may have signified, together the tricolors banners became universally known and recognized as a symbol of women's equality.
>
> (No date)

Applying an intersectional perspective allows us to see that the suffragists won women the vote in 1920, but it was not until the Voting Rights Act of 1965 did Black women have the ability to overcome barriers to the electoral process. This example of the right to vote versus ability illustrates white women's privilege, grounding the need for an intersectional feminism. The uproar over the initial name for the march, as well as the critiques of the pussyhat illustrate how issues of inclusion, privilege and oppression still challenge the movement and movement participants. Finally, drawing on the work of Verta Taylor and Leila Rupp (1987) we can see how the ideologies and organizations of suffrage continue to influence society long after the passage of the 19th amendment in 1920.

The Women's Marches of 2017 also stand as testament that feminist ideas, beliefs and policies have shaped the dominant culture even when we are not aware of it. The range of participants, issues and identities at the marches are the result of feminism changing society. Feminist gains altered the institutions of education, medicine, government, religion, family and the workplace. Cultural changes due to feminism submerged into the popular culture (Douglas 2010). Corporations draw on feminist ideas in the promotion of their products (Johnston and Taylor 2008, Messner 2002) and more and more female celebrities openly claim a feminist identity (Contrera 2014). Feminism continues to thrive in communities even in periods of "nowhere" (Reger 2012), and embeds itself in a range of places from OCCUPY mobilizations (Chapter 6 in this volume), anti-war protests (Kutz-Flamenbaum 2007), art groups (Raizada 2007), hip hop (Peoples 2007) and crafting (Pentney 2008; Kelly 2014). And it is this "everywhere" diffusion of the feminism that will continue to influence the women's movement activism yet to come.

The Organization of the Book

Many of the ideas and issues raised in this introduction are returned to in the chapters that follow. Divided into two segments, *Activists* and *Issues*, the authors tease out what is happening in contemporary feminism by taking a perspective that puts current activism in a historical context. Indeed, it is the linking of the historical with the contemporary that drove the title of this volume. In February 2017, Elizabeth Warren was warned by Mitch McConnell to end her speech in the Senate, he noted that "She was warned. She was given an explanation. Nevertheless, she persisted" (Wang 2017). Feminists quickly adopted the phrase, noting how activists, in particular women, have been historically silenced from speaking out. I alter the phrase to capture the multiplicity of activists who continue in contemporary feminism and the issues they address.

The Activists

The book opens with Fátima Suárez' work (Chapter 2 "Identifying with Inclusivity: Intersectional Chicana Feminisms") which draws on her participation in a 2017 Women's March to put the identity of an intersectional feminist into conversation with Chicana feminisms. She focuses on Chicana feminisms as a case study to assess how women of color have conceptualized and practiced intersectional feminism, and how it is being deployed by contemporary feminists.

Miriam Abelson takes a historical perspective to the relationship between feminism and transgender (Chapter 3 "Already Feminists Transfeminist Histories, Hurdles, and Futures") and argues that there have always been trans feminists and that to write them out of history is to miss important dialogues that can inform current debates. She notes that there have always been trans feminists, and that while some cisgender feminists have argued for their exclusion from the movement, many have included and, at times, fought for their inclusion.

Tracing the shorter history of online feminist activism, Alison Crossley argues (Chapter 4"Online Feminism is Just Feminism: Offline and Online Movement Persistence") that there should be no distinction between online and offline feminism. She finds that boundary between the two is permeable and that to focus the two as distinct ignores the reality of contemporary activism. Online feminism, she argues, is essential in carrying on feminist activism in the United States, supporting support the movement's continuity.

Kelsy Kretschmer and Kristen Barber take on an old question still is asked of contemporary feminism—Where are men in feminism? (Chapter 5 "The 'Man Question' in Feminism"). They examine men's diverse motivations for supporting feminism, acknowledging the importance of taking an intersectional perspective. Tracing back to the abolition movement, they find that the inclusion of men in feminism remains complicated and needs attention to issues of privilege, oppression and the constraints of patriarchy.

Lillian Junglieb draws on her research to tackle the ways in which feminist and gender-focused activism can leave out important activists (Chapter 6 "Anti-Trafficking and Feminism: Bringing in Survivors as Movement Activists"). She details how trafficking survivors are often restricted to the role of bringing authenticity to the anti-sex trafficking movement through their stories of their victimization and are shut out of more powerful roles.

Overall, these chapters address some of the question – who are contemporary feminists? They illustrate how race-ethnicity, gender identity, sex, and status (and more) create a multiplicity of activists who shape contemporary feminism and what it addresses.

The Issues

How feminist activism becomes embedded in other social movements is the focus of Heather McKee Hurwitz's analysis of recent protests (Chapter 7 "#FemGa,#SayHerName, #NotHereForBoys—Feminist Spillover in U.S. Social Movements 2011–2016"). She draws on the idea of social movement spillover to show how mechanisms, specific to feminism, account for new tactics, strategies, problems and opportunities in this latest cycle of protest.

Nancy Whittier addresses the tactics and strategies of campus activists on sexual assault and focuses on how colleges have a unique mechanism, in Title IX of the Civil Rights Act, for bringing legal pressure (Chapter 8 "Activism against Sexual Assault on Campus: Origins, Opportunities, and Outcomes). She traces the movement from its early roots and illustrates how political opportunities under the Obama administration facilitated this movement. She argues that while the Trump administration closed some political opportunities, it opened the door for cultural ones.

Chris Bobel and Breanne Fahs argue that it is much more than blood in their discussion of menstrual activism (Chapter 9 "The Messy Politics of Menstrual Activism"). Taking the feminist stance of the "personal is political," they link menstrual activism to critical embodiment work by questioning the relation between menstruation and cultural value systems. After an analysis of menstrual activism, they end by exploring the hazards and possibilities of doing menstrual activist work.

The body and issues related to control over the body continue to be feminist issues as detailed in Deana Rohlinger and Jessi Grace's overview of the battle over abortion and reproductive rights (Chapter 10 "The Continuing Battle over Abortion and Reproductive Rights"). They trace the four main areas of contestation, states and communities, the courts, Congress, and clinics, and find that efforts to increase restrictions disproportionately affect both/and poor women and women of color. They see the future of activism as occurring through hashtag storytelling to reduce abortion stigma (e.g., #ShoutYourAbortion), and a focus on reproductive rights with local and corporate-based initiatives.

Corrie Grosse takes on another core feminist issue and examines how women and ecofeminism have shaped the movement for climate justice (Chapter 11 "Ecofeminism and Climate Justice"). After a brief review of ecofeminism's history, she centers her discussion on the 2016 battle to stop the Dakota Access Pipeline at Standing Rock by a coalition of activists and highlights the role of ecofeminism, intersectionality and community building in contemporary activism on climate justice and beyond.

Allison Elias brings the volume to a close with one of the oldest and most persistent issues that feminists have addressed—equality in the workplace (Chapter 12 "Women, Gender, and Feminism at Work"). She takes a look at how women have turned to unions and the law as a way to make progress for income equality (among other workplace issues.) Adopting an intersectional perspective, she concludes that contemporary feminists still struggle to dismantle subtle inequities arising from embedded gender norms and institutional structures.

Notes

1 Data collected by Jeremy Pressmen, University of Connecticut and Erica Chenoweth, University of Denver.
2 In the United States, slut walks were planned in every region of the country, including both blue and red states. For example, not only did the East (New York City, Baltimore) and West and Northwest (Portland, Los Angeles, San Diego, San Francisco) plan or hold slut walks, but also did the South (Tampa, Dallas, Houston), Southwest (Reno, Tucson), and mid-regions (Nashville, Kansas City, Milwaukee). Globally, slut walks happened in Australia, Great Britain, Germany, the Netherlands, India and South Africa, among other countries.

3 In the anniversary marches held in 2018, many participants chose not to wear their pussyhats because of concerns and critiques raised by trans women and women of color. In a statement from Women's March Lansing (MI) organizers, they wrote that "We encourage daring discussions with people who experience the world and their personhood differently. Women's March Michigan is excited to experience the conversation around pussyhats as a part of that open dialogue" (https://womensmarchmichigan.org/the-movement-continues/).

4 Forward Action Michigan, January 12, 2018, https://www.forwardactionmichiga n.org/2018/01/reflecting-on-pink-pussy-hats/.

5 https://www.cnn.com/election/2016/results/exit-polls.

References

Alfonso, Rita, and Jo Trigilio. 1997. "Surfing the Third Wave: A Dialogue between Two Third Wave Feminists." *Hypatia: A Journal of Feminist Philosophy* 12(3):7–16.

Bellafante, Ginia. 1998. "Feminism: It's all about Me." *Time Magazine.* http://con tent.time.com/time/magazine/article/0,9171,988616,00.html.

Black, Shannon. 2017. "Knit + Resist: Placing the Pussyhat Project in the Context of Craft Activism," *Gender, Place & Culture: A Journal of Feminist Geography* 24 (5):696–710.

Collins, Patricia Hill. 1991. *Black Feminist Thought: Knowledge, Consciousness, and the Politics of Empowerment.* Boston: Unwin Hyman.

Combahee River Collective. 1978. "The Combahee River Collective State-ment." Copyright by Zillah Eisenstein. http://circuitous.org/scraps/combahee. html.

Contrera, Jessica. 2014. "Can Stars Mix Fame and Feminism?; Female Celebrities being asked about 'F-word' More and More," *The Toronto Star*, p.E1.

Crossley, Alison Dahl. 2017. *Finding Feminism: Millennial Activists and the Unfinished Gender Revolution.* New York: NYU Press.

Crossley, Alison Dahl. 2015. "Facebook Feminism: Social Media, Blogs, and New Technologies of Contemporary Feminism." *Mobilization* 20(2): 253–268.

Crenshaw, Kimberle. 1991. "Mapping the Margins: Intersectionality, Identity Poli-tics and Violence Against Women of Color." *Stanford Law Review* 43(6):1241–1299.

Daniels, Jesse. 2009. "Rethinking Cyberfeminism(s): Race, Gender and Embodi-ment." *WSQ: Women's Studies Quarterly* 37(1–2):101–124.

Douglas, Susan J. 2010. *Enlightened Sexism: The Seductive Message That Feminism's Work is Done.* New York: Times Books.

Ensler, Eve. 1998. *The Vagina Monologues*, New York: Villard Press.

Everett, Anna. 2004. "On Cyberfeminism and Cyberwomanism: High-Tech Med-iations of Feminism's Discontents." *Signs: Journal of Women in Culture and Society* 30(1):1278–1286.

Fisher, Dana. 2017. "100 Days of Resistance and Still Counting: Innovating How We Study Protest." *Critical Mass Bulletin* 42(1):3–4.

Fisher, Dana, Dawn M. Dow, and Rashawn Ray. 2017. "Intersectionality takes it to the streets: Mobilizing across diverse interests for the Women's March." *Science Advances* 3:1–8. Retrieved June 12, 2018. http://advances.sciencemag.org/con tent/3/9/eaao1390.

Freeman, Jo. 1973. "The Origins of the Women's Liberation Movement." *American Journal of Sociology* 78:792–811.

Freeman, Jo. 1998. "On the Origins of the Women's Liberation Movement from a Strictly Personal Perspective." Pp. 171–196 in *The Feminist Memoir Project*, edited by R. Blau DuPlessis and A. Snitow. New York: Three Rivers Press.

Ghaziani, Amin. 2008. *The Dividends of Dissent: How Conflict and Culture Work in Lesbian and Gay Marches on Washington.* Chicago: University of Chicago Press.

Gibson, Megan. 2011. "The Suffrage Movement." *Time Magazine.* Retrieved August 12, 2017. http://content.time.com/time/specials/packages/article/0,28804,2088114_2087975_2087964,00.html.

Hawkesworth, Mary. 2004. "The Semiotics of Premature Burial: Feminism in a Postfeminist Age." *Signs: Journal of Culture and Society* 29:961–986.

Jenkins, J.Craig. 1983. "Resource Mobilization Theory and the Study of Social Movements." *Annual Review of Sociology* 9:527–553.

Johnston, Josee and Judith Taylor. 2008. "Feminist Consumerism and Fat Activists: A Comparative Study of Grassroots Activism and the Dove Real Beauty Campaign." *Signs: Journal of Women in Culture and Society* 33(4):941–966.

Kelly, Maura. 2015. "Feminist Identity, Collective Action, and Individual Resistance Among Contemporary U.S. Feminists." *Women's Studies International Forum* 48 (Jan–Feb):81–92.

Kelly, Maura. 2014. "Knitting as a Feminist Project?" *Women's Studies International Forum* 4 (May–June):133–144.

Kretschmer, Kelsy. 2019. *Not NOW: Factionalism and Splitting in the National Organization for Women.* Minneapolis, MN: University of Minnesota Press.

Kutz-Flamenbaum, Rachel. 2007. "Code Pink, Raging Grannies, and the Missile Dick Chicks: Feminist Performance Activism in the Contemporary Anti-War Movement." *NWSA Journal* 19(1, Spring):89–105.

LaCroix, Alison. (No date.) "The National Women's Party and the Meaning Behind their Purple, White and Gold Textiles," National Women's Party website. Retrieved June 12, 2018. http://nationalwomansparty.org/the-national-womans-party-and-the-meaning-behind-their-purple-white-and-gold-textiles/.

Livingston, Josephine. 2017. "The Problem with 'Pussy': Feminism under Trump Must Remember the Body but not be Limited by It." *New Republic Magazine.* Retrieved January 24, 2017. https://newrepublic.com/article/140063/problem-pussy.

Martin, Courtney. 2009. "The End of the Women's Movement." *The American Prospect.* Retrieved March 30, 2009. http://prospect.org/cs/articles.

Messner, Michael. 2002. *Taking the Field: Women, Men and Sports.* Minneapolis, MN: University of Minnesota Press.

Meyer, David S. 1993. "Protest Cycles and Political Process: American Peace Movements in the Nuclear Age." *Political Research Quarterly* 46(3):451–479.

Meyer, David S. 2003. "How Movements Matter." *Contexts* 2(4):30–35.

Meyer, David S., and Nancy Whittier. 1994. "Social Movement Spillover." *Social Problems* 41(2):277–298.

Million Women March. 2018. Retrieved March 5, 2018. http://millionwomanmarch20.com/.

Papachristou, Judith. 1976. *Women Together: A History in Documents of the Women's Movement in the United States: A Ms. Book.* New York: Alfred J. Knopf.

Peoples, Whitney. 2007. "'Under Construction:' Identifying Foundations of Hip-Hop Feminism and Exploring Bridges Between Black Second-Wave and Hip-Hop Feminism." *Meridians: Feminism, Race, Transnationalism* 8(1):19–52.

Pentney, Beth Ann. 2008. "Feminist Activism And Knitting: Are Fibre Arts a Viable Mode for Feminist Political Action?" *thirdspace: a journal of feminist theory & culture* 8(1, summer). Online.

Raizada, Kristen. 2007. "An Interview with the Guerilla Girls, Dyke Action Machine (DAM!), and the Toxic Titties." *NWSA Journal* 19 (1, Spring):39–58.

Reger, Jo. 2014. "Micro Cohorts, Feminist Generations and the Making of the Toronto Slutwalk." *Feminist Formations* 26(1):49–69.

Reger, Jo. 2012. *Everywhere and Nowhere: Contemporary Feminism in the United States.* New York: Oxford University Press.

Reger, Jo, and Suzanne Staggenborg. 2006. "Patterns of Mobilization in Local Movement Organizations: Leadership and Strategy in Four National Organization for Women Chapters." *Sociological Perspectives* 49(3):297–323.

Reger, Jo, and Lacey Story. 2005. "Talking about My Vagina: Two College Campuses and the Influence of the Vagina Monologues." Pp. 139–160 in *Different Wavelengths: Studies of the Contemporary Women's Movement*, edited by J. Reger. New York: Routledge.

Robnett, Belinda. 1997. *How Long? How Long? African-American Women in the Struggle for Civil Rights.* New York: Oxford University Press.

Rose-Redwood, CindyAnn and Reuben Rose-Redwood. 2017. "'It Definitely Felt Very White:' Race, Gender, and the Performative Politics of Assembly at the Women's March in Victoria, British Columbia." *Gender, Place & Culture* 24 (5):645–654.

Roth, Benita. 2017. "Intersectionality: Origins, Travels, Questions, and Contributions." Pp. 129–149 in *The Oxford Handbook of U.S. Women's Social Movement Activism*, edited by H. McCammon, V. Taylor, J. Reger, and R. Einwohner. New York: Oxford University Press.

Roth, Benita. 2002. *Separate Roads to Feminism: Black Chicana and White Feminist Movements in America's Second Wave.* New York: Cambridge University Press.

Rupp, Leila J. and Verta Taylor. 1987. *Survival in the Doldrums: The American Women's Rights Movement, 1945 to 1960s.* New York: Oxford University Press.

Rush, Curtis. 2011. "Cop Apologizes for 'Sluts' Remark at Law School." *Toronto Star.* Retrieved February 11, 2011.https://www.thestar.com/news/gta/2011/02/18/cop_apologizes_for_sluts_remark_at_law_school.html.

Sassen, Saskia. 2002. "Towards a Sociology of Information Technology." *Current Sociology* 50(3):365–388.

Staggenborg, Suzanne and Verta Taylor. 2005. "Whatever Happened to the Women's Movement?" *Mobilization: The International Journal of Research and Theory about Social Movements, Protest and Collective Behavior.* 10(1):37–52.

Suh, Krista and Jayna Zweiman, 2016, "Pussyhat Project: Design Interventions for Social Change." Retrieved March 6, 2018. https://www.pussyhatproject.com/.

Taylor, Verta and Nancy Whittier. 1992. "Collective Identity in Social Movement Communities: Lesbian Feminist Mobilization." Pp. 104–129 in *Frontiers in Social Movement Theory*, edited by A. D. Morris and C. M. Mueller. New Haven and London: Yale University Press.

Thompson, Becky. 2002. "Multiracial Feminism: Recasting the Chronology of Second Wave Feminism." *Feminist Studies* 28(2):336–360.

Tilly, Charles. 1978. *From Mobilization to Revolution*. Reading, MA: Addison-Wesley.

Walker, Rob. 2017. "The D.I.Y. Revolutionaries of the Pussyhat Project," *The New Yorker*. Retrieved March 13, 2018. https://www.newyorker.com/culture/cul ture-desk/the-d-i-y-revolutionaries-of-the-pussyhat-project.

Wang, Amy B. 2017. "'Nevertheless, she persisted' becomes new battle cry after McConnell silences Elizabeth Warren," *Washington Post*. Retrieved July 5, 2018. https://www.washingtonpost.com/news/the-fix/wp/2017/02/08/never theless-she-persisted-becomes-new-battle-cry-after-mcconnell-silences-eliza beth-warren/?utm_term=.484aa9d0579c.

Winerip, Michael. 2009. "Where to Pass the Torch," *The New York Times*. Retrieved March 8, 2009. http://nytimes.com/2009/03/08/fashion/08genera tionb.html.

Part I
Activists

2 Identifying with Inclusivity
Intersectional Chicana Feminisms

Fátima Suárez

On January 21, 2017, the day after the Presidential Inauguration, I joined the 750,000 people who gathered in downtown Los Angeles to march in solidarity against the Trump presidency. Although I participated in protests in the past, I had never been surrounded by this kind of hopeful, passionate, empowered, and fearless energy. Some of the protestors wore pink "pussy" hats, while others carried signs that read of messages of love and justice, and many more chanted words of solidarity while marching with their families. This was one of the Women's Marches and although the term "women" was in the title of this global mobilization, it was a march for human rights and social justice. (See Chapter 1 on the 2017 and 2018 Women's Marches.)

Despite this mass mobilization, there were many people, particularly women of color, who were critical about the lack of inclusivity and the organizers' neoliberal tactics at the organizational level. Some of the critiques included calling women of color "divisive" for raising issues such as race, class and immigration; solidarity with law enforcement despite their aggressive responses to movements led by people of color like #blacklivesmatter; lack of acknowledgment of longtime activists and organizers, most of whom have been women of color; and the removal of sex workers from the Women's March platform (Lemieux 2017; Mosthof 2017). Others were concerned with how the march alienated transwomen by relying on essentialism to define womanhood (Solis 2017). These critiques are neither new to feminism nor unfounded. Historical accounts of the women's rights movement acknowledge the movement's lack of inclusivity and diversity with regards to race, class, and sexuality (e.g., Reger 2012; Roth 2004, 2017; Thompson 2002; Whittier 1995).

As I marched, however, I was struck by how people, especially Latinas/os, made this march their own regardless of the politics at the organizational level. Some brought live bands and dancers who danced the *Concheros*, [1] while others chanted in multiple languages including indigenous ones. Many carried signs that had messages such as "The Revolution Will Be Intersectional Or It Won't Be My Revolution" and others connected feminism to other social movements such as #blacklivesmatter and the immigrant rights movement. Both the participation and critiques of the

Women's Marches illustrate the importance of the concept of intersectionality in U.S. feminism and in this chapter, I review the intellectual history of the concept and the contemporary claims of an "intersectional feminist" identity. I focus on Chicana[2] feminisms as a case study to assess how women of color have conceptualized and practiced intersectional feminism.

Intersectionality: The Intellectual Revolution in Women's Studies

At the Women's March, many participants carried signs in which they claimed an "intersectional feminist" identity and called for an "intersectional revolution." So what does it mean to draw on intersectionality as an identity? The roots of intersectionality come from feminists of color engaged in activism during the political and cultural revolutions of the 1960s and 1970s (Blackwell 2011; Combahee River Collective 2015; Cornell 2000; Espinoza 2001; García 1997; Gutiérrez 2008; Nieto-Gómez 1997; Robnett 1997; Roth 2004; Thompson 2002). These activists conceptualized their lived experiences as bodies of knowledge to write about the ways in which race, class, gender, and sexuality are mutually reinforcing axes of power (Anzaldúa 1987; Collins 2000; Cotera 1976; Hull et al. 1982; Moraga and Anzaldúa 1983; Smith 1987). However, it was not until Kimberlé Crenshaw (1989, 1991) coined the term "intersectionality" that this theoretical paradigm proliferated in the academy and women's studies in particular. Using legal cases of discrimination as empirical evidence, Crenshaw (1989:140) described intersectionality as a metaphor to illustrate how Black women are "excluded from feminist theory and antiracist policy discourse because both are predicated on a discrete set of experiences that often does not accurately reflect the interaction of race and gender." Furthermore, Crenshaw suggested that the law's treatment of race and gender as mutually exclusive categories actually limited its reach to the experiences of privileged members of the group. In other words, the law's definition of sex discrimination was based on the experiences of white women and racial discrimination policy was grounded on the experiences of Black men or the Black middle-class. Intersectionality then is the *relationship* between overlapping systems of oppression which shapes lived experiences in multidimensional ways. Crenshaw did not endorse an "add Black women and stir" approach because "the intersectional experience is greater than the sum of racism and sexism" (p. 140). As such, to think "intersectionally" is to understand that all people have a matrix of overlapping identities that are in constant relation to each other as they experience the social world.

So what does it mean to understand the world through an intersectional lens? HaeYeon Choo and Myra Marx Ferree (2010: 130–131) view intersectional practices as being focused on "inclusion, analytical interactions, and institutional primacy." To use an inclusive intersectional lens is to focus on "giving voice to the oppressed." Drawing on analytical intersectionality moves beyond listing and adding race, class, gender and other types of social identities as separate factors. A systemic intersectional approach sees "gender and race [as] fundamentally embedded in, working through, and determining the organization of ownership, profit, and commodification of labor" (135). Given its history in the public sphere and in the academy, intersectionality is a political, theoretical, and methodological approach. Luft and Ward (2009) stress the importance of bringing intersectionality back to its social justice roots to render the work of women of color, especially Black women, visible. So what does it mean to say you are intersectional?

Claiming an Intersectional Feminist Identity

What does it mean to claim an intersectional feminist identity? Is the goal of contemporary U.S. feminist activity to achieve an intersectional feminist identity? Social movement scholars argue that collective identity is a precursor to movement participation, a positive movement outcome, and an important factor in establishing social movement communities (Gamson 1992; Hunt and Benford 2007; Klandermans 2014; Rupp and Taylor 1999; Staggenborg and Taylor 2005; Taylor and Whittier 1992). Polletta and Jasper (2001:285) conceptualize collective identity as an individual's perceived "cognitive, moral and emotional" relationship with a community and this connection can impact the individual's personal identity. Overall, collective identities are grounded in attachment to social groups and interpretation of shared lived experiences due to the group's structural location. In the words of the political scientist Lisa García Bedolla (1995: 7), collective identities are "shifting, situational, [and] contextually driven understandings of self and place in particular historical moments."

Leila Rupp and Verta Taylor (1999) argue that feminism is a collective identity that is constantly being revised and negotiated. This redefinition of feminism allows us to consider intersectional feminist identity as a "politicized collective identity" (Simon and Klandermans 2001). According to Klandermans (2014:20) collective identities are politicized "when grievances are turned into claims and citizens begin to campaign and mobilize to win for their cause." At the Women's Marches, many marchers deployed a politicized intersectional feminist identity to express their shared grievances, mobilizing to challenge the new administration and its establishment. I argue that this identity is historically situated in a time where ethnic and women's studies departments and programs are flourishing, the access to different forms of media is wide ranging, and advocates seek to unite theory and practice.

Intersectional feminism is set in a time when feminism, is "shaped by the politicized experience of being an aged, gendered, and sexed being, among other social categories made relevant in a particular social context" (Reger 2017: 113). Feminists identify the current social context as in a state of social, political, economic, and environmental crises, and draw on intersectionality as a framework to make sense of what is happening and why. In this setting, intersectionality operates both as a "frame" (Benford and Snow 2000) to construct meaning and as an identity marker. The 2017 Women's Marches are evidence that a goal of U.S. contemporary feminism is the achievement of an intersectional feminist identity to address a range of social inequality. At the cultural level, intersectional feminist identity challenges what Chela Sandoval (1991) calls "the great hegemonic model" of feminism based on four types of feminist consciousness: liberal, Marxist, cultural, and socialist. Moreover, it is publicly expressed through language and symbols such as wearing pin buttons that read "intersectional feminist" or carrying the images of iconic feminists of color such as Angela Davis.

Practicing intersectionality in the women's movement is a form of "solidarity politics" (Luft and Ward 2009) or "coalition politics" (Cole 2008). When one claims to be an intersectional feminist, one is signaling one's desire and commitment to stand in solidarity and work in collaboration with *all* people. This identity claim can enlarge one's personal identity and offer a sense of contentment and self-realization via one's connection with others (Friedman and McAdam 1992; Gamson 1992). Claiming an intersectional feminist identity is a movement tactic that can go beyond racial and/or ethnic-linked feminist identities, such as Asian, Black, Chicana, allowing women to experience their racialized gender identities differently. Since these collective identities are based on different boundaries (Taylor and Whittier 1992), an intersectional feminist identity can expand those boundaries. This is because our lives are multifaceted and feminist activism cannot be completely described only by racial and ethnic labels, yet it still acknowledges their power and historical influence. Furthermore, claiming an intersectional feminist identity incorporates a willingness to be self-reflexive and confront one's power and privilege, vis-à-vis other women, as well as one's oppression. The claiming of an intersectional feminist identity is reminiscent of those who claimed a U.S. Third World feminist identity during the 1980s. This feminist identity was framed by an oppositional, decolonizing consciousness in the United States. U.S. Third World feminists postulate a differential consciousness which they use to determine which actions or movements to engage in based upon the types of oppression they confront (Sandoval 1991).

The claims of an intersectional feminist identity are preceded by women's efforts to create a new feminist identity that is inclusive and all-encompassing. One example includes "Xicanisma" (Castillo 1994), which acts as a decolonial label for Chicana feminism, and "Womanist" (Ogunyemi 1985; Walker 1983), which is both a philosophy and consciousness of unity and equity through intersectional considerations. These efforts are part of the struggle to create a social movement community that is accessible to those who are in search of a community outside of the margins in which they live. Black lesbian feminists in the Combahee River Collective (2015:212) believed that "the most profound and potentially most radical politics come directly out of our own identity, as opposed to working to end somebody else's oppression." During the same time the Combahee River Collective wrote what is now considered as a classic example of intersectional praxis, Chicanas were in the process of crafting their own radical politics out of their own intersectional experience. I now turn to the herstory of Chicana feminisms as a way to illustrate how an intersectional identity emerges and engenders theories that reflect Chicanas' complex lived experiences due to their community's history of colonial domination. A focus on Chicana feminisms also illustrates how women of color's political histories shape their personal and collective response to interlocking systems of power.

Borderlands and the Intersectional Activism of Chicana Feminisms

Chicana feminisms flourished during a period of cultural and political movements in the United States during the 1960s and 1970s. Becky Thompson (2002: 338) defines Chicana feminisms as part of the larger identity of "multiracial feminism" that emerged in the period and argues that feminists of color worked in both women-only and in mixed-gender organizations across diverse issues and causes. This new form of consciousness emerged when Chicanas began to question their roles in the Chicano movement and the patriarchal elements of Chicano nationalism.[3] When they challenged the gendered structure of the movement, Chicanas were criticized and isolated by their fellow Chicanos and "loyalists"[4] because they were perceived as "traitors," "sell outs to white feminism" and "anti-Chicano movement" (Nieto-Gómez 1974: 35).

Chicana feminists were working within a cultural context and were concerned with sexism, racism, and classism (Blackwell 2011; Espinoza 2001; García 1997; Guttiérrez 2008; Nieto-Gómez 1997; Segura and Facio 2008). According to Benita Roth (2004:167), "the desire to stay linked to activist Chicano males shaped the way that Chicanas saw their feminism" and Chicana feminists "continually asserted that the proper site of Chicana feminism was the Chicano movement." Chicana feminists argued that Chicana, Mexican, and Indigenous women in Mexico shared a long history of feminist activism and they framed the Chicana/o family as a potential site of resistance against white supremacist domination (Cotera 1976; Hurtado 2003; Roth 2004). Chicana feminists also highlighted class because of their participation in the work force where they were denied access to decent wages and safe working conditions (Glenn 1992; Pardo 2017; Ruiz 2008; Segura 1994, 1984; Zavella 1987). Chicanas felt that the white feminist movement had also failed to speak to their lived experiences as working class and as women of color. Chicana feminists understood that their subordination was the result of what the sociologist Patricia Hill Collins (2000) refers to as "the matrix of domination" characterized by interlocking race-ethnic, class, and gender/sexuality systems of oppression. In sum, they were doing intersectional thinking without the language to frame their activity as such.

Theorizing Chicana Feminisms

In *Making Face, Making Soul/ Haciendo Caras,* Gloria Anzaldúa argues for the need to create theories that reflect the lives of women of color. She wrote, "*necesitamos teorías* (we need theories) that will rewrite history using race, class, gender and ethnicity as categories of analysis, theories that cross borders, that blur boundaries" (1990: xxv). Chicana feminists have taken heed of Anzaldúa's call by using their lived experiences as foundational blocks for theory building. Due to the marginalization of gender within the Chicano Movement, race within the white feminist movement, and sexuality in both movements, Chicana feminist production is concerned with (re)claiming a language and a space (Castillo 1994; Hurtado 1998; Moraga and Anzaldúa 1983; Pérez 1999, 1991; Trujillo 1998).

(Re)claiming a language meant claiming a discourse and the Spanish language. Chicana feminisms are concerned with taking control of the narratives that are told about Chicanas and Latinas in the United States. Furthermore, according to Hurtado (2003: 8), Chicana feminists' use of Spanish in their scholarly work is "a political assertion of the value of their heritage and the means to create feminist discourses that was directly tied to a Chicana experience." Claiming a language is part of the Chicana feminisms' project as a way to also claim sexuality and to speak to the invisibility of Chicana lesbians in the Chicano, white feminist, and gay rights movements (Moraga and Anzaldúa 1983; Saldívar-Hull 1991; Trujillo 1997).

The (re)claiming of a space is multidimensional in that it can mean claiming "a historical place, a geographical location, and a philosophical space" (Hurtado 2003: 6). Chicana feminists have sought to recuperate their history as women and as members of a marginalized ethnic and racial group (Cotera 1976, Pérez 1999; Ruiz 2008). An integral part of this project involves rewriting the dominant historical narrative about the colonization of Mexicans; first by the Spanish and then by the United States. The site of colonization from which Chicana feminists theorize is geographically specific to the U.S.-Mexico border. Chicana feminisms are based in *la frontera* (the borderlands) to emphasize a border culture and language which stands between two countries- Mexico and the United States-but not belonging fully to either one (Anzaldúa 1987). It is at this border where Chicanas learned that the categories of race, class, gender, and sexuality are arbitrary and socially constructed and where a feminist consciousness is born. The borderlands exemplify the cultural hybridity that Crenshaw's concept of intersectionality seeks to capture.

The ability to observe and act on the arbitrary nature of their social categorization and articulate individual and collective agency is integral to what Anzaldúa (1987) refers to as Chicanas' *mestiza consciousness*. For

Anzaldúa, Chicanas are women who experience a "struggle of borders," they are "betwixt and between" in terms of the range of life choices they have had historically and in contemporary times (78–79). Chicanas' *mestiza consciousness* is not uniform as each woman experiences a distinct "struggle of borders" that develops a "tolerance for contradictions [and ambiguities]" (79). Having a *mestiza consciousness* means having the ability to hold multiple social perspectives while simultaneously maintaining a center located on the border which exists when more than one culture meets. *Mestiza consciousness* is a Chicana-centered intersectionality framework (Segura and Zavella 2016).

Chicana feminists theorize about a collective liberation because they understand that their subordination cannot be overcome without an intersectional analysis. Theorizing "outsider" (Collins 1986), "*mestiza*" (Anzaldúa 1987), and "transgressive" (hooks 1994) knowledges can "value the presence of people of color, and can re-envision the margins places empowered by transformative resistance" (Yosso 2005: 70). This collective approach to liberation has allowed Chicana feminists to form coalitions with other women of color, lesbians, and working-class women who are also politically and socially marginalized. Moreover, contemporary Chicana and Latina[5] feminist writers and activists continue to bring an intersectional lens to the struggle for social justice.

Chicana and Latina Feminisms in Action

Chicana and Latina organizing and activism are important sites for Chicana feminisms. Grassroots activism lies at the heart of Chicana and Latina activism across the Americas (Hardy-Fanta 1993; Naples 1992; Pardo 1999; Peña 2007; Taft 2010; Viterna 2013). According to Mary Pardo (2017), Chicanas' political activism has challenged racism and discrimination in the workplace and in the community. Chicanas and Latinas including Dolores Huerta and Maria Elena Duranzo fought for the right to unionize, safe working conditions, and livable wages (Cotera 1976; Segura and Facio 2001). They formed labor unions like the United Farm Workers and Domestic Workers Association (Hondagneu-Sotelo 2001; Ruiz 2008). Along with Antonia Hernandez and Gloria Arellanes, they are instrumental in the struggle for reproductive justice and access to health care (Espinoza 2001; Gutiérrez 2008; Luna 2009). Chicanas and Latinas in immigrant rights organizations such as National Network for Immigrant and Refugee Rights[6] have fought anti-immigrant state policies like Operation Streamline. Chicanas and Latinas such as Lucy Ramos and Aurora Castillo have also organized against environmental racism (Pardo 2017; 1999). These social justice movements continue the work of activists including Anna Nieto-Gómez and the *Hijas de Cuauhtémoc* [7] who fought for respect, dignity, and a space for women's political participation in the Chicano Movement of the late 1960s and 1970s (Blackwell 2011).

In struggling to resist the oppressive forces that impede their abilities to thrive and their families to prosper, Chicanas and Latinas opened the boundaries of what can be considered "political," expanding the fields of gender, politics, and social movement research. For example, political scientist Carol Hardy-Fanta (1993) argues that "being political" is a complex process for women of Latin American ancestry. Excluded from electoral politics, Chicanas and Latinas have expanded the notion of "political work," illustrating their unwillingness to be restricted to one political arena. For Chicanas and other historically disenfranchised women, "being political involves the intense and far-ranging exchange of ideas" and it is connected to taking action, both as an individual and as a collective by not merely following a designated leader but by seeing themselves as leaders (133–134).

Similarly, Mary Pardo's (1999: 59) work on the Mothers of East Los Angeles demonstrates how the intersections of gender, race and class shape political participation to produce a form of "gendered citizenship." Gendered citizenship acknowledges the process in which political participation and citizenship are gendered, as well as how gender is mediated by other systems of stratification such as race, class, nationality, and language. The women who were part of Mothers of East Los Angeles also transformed the meaning of motherhood into an oppositional identity to challenge a state-proposed project to build a prison in their community. Chicanas' *mestiza consciousness* allowed them to merge what appeared to be opposing identities- the "activist" and the "mother"- into an empowering and culturally accessible identity and practice which Nancy Naples (1992) calls "activist mothering." As a result of these key theoretical interventions, mothering can now be considered political work with Mothers of East Los Angeles's framing of motherhood and the role of the family in social justice struggles. Through their groundbreaking works on Chicana and Latina organizing, both Hardy-Fanta and Pardo reveal that "being political and becoming political may develop out of actions begun with women's traditional roles," thus changing the meanings that academics attach to traditional gender practices in the family (Hardy-Fanta 1993:147).

As Chicanas navigate the borderlands they bridge different issues and transform cultural traditions in their political work. Milagros Peña (2007: 149) asserts that the struggles for "connecting health, education, social, political, economic, and environmental concerns to human rights is an important contribution of grassroots women's activism." The women activists in Peña's study bridge spiritual and physical borders as they work in faith-based and grassroots nongovernmental organizations that craft agendas focused on women's issues and needs in the United States and Mexico. While the term "feminism" is often associated with progressive politics and social movements to eradicate structural violence against women, for Peña's participants, that term had meaning only when reframed as "fe-en-mi-mismo" or having faith in themselves. Their faith in themselves allowed the women to collectively organize against labor exploitation, domestic

violence, and *feminicidio*, all of which significantly impacted their relationships to their families and to the state. Chicanas and Latinas use their *mestiza
consciousness* and politicized collective identity to overcome the structural
barriers of U.S. racialization, idealized femininity, class status, educational
and employment discrimination, and citizenship. They engage in acts of
resistance that range from challenging patriarchal arrangements in the family
to large mobilizations against the state. Chicanas and Latinas have been
denied access to pivotal resources such as fair wages, education, and health
care, which would improve not only their lives and that of their families but
also of their communities. Younger women build on the legacy they
inherited, visible at the 2017 Women's Marches.

Returning to the Women's March

By drawing on a history of Chicana and Latina feminisms and their activism,
we can begin to understand contemporary Chicanas and Latinas struggle for
social justice and equality as reflected at the Women's March. Through the
borderlands, the intersection where two cultures, nations, languages and
identities meet, Chicanas and Latinas challenge arbitrary categories and
binaries thus reaffirming the multidimensionality of human existence. This
space shapes and is shaped by a consciousness and identity that is intersectional. Contemporary Chicana and Latina advocacy is informed by the
election of Donald Trump, the resurgence of anti-Mexican, anti-immigrant,
and anti-feminist sentiments as well as the rollback of social welfare. Whether it is through literature, social media, visual and performing arts, academic scholarship, or social movements, young Chicanas and Latinas
continue to develop their political subjectivities that are intimately tied to
previous Chicana and Latina theorizing and organizing.

At the Women's March, Chicanas and Latinas used their community's
cultural wealth[8] (Yosso 2005) and their position in the borderlands to speak
on key feminist issues: reproductive justice, pay equity, body positivity, and
violence against women.[9] Like their political foremothers, they also practiced intersectional thinking by addressing how immigration, environmental
racism, labor exploitation, and mass incarceration are also feminist concerns.[10] Some centered on their community's value of education and jux-
taposed it with the rise of deportations. They argued that women's
liberation is tied to education not deportations, thus demonstrating how
these are interlocking feminist issues (See Image 2.1). By using a *calavera* [11]
version of "Rosie the Riveter," this protestor updated a feminist icon to
critique the continued invisibility of Latinas and Chicanas in mainstream
feminist discourses and to render it more relatable and accessible to Chicanas
and Latinas.

Other protestors carried images of Chicana lesbian feminist icons such as
Gloria Anzaldúa, drawing on cultural memory to make visible and exalt
Chicana and Latina feminist theorists who have been ignored in the

Image 2.1 Education and deportations
Photo taken by author.

academia, even by scholars of intersectionality[12] (see Image 2.2). The caption under the image of Anzaldúa also reminds us that if women are empowered, then their families and communities are also empowered. As we have seen through Chicanas and Latinas' activism, if women feel capable to participate in, negotiate with, control, influence and hold institutions and institutional actors accountable for how they affect their lives, then that will also expand the assets and capabilities of their entire communities.

Image 2.2 Protestor with image of Gloria Anzaldúa: "A Woman with Power is Power!"
Photo taken by Esmeralda Suárez. Used with permission.

Part of this empowerment rests on being aware and proud of one's cultural and political history (see Image 2.3). The Chicana in this image carries a sign in Spanish that reads, "I am capable, I am strong, I am invincible, I am woman." "Woman" is equated with "power" as a way to foster a political consciousness that will engender mobilization against the structural forces that impede women from realizing their full potential.

Image 2.3 Bringing Chicana feminisms to the revolution
Photo taken by Esmeralda Suárez. Used with permission.

In sum, the herstory of Chicana feminisms and activism and the radical project of intersectionality was present on January 21, 2017. One of the consequences is the creation of a new politicized collective identity: an intersectional feminist identity. One of the contributions of contemporary feminists to the women's movement is the transformation of intersectionality from a theoretical and methodological paradigm into an activist identity. This transformation symbolizes contemporary feminist aims to describe their feminisms as different from previous political generations of activists who excluded other feminisms (Reger 2012). Claiming an intersectional feminist identity can also signify solidarity and commitment to work collaboratively for social justice and such claims can also act as a frame or movement tactic for the purposes of coalition building. Claiming this political identity can also signify one's pledge to reflect on one's position in the matrix of domination (Collins 2000) since one can be both the oppressed and the oppressor.

The contemporary claims of an intersectional feminist identity expose a new avenue of scholarship. Future research that interrogates whether this claim has different meanings for different groups of women (especially to white women) is imperative. Do white women claim to be intersectional feminists as a way to distance themselves from "white feminism," which does not acknowledge privilege? Or do these claims craft an authentic feminist identity among white feminists? Are these claims a form of "activist capital" that symbolizes their solidarity with women of color? Even though the roots of intersectionality are in the political work and lived experiences of women of color, are contemporary women of color inclined to explicitly identify their feminism as "intersectional"? Or do they continue to signify their feminism within racial or ethnic traditions?

There are also concerning ramifications of transforming intersectionality into an identity. Due to increasing access to information and the popularity of social media, intersectionality has become a "buzzword" (Davis 2008) and has proliferated in the public consciousness and in the vernacular of contemporary activist circles. Although this might be a positive movement outcome, it can also have unintended, negative consequences for the concept itself. Intersectionality scholars such as Luft and Ward (2009) caution against the misidentification and appropriation of intersectionality because it dilutes the potential of what was originally a political and theoretical intervention. The authors argue that misidentification is an "apparatus that avoid[s] accountability to social justice outcomes" and appropriation means to "claim the intellectual political, or moral virtue the term has come to imbue, without supporting the work of intersectional resistance" (15–16). Are intersectional feminist claims both a form of empowerment and appropriation? To what or whom are intersectional feminists accountable? At what point and to what ends is an intersectional feminist consciousness put into practice?

Contemporary massive mobilizations are evidence that the world may be on the brink of a radical social transformation. Part of this political work entails creating an activist identity that will continue to engender action, and for some, an intersectional feminist identity may be a collective identity that will motivate them to fight for social justice. However, in our appreciation of the concept, we must not ignore the genealogies of intersectionality. We must remember what Chicanas, Latinas and other women of color activists have taught us: despite the oppressions that frame our lived experiences, the love and respect we feel for ourselves, our (her)stories, families, and communities will inspire us to be creative in our resistance.

Notes

1 The *Concheros* dance is a traditional dance and ceremony performed in Mexico since before the Spanish colonial period. Current performances are aimed to preserve and celebrate Mexican and Mexican Americans' Indigenous heritages.

2 Chicanas are women of Mexican descent in the United States who are from diverse class, sexualities, education, occupations, generation from Mexico, language proficiencies, and political perspectives, all of which contribute to how they express their identities. Depending on the situation and context, Mexican descent women may refer to themselves as "Chicanas," "Mexican Americans," "Mexican women," "Hispanic" or "Latina."

3 See García's (1997) exceptional anthology on early Chicana feminist writings for an overview.

4 "Loyalists" were Chicanas who agreed to prioritize the issue of race over gender in their community's struggle for liberation.

5 Although my focus is on Chicana feminisms, I am also including Latina feminist activism in this discussion. Due to their history in the United States, Chicanas have been critical political actors who often collaborate with other Latina women. Latinas have also been highly influenced by Chicana feminist work. Therefore, any discussion about Chicana feminist theorizing and activism must also engage Latinas' activism.

6 Visit http://www.nnirr.org/drupal/just-borders for more information.

7 In 1971, *Las Hijas de Cuauhtémoc* was established at California State University, Long Beach making it one of the first Chicana and Latina feminist organizations. For a historical overview of this organization, see Balckwell's (2011) outstanding text on the Chicana feminist movement.

8 Community cultural wealth is the cultural capital that communities of color possess which includes linguistic, familial, navigational, social, aspirational, and resistant capital.

9 https://www.buzzfeed.com/norbertobriceno/chingxs-all-day-every-day?utm_term=.lwQYxOK2o#.jbRw3QjPV.

10 https://www.buzzfeed.com/pablovaldivia/viva-la-mujer?utm_term=.taZ8p2p lk#.kdjdeBeoG.

11 A *calavera* is a decorative human skull used during the Day of the Dead celebrations in Mexico.

12 I surmise there are three reasons that explain the absence of Chicanas and Latinas in intersectional work. First, despite its racial diversity, race in the United States still operates within the black/white binary which obscures Latinas/os, Asians and Indigenous people's racialized experiences. Second, earlier writings on intersectionality were written by Black women based on their racialized, gendered, and classed experiences. Although, their writings have been fundamental to our understanding of intersectionality, their work is situated within the black/white binary. Third, activists and scholars in the humanities- poets, writers, artists- pioneered the work on Chicana feminisms, which is not often cited by

scholars in the social sciences and vice versa. Therefore, the boundaries that surround disciplines may impact the level of intellectual engagement with Chicana and Latina feminisms.

References

Anzaldúa, Gloria. ed. 1990. *Making Face, Making Soul/Haciendo Caras: Creative and Critical Perspectives by Women of Color.* San Francisco, CA: Aunt Lute Books.

Anzaldúa, Gloria .1987. *Borderlands/La Frontera: The New Mestiza.* San Francisco, CA: Aunt Lute Books.

Benford, Robert D. and David A. Snow. 2000. "Framing Processes and Social Movements: An Overview and Assessment." *Annual Review of Sociology* 26:611–639.

Blackwell, Maylei. 2011. *Chicana Power!: Contested Histories of Feminism in the Chicano Movement.* Austin, TX: University of Texas Press.

Choo, HaeYeon and Mayra Marx Ferree. 2010. "Practicing Intersectionality in Sociological Research: A Critical Analysis of Inclusions, Interactions, and Institutions in the Study of Inequalities." *Sociological Theory* 28(2):129–149.

Castillo, Ana. 1994. *Massacre of the Dreamers: Essays on Xicanisma.* New York, NY: Plume.

Cole, Elizabeth R. 2008. "Coalitions as a Model for Intersectionality: From Practice to Theory." *Sex Roles* 59:443–453.

Collins, Patricia Hill. 2000 [1990]. *Black Feminist Thought: Knowledge, Consciousness, and the Politics of Empowerment.* New York: Routledge.

Collins, Patricia Hill. 1986. "Learning from the Outsider Within: The Sociological Significance of Black Feminist Thought." *Social Problems* 33(6):S14–S30.

Combahee River Collective. 2015. "A Black Feminist Statement." Pp. 210–218 in *This Bridge Called My Back: Writings by Radical Women of Color*, edited by C. Moraga and G. Anzaldúa. Albany, NY: SUNY Press.

Cornell, Drucilla. 2000. "Las Greñudas: Recollections on Consciousness-Raising." *Signs* 25(4):1033–1039.

Cotera, Martha P. 1976. *Diosa Y Hembra: The History and Heritage of Chicanas in the U.S.* Austin, Texas: Statehouse Printing.

Crenshaw, Kimberlé. 1991. "Mapping the Margins: Intersectionality, Identity Politics, and Violence against Women of Color." *Stanford Law Review* 43(6):1241–1299.

Crenshaw, Kimberlé. 1989. "Demarginalizing the Intersection of Race and Sex: A Black Feminist Critique of Antidiscrimination Doctrine, Feminist Theory and Antiracist Policies." *University of Chicago Legal Forum* 1989(1):139–167.

Crossley, Alison Dahl. 2017a. *Finding Feminism: Millennial Activists and the Unfinished Gender Revolution.* New York: New York University Press.

Crossley, Alison Dahl. 2017b. "Women's Activism and Educational Institutions." Pp. 582–601 in *The Oxford Handbook of U.S. Women's Social Movement Activism*, edited by H. J. McCammon, V. Taylor, J. Reger and R. L. Einwohner. Oxford, UK: Oxford University Press.

Davis, Kathy. 2008. "Intersectionality as Buzzword: A Sociology of Science Perspective on What Makes a Feminist Theory Successful." *Feminist Theory* 9(1):67–85.

Espinoza, Dionne. 2001. "'Revolutionary Sisters': Women's Solidarity and Collective Identification among Chicana Brown Berets in East Los Angeles, 1967–1970." *Aztlán* 26:17.

Friedman, Debra and Doug McAdam. 1992. "Collective Identity and Activism: Networks, Choices, and the Life of a Social Movement." Pp. 156–173 in *Frontiers in Social Movement Theory*, edited by A. D. Morris and C. M. Mueller. New Haven, CT: Yale University Press.

Gamson, William A. 1992. "The Social Psychology of Collective Action." Pp. 53–76 in *Frontiers in Social Movement Theory*, edited by A. D. Morris and C. M. Mueller. New Haven, CT: Yale University Press.

García, Elena H. 1997. "Chicana Consciousness: A New Perspective, A New Hope." Pp. 39–40 in *Chicana Feminist Thought: The Basic Historical Writings*, edited by A. M. García. New York, NY: Routledge.

García Bedolla, Lisa. 2005. *Fluid Borders: Latino Power, Identity, and Politics in Los Angeles*. Berkeley, CA: University of California Press.

Glenn, Evelyn Nakano. 1992. "From Servitude to Service Work: Historical Continuities in the Racial Division of Paid Reproductive Labor." *Signs* 18(1):1–43.

Gutiérrez, Elena R. 2008. *Fertile Matters: The Politics of Mexican-Origin Women's Reproduction*. Austin, TX: University of Texas Press.

Hardy-Fanta, Carol. 1993. *Latina Politics, Latino Politics: Gender, Culture, and Political Participation in Boston*. Philadelphia, PA: Temple University Press.

Hondagneu-Sotelo, Pierrette. 2001. *Doméstica: Immigrant Workers Cleaning and Caring in the Shadows of Affluence*. Berkeley, CA: University of California Press.

hooks, bell. 1994. *Teaching to Transgress: Education as the Practice of Freedom*. New York, NY: Routledge.

Hull, Gloria T., Patricia Bell Scott and Barbara Smith, eds. 1982. *All the Women Are White, All the Men Are Black, but Some of Us Are Brave: Black Women's Studies*. Old Westbury, NY: Feminist Press.

Hunt, Scott A. and Robert D. Benford. 2007. "Collective Identity, Solidarity, and Commitment." Pp. 433–457 in *The Blackwell Companion to Social Movements*, edited by D. A. Snow, S. A. Soule and H. Kriesi. Oxford, UK: Wiley-Blackwell.

Hurtado, Aída. 2003. *Voicing Chicana Feminisms: Young Women Speak Out on Sexuality and Identity*. New York: New York University Press.

Hurtado, Aída. 1998. "Sitios y Lenguas: Chicanas Theorize Feminisms." *Hypatia* 13 (2):134–161.

Klandermans, Bert. 2014. "Identity Politics and Politicized Identities: Identity Processes and the Dynamics of Protest." *Political Psychology* 35(1):1–22.

Lemieux, Jamilah. 2017, "Why I'm Skipping the Women's March on Washington": COLORLINES. Retrieved January 17, 2017. http://www.colorlines.com/arti cles/why-im-skipping-womens-march-washington-opinion.

Lozano, Adele, ed. 2015. *Latina/o College Student Leadership: Emerging Theory, Promising Practice*. Lanham, MD: Lexington Books.

Luft, Rachel E. and Jane Ward. 2009. "Toward an Intersectionality Just out of Reach: Confronting Challenges to Intersectional Practice." *Advances in Gender Research* 13:9–37.

Luna, Zakiya. 2009. "From Rights to Justice: Women of Color Changing the Face of Reproductive Justice Organizing." *Societies Without Borders* 4:343–365.

Moraga, Cherríe and Gloria Anzaldúa, eds. 1983 [1981]. *This Bridge Called My Back Writings by Radical Women of Color*. New York: Kitchen Table Women of Color Press.

Mosthof, Mariella. 2017, "If You're Not Talking About the Criticism Surrounding the Women's March Then You're Part of the Problem." *Bustle*. Retrieved January 30, 2017. https://www.bustle.com/p/if-youre-not-talking-about-the-criti cism-surrounding-the-womens-march-then-youre-part-of-the-problem-33491.

Naples, Nancy. 1992. "Activist Mothering: Cross-Generational Continuity in the Community Work of Women from Low Income Urban Neighborhoods." *Gender & Society* 6(3):441–463.

Nieto-Gómez, Ana. 1997. "Chicana Feminism" Pp. 52–57 in *Chicana Feminist Thought: The Basic Historical Writings*, edited by A. M. García. New York: Routledge.

Nieto-Gómez, Ana. 1974. "La Feminista." *Encuentro Femenil* 1(2):34–47.

Ogunyemi, Chikwenye Okonjo 1985. "Womanism: The Dynamics of the Contemporary Black Female Novel in English." *Signs* 11(1):63–80.

Pardo, Mary. 2017. "Latinas in U.S. Social Movements." Pp. 643–663 in *The Oxford Handbook of U.S. Women's Social Movement Activism*, edited by H. J. McCammon, V. Taylor, J. Reger and R. L. Einwohner. Oxford, UK: Oxford University Press.

Pardo, Mary. 1999. "Gendered Citizenship: Mexican American Women and Grassroots Activism in East Los Angeles, 1986–1992." Pp. 58–79 in *Chicano Politics and Society in the Late 20th Century*, edited by D. Montejano. Austin, TX: University of Austin Press.

Peña, Milagros. 2007. *Latina Activists Across Borders: Women's Grassroots Organizing in Mexico and Texas*. Durham, NC: Duke University Press.

Pérez, Emma. 1999. *The Decolonial Imaginary: Writing Chicanas into History*. Bloomington, IN: Indiana University Press.

Pérez, Emma. 1991. "Sexuality and Discourse: Notes from a Chicana Survivor." Pp. 159–184 in *Chicana Lesbians: The Girls Our Mothers Warned Us About*, edited by C. Trujillo. Berkeley, CA: Third Woman Press.

Polletta, Francesca and James M. Jasper. 2001. "Collective Identity and Social Movements." *Annual Review of Sociology* 27:283–305.

Reger, Jo. 2017. "Contemporary Feminism and Beyond." Pp. 109–128 in *The Oxford Handbook of U.S. Women's Social Movement Activism*, edited by H. J. McCammon, V. Taylor, J. Reger and R. L. Einwohner. Oxford, UK: Oxford University Press.

Reger, Jo. 2012. *Everywhere and Nowhere: Contemporary Feminism in the United States*. Oxford, UK: Oxford University Press.

Robnett, Belinda. 1997. *How Long? How Long?: African American Women in the Struggle for Civil Rights*. Oxford, UK: Oxford University Press.

Roth, Benita. 2017. "Intersectionality: Origins, Travels, Questions, and Contributions." Pp. 129–149 in *The Oxford Handbook of U.S. Women's Social Movement Activism*, edited by H. J. McCammon, V. Taylor, J. Reger and R. L. Einwohner. Oxford, UK: Oxford University Press.

Roth, Benita. 2004. *Separate Roads to Feminism: Black, Chicana, and White Feminist Movements in America's Second Wave*. Cambridge, UK: Cambridge University Press.

Ruiz, Vicki L. 2008 [1998]. *From out of the Shadows: Mexican American Women in Twentieth-Century America*. Oxford, UK: Oxford University Press.

Rupp, Leila J. and Verta Taylor. 1999. "Forging Feminist Identity in an International Movement: A Collective Identity Approach to Feminism." *Signs* 24:363–386.

Saldívar-Hull, Sonia. 1991. "Feminism on the Border: From gender politics to geopolitics" Pp. 203–220 in *Criticism in the Borderlands: Studies in Chicano Literature, Culture, and Ideology*, edited by H. Calderón and J.D. Saldívar. Durham, NC: Duke University Press.

Sandoval, Chela. 1991. "Us Third World Feminism: The Theory and Method of Oppositional Consciousness in the Postmodern World." *Genders* 10:1–24.

Segura, Denise A. 2001. "Challenging the ChicanO Text: Towards a More Inclusive Contemporary 'Causa'." *Signs* 26(2):542–550.

Segura, Denise A. 1994. "Beyond Machismo: Chicanas, Work and Family." Paper presented at the Sixth European Conference on Latino Cultures in the United States, July 7–10, Bordeaux.

Segura, Denise A. 1984. "Chicanas and Triple Oppression in the Labor Force." Paper presented at the National Association for Chicana and Chicano Studies Annual Conference, Austin, Texas.

Segura, Denise A. and Patricia Zavella. 2016. "Borderlands." Pp 1–5 in *The Wiley Blackwell Encyclopedia of Gender and Sexuality Studies* edited by N. A. Naples, R. C. Hoogland, M. Wickramasinghe and W. C. A. Wong. Hoboken, NJ: John Wiley & Sons.

Segura, Denise A. and Elisa Facio. 2008. "Adelante Mujer: Latina Activism, Feminism, and Empowerment." Pp. 294–307 in *Latinas/os in the United States: Changing the Face of America*, edited by H. Rodríguez, R. Sáenz and C. Menjívar. New York, NY: Springer.

Simon, Bernd and Bert Klandermans. 2001. "Politicized Collective Identity." *American Psychologist* 56(4):319–331.

Smith, Dorothy E. 1987. *The Everyday World as Problematic: A Feminist Sociology.* Boston, MA: Northeastern University Press.

Solis, Marie. 2017, "How the Women's March's "Genital-Based" Feminism Isolated the Transgender Community." *Mic.* Retrieved January 23, 2017. https://mic.com/articles/166273/how-the-women-s-march-s-genital-based-feminism-isolated-the-transgender-community#.UaUlMdwu4.

Staggenborg, Suzanne and Verta Taylor. 2005. "Whatever Happened to the Women's Movement?" *Mobilization: The International Journal of Research and Theory about Social Movements, Protest, and Collective Behavior* 10(1):37–52.

Taft, Jessica. 2010. *Rebel Girls: Youth Activism and Social Change Across the Americas.* New York, NY: New York University Press.

Taylor, Verta and Nancy E. Whittier. 1992. "Collective Identity in Social Movement Communities: Lesbian Feminist Mobilization." Pp. 104–129 in *Frontiers in Social Movement Theory*, edited by A. D. Morris and C. M. Mueller. New Haven, CT: Yale University Press.

Thompson, Becky. 2002. "Multiracial Feminism: Recasting the Chronology of Second Wave Feminism." *Feminist Studies* 28(2):337–360.

Trujillo, Carla, ed. 1998. *Living Chicana Theory.* Berkeley, CA: Third Woman Press.

Trujillo, Carla. 1997. "Chicana Lesbians: Fear and Loathing in the Chicano Community." Pp. 281–287 in *Chicana Feminist Thought: The Basic Historical Writings*, edited by A. M. García. New York, NY: Routledge.

Viterna, Jocelyn. 2013. *Women in War: The Micro-Processes of Mobilization in El Salvador.* Oxford, UK: Oxford University Press.

Walker, Alice. 1983. *In Search of Our Mothers' Gardens: Womanist Prose.* New York, NY: Harcourt Brace Jovanovich.

Whittier, Nancy. 1995. *Feminist Generations: The Persistence of the Radical Women's Movement.* Philadelphia, PA: Temple University Press.

Yosso, Tara J. 2005. "Whose Culture Has Capital? A Critical Race Theory Discussion of Community Cultural Wealth." *Race, Ethnicity, and Education* 8(1):69–91.

Zavella, Patricia. 1987. *Women's Work and Chicano Families: Cannery Workers of the Santa Clara Valley.* Ithaca, NY: Cornell University Press.

3 Already Feminists

Transfeminist Histories, Hurdles and Futures

Miriam J. Abelson

Some feminists seem to imagine that transgender people exist at one end or another of two extremes. One end suggests that trans people are gender warriors who will ultimately breakdown long-standing restrictive ideas of binary gender (e.g., Butler 2004; Risman, Lorber and Sherwood 2012). The other end assumes that trans people reinforce traditional notions of gender, either by existing in a binary or through reemphasizing gender difference (see Connell 2012 for examples). In reality, neither of these extremes captures the complicated relationship that transgender people have to gender and to feminist movements. As Susan Stryker (2017: 5) writes, "It is neither radical or reactionary to embrace a trans identity." Yet, trans people have found themselves in the middle of some of the most contentious debates among 20th- and 21st-century feminists. Further, trans people's lives have been at the center of feminist theorizing for decades, often as objects of study rather than active subjects or agents in their own lives (Schilt and Lagos 2017). What these debates and this theorizing tend to forget is that, through all of this, some trans people have been feminists all along. In fact, they have been creating their own gender theories and politics that are at the forefront of feminist futures.

The dominant narrative of trans people and feminist movements usually focuses on tensions between radical feminists and trans people from the 1970s to today. This centers on how some radical feminists' politics and particular understandings of gender exclude transgender people from feminist spaces. This frequent retelling is important because it demonstrates a key tension around inclusion and exclusion in feminist movements and the damages the exclusion of trans people can do. While likely giving undue attention to what is often a small minority of feminists, the way this narrative is typically framed ignores two crucial things: First, that as long as there have been transgender people and feminist movements, there have been trans people active in them. In other words, trans people have already and always been feminists. Second, while the trans exclusionary feminists have been particularly vocal, there were often just as many, if not more, cisgender feminists who did not seek to exclude, and even fought to include, trans people in the movements. That said, even when feminist movements have been inclusive towards trans people, the movements and politics often center cisgender women and their concerns.

Through an examination of both historical and contemporary trans feminist issues and activism, along with the everyday experiences of trans men, this chapter complicates the relationship between trans people and feminism. I use trans to refer both to people who identify as transgender and, in a broader sense, to mean a crossing of gendered and other boundaries. Using this understanding, the chapter documents how there have always been trans feminists. Further, that the divisions that do exist between some feminists and trans people are not as clear in the past or today as some stories would have us believe. Trans people do not have one connection to feminist movements, but have many different relationships with feminisms. Finally, trans people are creating transfeminist futures both for themselves and for all people who embrace transfeminist ideologies.

Trans Feminist Histories and Tensions

Pauli Murray, while never working under the banner of transfeminism, is one example of a historical trans figure that undertook the work of feminism at the intersections of race, gender, and economic justice. Murray was a feminist and civil rights activist who battled against both the racial segregation of Jim Crow and what she termed "Jane Crow," meaning the unequal status of women in U.S. society. According to Susan Ware (2002:55), "Pauli Murray was involved in practically all the major developments that historians write about when they try to make sense of the twentieth century, especially the movements for social change that have been so central to its history. Pauli Murray was a nexus of activism and history on civil rights, feminism, religion, literature, law, and sexuality." While never labeling herself transgender, though that term existed in Murray's lifetime, she is considered by many scholars and activists to be part of the broader trans experience due to her life-long gender nonconformity and efforts to access medical transition earlier in her life.[1]

Murray began her activism in the years between what is thought of as the first and second wave of U.S. feminist activism. She started combatting racial segregation in the 1930s and was eventually arrested for refusing to leave the whites' only section of a segregated bus. She also challenged the exclusion of people of color from prominent white universities and women from men's-only institutions. However, she herself was unsuccessful in her attempts to attend graduate school at the University of North Carolina due to her race and Harvard Law due to her gender. Finally accepted to Howard Law School in 1941, in her time there Murray developed the legal theory that would underlie the NAACP's successful case in *Brown v. Board of Education*. However, she developed her idea of Jane Crow and a burgeoning feminist politics when she faced gender discrimination at Howard, even though she was the top student in the program and had a brilliant legal mind (Mack 2012). Later, she was a founding member of the National Organization for Women (NOW) and brought feminist issues into the work of the American Civil Liberties Union (ACLU) in the late 1960s and early 1970s (Rosenberg 2002). Ruth Bader Ginsburg, long before she was a Supreme Court Justice herself, credits her work with Pauli Murray at the ACLU as one of the key influences on her early legal victories for women's rights.

Through her diaries, Murray acknowledged that in her own life she defied easy racial, gender, and class categorization. Long before Kimberlé Crenshaw coined the term "intersectionality," Murray named the impossibility of separating her identities and that she could not "be fragmented into Negro at one time, woman at another, or worker at another" (Hartmann 2002:76). Intensely private about her gender and sexuality, she confided in a few others that she "felt more male than female." She tried to seek access to masculinizing hormone therapy and surgery in the 1930s and 1940s, and expressed a specific desire for "monogamous married life" with a heterosexual woman (Mack 2012). Her gender and sexuality were the cause of much distress and she was hospitalized due to related emotional problems several times in this period. Murray had relationships with women and expressed her gender in a nonconforming way throughout her life, but never used the words lesbian or transgender to describe herself. In addition to having a somewhat ambiguous gender presentation and identity, her racial identity was also difficult to classify. She was light-skinned with a mixed-race background, though she did identify heavily with her African American heritage.

Regardless of her own identities, she found that her race and gender were categorized differently based on local norms of race and gender as she travelled around the United States (Fisher 2016). Much of Murray's activism and legal thinking was based on a frustration with what she saw as arbitrary but rigid categorizations based on race, gender, and class that formed the basis for broader inequalities (Rosenberg 2002). She spent much of her life in poverty, due to difficulty in finding well-paying work. For example, her gender nonconforming presentation and relationships with women were likely the reason that she was never offered a paid position at the NAACP (Mack 2012). Thus, Murray's own gender nonconformity and sexuality affected her psychological and economic well-being. As a historical trans figure she faced many similar difficulties that transgender-identified activists faced when engaging in movements for social justice, especially trans women in the United States women's movement from the 1970s to today.

Lesbian Feminism

Lesbian feminism is a particular kind of radical feminism that gained prominence in the 1970s in a number of Anglophone countries. Exemplified in the 1970 manifesto by Radicalesbians, "The Woman-Identified-Woman," lesbian feminism called on women to turn from a patriarchal and male-centric existence to new lives centered on other women. Beyond understanding lesbian as simply a description of a sexual orientation, this was a political lesbianism where women chose to put their social and political energies fully into other women. Central to this ideology was a focus on creating women-only, and sometimes lesbian-only, spaces and cultures (Echols 1989). These women, often called separatists, were interested in withdrawing from the patriarchal male-centric world and forming new radical ways of living (Shugar 1995).

Lesbian feminists faced many critiques due to their separatist ideology, including from women of color, who were often not willing to give up organizing with men of color to work solely with white women (Combahee River Collective 1983). In addition to these critiques, the other practical problem that quickly emerged with this ideology was the question of where to draw the line of separatism. This meant grappling with the issue of who counts as a woman and who does not. While both trans and cisgender women were radical feminists and lesbian feminists, contention over how to define the boundaries of womanhood caused a series of controversies around the inclusion and exclusion of transgender people, particularly trans women, in women's spaces.

Despite narratives that paint all radical feminists as hostile to the idea of recognizing trans women as women, feminists in the second wave generation were both welcoming and hostile to transgender people. For example, radical socialist feminist Shalumith Firestone saw revolutionary possibilities in the use of medical technology, unlike trans exclusionary writers, such as Mary Daly and Janice Raymond, who saw trans people as, at best, dupes of the medical industry, and at worst as agents of patriarchy trying to sow dissension in feminist movements. Firestone thought that medical innovation could lead to new possibilities, such as people of all sexes giving birth to children, which would be a means for the "underclass" of women to ultimately undermine the larger system of gender (Stryker 2017: 136). Other prominent radical feminists, such as Andrea Dworkin and Catherine MacKinnon, who aligned with conservatives in their anti-pornography work, saw "woman" as a political rather than biological designation. They supported free access to transition-related medical care for trans people (Williams 2016).

Noting that not all radical feminists were hostile to trans women does not erase the harm caused by exclusionary feminists, such as Janice Raymond, who encouraged others to exclude and demonize trans people. Raymond and other exclusionary lesbian feminists claimed at times that the very presence of trans women in women's spaces was an act of rape. This hostility has caused documented negative impacts on trans people's mental and physical well-being. Further, Raymond's writing was at least partially responsible for framing medical transitions as controversial, which was used to change U.S. health policy in the early 1980s so that public funds and private insurers were not required to provide transition-related care (Williams 2014). There was immediate resistance to Raymond's work by trans feminists, such as Carol Riddell. Riddell showed that by attacking trans people, Raymond scapegoated a relatively small group of people instead of addressing larger patriarchal relations. Further, she showed that this analysis ignored the experiences of transgender people, as well as rigidly defined who could be feminist and who could not (Riddell 1980).

By examining a few well-known controversies from this time, centered around Beth Elliott, Sandy Stone, and Sylvia Rivera, it becomes clear that the inclusion and exclusion of trans women and trans issues more broadly was more complicated in this early period than common historical narratives would suggest. While there were lesbian feminists who fought to exclude trans women, there were both cisgender and trans feminists who fought for their inclusion.

Beth Elliott

Beth Elliott was a politically-oriented trans folk singer in the 1970s and a participant in lesbian and feminist organizations, even serving as vice president of the San Francisco chapter of the Daughters of Billitis (DOB), an early lesbian social and political organization. Elliot had transitioned in her late teens and identified as a lesbian and a feminist, in addition to participating in the anti-war movement. After questions arose over trans women being welcome in DOB, Elliot and another trans woman were ousted from the organization after a close vote. Several cisgender members resigned in protest of the exclusion, including the entire cisgender staff of the organization's newsletter, *Sisters* (The Tide Collective 2016). In fact, the Tide Collective, another lesbian feminist organization that published the magazine *Lesbian Tide*, voted to include trans women earlier that same day and sent a telegram urging the members of DOB to do the same. The Tide Collective wrote:

> Those who vote no tonight vote with our oppressors. Those who vote yes recognize that none of us is free unless all of us are free. Please advise our transsexual sisters that, if they are not welcome in the liberal city of San Francisco, they are most welcome in the city of Los Angeles.
>
> (2016: 277)

While DOB did not heed the words of the Tide Collective, this illustrates that some organizations had a wider view of lesbian feminist sisterhood.

Elliott again was at the center of controversy when she was invited to perform at the 1973 West Coast Lesbian Feminist Conference, one of the largest early gatherings of lesbian feminists. Some exclusionary feminists did not want Elliot to be allowed at the conference because they did not accept that she was a woman. According to organizer Jeanne Córdova, the organizers of the conference held a trans inclusive stance before, during, and after the event, but the keynote speaker, feminist Robin Morgan, used violent rhetoric to advocate for excluding Elliott. Despite Morgan's speech, the majority of the attendees actually voted to allow Elliott to perform (Bettcher 2016; Stryker 2017). The controversy deepened when a college friend, also a lesbian feminist, accused Elliot of sexually harassing her years before. Elliott performed, but did not participate further in the conference.

Regardless of the truth of the allegations, it is clear this incident became the basis for the damaging myth that transgender women join feminist movements to sexually assault and control other women. The framing by some feminists of Elliot being a man invading women spaces and of trans women as sexually threatening during these events have remained in some feminist spaces to the current day (Phipps 2016). However, there is no evidence that transgender people are more likely to commit sexual assault in general or in feminist communities, but there is plenty of evidence that transgender people experience high rates of sexual assault and other forms of violence (James et al. 2016). Unwelcome in some lesbian-feminist circles, Beth Elliott continued her feminist activism, focusing on transgender and bisexual inclusion, as well as sex positivity (Sides 2009).

Sandy Stone

Perhaps the most well-known controversy between trans exclusionary lesbian feminists and transgender lesbian feminists erupted in the late 1970s around a recording engineer for Olivia Records, Sandy Stone. Olivia was an all-women collectively run record label whose members reached out to Stone to join the collective and, due to the lack of well-trained women sound engineers, planned to set up a sort of school to train other aspiring women engineers. Prior to coming to Olivia Records, Stone had worked as a recording engineer for A&M records and had engineered albums for artists such as Jimi Hendrix and Van Morrison (Gabriel 1995). Stone had always been open as trans to the other women in the collective, but when this fact was publicized to a wider audience, at least partially through Raymond's book *The Transsexual Empire* in 1979, Olivia started receiving complaints and threats about Stone being part of an all-women record label.

The Olivia collective was supportive of Stone and tried to respond to the controversy through dialogue with the broader feminist community. As Stone explained, "Of course, there was a tremendous amount of support. There was no question of that, but there was this absolutely intractable, small, but extremely 'moral majority,' that never let up, and eventually began to do things like threaten boycotts" (Gabriel 1995: 18). In addition to the boycott, the collective received threats of violence, going so far as to threaten murdering Stone if she was allowed to remain in the collective. In another moment of confrontation, a separatist group in Seattle called the

Gorgons showed up armed with guns to an Olivia show where Stone was running the soundboard. Olivia's security disarmed the Gorgons and kept a semblance of peace, but it was a harrowing experience for Stone and the rest of the collective (Williams 2016).

After choosing to leave the collective and protect them from what could have been a disastrous boycott, Stone returned to Santa Cruz. There she had a similar experience with divisions in the local feminist community where some feminists accepted her and others did not. Stone eventually completed a PhD at the University of California Santa Cruz, working with feminist scholar Donna Haraway. In 1989, she published "The Post-Transsexual Manifesto," a reply to Raymond's book, and that essay is considered one of the central founding texts of transgender studies (Stryker 2006).

Sylvia Rivera

Since lesbian feminists were a vocal part of both feminist and gay liberation movements, the controversies over who counted as a woman and a lesbian were prominent in both movements. Sylvia Rivera, a Puerto Rican and Venezuelan trans activist, had been organizing under gay liberation since the Stonewall Riots in June of 1969. She founded an organization, STAR, along with her friend Marsha P. Johnson, to support gay and gender-variant street kids with an explicit focus on racial, economic, gender, and sexual justice. While Rivera and STAR worked well with revolutionary groups, such as the Young Lords and the Black Panthers, her outspoken and sometimes coarse style created friction with radical gay and lesbian organizers. This tension came to a head at the 1973 Christopher Street Liberation Day March, when lesbian feminists worked to ban trans individuals, such as Rivera, from speaking (Lewis 2017).[2] Lesbian feminist Jean O'Leary took to the stage to critique the inclusion of people who at the time identified as drag queens or crossdressers, because, according to the lesbian feminist groups, they were parodying women. The event devolved into chaos, and, partly in response to O'Leary, Rivera took to the stage, even though she had been denied permission earlier to speak. Amid boos from the crowd, Rivera spoke to the relevance of her experiences in relation to other women, specifically that she too had been raped and beaten by heterosexual men. She gave an incisive critique of the gay and feminist movements' exclusions of poor people, people of color and transgender people and then spoke on the work of STAR, calling for the kind of broad-based revolutionary solidarity that is at the core of many feminisms today. While Rivera continued her activism on and off throughout her life, these events left her disillusioned with the radical gay movement (Gan 2013). More recently, Rivera has been recuperated as a hero of queer and trans politics by newer generations of activists, including having the Sylvia Rivera Law Project named after her. This organization works to provide legal, health, and other low-income services to transgender, intersex, and gender nonconforming people of color.

While feminists such as Janice Raymond have not changed their views and Sylvia Rivera never got the support of cisgender feminists that she deserved, some lesbian feminists, including Jean O'Leary, did come around. Years later, reflecting on the events of the march in 1973 and also a later campaign that excluded trans people, O'Leary said, "I found this so embarrassing because my views have changed so much since then" (Marcus 1992: 267). After spending more time around transgender people, O'Leary had realized her earlier shortsightedness. This change of heart does not undo the harm caused by her exclusionary practices, but illustrates how activists have the capacity for growth and change.

The more well-known moments of exclusion by lesbian feminists center on the question of whether trans woman should be included in women-only spaces. However, their strict definitions of gender excluded others as well. Radical and lesbian feminists also critiqued any gendered roles, including the butch-femme roles that had been so central to earlier lesbian communities. This critique had the effect of excluding some people who were assigned female at birth but expressed a masculine presentation, whether or not they identified themselves as transgender or not. Thus, these narrow definitions of gender excluded trans-masculine people as well as trans feminine people, for example as illustrated in Leslie Feinberg's (1993) novel *Stone Butch Blues*.[3] Indeed, the notion of women-only spaces in general often leads to the exclusion of non-binary people. Where might Pauli Murray's gender nonconformity and feminist activism fit in the separatist logic? Both in the past and today, binary and exclusionary feminist ideologies seem to narrow the scope and transformative possibilities of feminist politics.

Ongoing Tensions

Debates among feminists about the inclusion of trans people in women-only spaces did not end in the 1970s, but continue to today. It is true that there are fewer strict women-only feminist spaces than in the past. However, these tensions of inclusion and exclusion still play out, because essentialist ideas about gender persist that do not recognize trans women as women, trans men as men, and other trans people as having valid genders. Even the long-running controversy over the "women-born-women" policy at the Michigan's Women's Music Festival, which excluded trans women, concluded when the organizers decided to end the event in 2015 rather than changing their policy. At the same time, both exclusionary feminists and conservative politicians have made transgender people's access to public sex-segregated bathrooms the most prominent contemporary battleground of this conflict. These tensions and exclusions are not just evident in the United States, Canada, and the United Kingdom, but they echo globally, such as in recent skirmishes between trans and cisgender feminists on the streets of Istanbul, Turkey (Zengin 2016).

A small but vocal group of feminists still organize today to exclude and critique trans people. The term TERF, meaning Trans Exclusionary Radical Feminist, gained popularity among trans activists in the late 2000s, especially in online spaces, to describe exclusionary feminists such as Raymond and Sheila Jeffreys. Meant as a neutral descriptive term, many of the individuals who are labeled as TERFS find it to be offensive and prefer to be called "gender critical." However, as Sara Ahmed (2016) points out, this naming implies that somehow trans feminists and activists are "uncritical" of gender and associated power relations. This framing of transfeminist activism is another example, according to Ahmed, of the ways that transphobia chips away at the existence of trans people and how cisgender privilege allows some feminists to avoid this "hammering." Through an analysis of several recent controversies in Britain involving exclusionary feminists who publicly assert that trans women are not women, Sally Hines (2005, 2017) documents how this group of feminists represent a stream in contemporary feminist thought that relies on an essentialist biological understanding of gender and what it means to be a woman. While these extreme views are marginal among most feminists, they have gained ample media coverage and been subject to considerable online discussion. Exclusionary feminists' notoriety is also likely a partial backlash against greater trans visibility. In response, there have been efforts in Britain and the United States by cisgender and trans feminists to protest and even seek to cancel speaking engagements by some exclusionary feminists. The controversy is likely amplified by exclusionary feminists' efforts to connect the criticism they receive about their views to larger debates about censorship and free speech (Hines 2017). Ahmed (2016) notes that rather than acknowledging that trans activists' critiques are also an expression of free speech, trans people and allies are labeled as censors and made out to be unreasonable and unfairly silencing when they point out the violent effects of the transphobia of exclusionary feminists.

Everyday Trans Feminist Engagement and Resistance

Thus far, this chapter has focused mostly on trans women and on public and well-known controversies of the past, but how do these tensions among feminists play out in the experiences of everyday trans people? The lives of most trans individuals and most feminists do not become major controversies that get extensive media coverage. Yet, individuals grapple with the effects of those larger tensions along with a myriad of individual and historical factors as they attempt to make sense of their own relationship to feminism. In interviews with everyday trans people, Hines (2005) found that trans women reported experiencing rejection from lesbian and feminist communities and women-only spaces. Trans women also feel pressures to perform normative femininity to gain access to medical transition. At the same time, trans women are aware of critiques of trans femininity. Many trans women consciously work against these stereotypes to reject normative femininity and embrace a wider range of gender presentations. They even sometimes critique other trans women for performing normative femininity. Like many people, they are navigating the difficulties of managing to exist between trying to achieve feminist ideals and the very real pressures of trying to survive in a patriarchal (not to mention white supremacist and heteronormative) society.

Trans men have their own unique experiences and relationships to feminist identities and movements. From 2009 to 2013, I interviewed 66 trans men, people who were assigned female at birth and transition to live as men, living in the U.S. South, Midwest and West, to better understand their lives as men. Their relationships to feminism kept popping up in the interviews, even though I had not planned on asking them about it. Like one would find with most groups of people, some of the men identified as feminists and others did not. Further, as men and as trans people, they had particularly complicated relationships to feminist movements. In all, they were more likely to engage in and support feminist politics if they understood feminism as multiple, that is, as varied feminisms versus a monolithic feminist politic or movement. When the interviewees understood feminism as singular with a fairly rigid political view, they were more likely to reject feminism as outdated and too narrow. Trans men's engagements with and resistance to feminism provide some important lessons for trans and cis feminists who are interested in building broader movements.

Engaging Feminisms

As I have written elsewhere (Abelson 2016), a majority of the men I interviewed identified as feminists, though the individual form of that feminism was highly varied. Like many trans-masculine people who have written about their relationship to feminism, most of this group spent part of their lives in feminist or women-centric communities. These men embody Bobby Noble's (2006) framing of trans-masculine people as "sons of the movement." The "sons" do not infiltrate feminist movements, but are instead a vibrant part of the movement, acting as emissaries to bring feminism into the rest of the world through masculine bodies. That is not to say that these men did not have conflicts with other feminists or some aspect of feminist politics, but their personal articulations of feminist commitments meshed with trans and/or masculine identities.

For Saul, positive encounters with feminism and his development of a feminist identity were made possible through time living as a woman, and strengthened through his experience in trans politics and communities. He said, "I think if I had been born male I would have been a chauvinist like my father [he laughs] but it's like I had this other experience and other exposures and that was a really good thing." Saul's experience is a commonly reported route to feminist identity for trans-masculine people, but certainly does not guarantee an individual's investment in feminist or trans politics (Hale 1998).

The key for many of these men in maintaining a feminist identity was their ability to recognize that there is not one definition of feminism or way to be a feminist, but instead there are *feminisms*, through which to build politics and identity. Many trans men had positive experiences with other feminists, and also had interactions with feminists who were hostile to trans men. Some feminists denied that trans men were or could possibly be men, and others ostracized them from organizations and larger communities either because they were transgender, men, or both. According to Alan, another trans man in his community was pushed to commit suicide after engaging with a group of feminists who said he could never be a man and implied that taking testosterone would make him hurt women. Alan worked to resist this group's ideologies and despite this struggle, he did not see all feminists as bad. He explained, "It's only a small subset of feminists that do that, but there's enough of them and they're loud enough and they put that agenda out there. But there are other feminists that are like, 'I don't care what you are as long as you treat everyone fair.'" Like Alan, many of the men I interviewed clearly understood that no one group represented all feminists. The interviewees described these feminists as "second wave" and "lesbian feminists" and contrasted them to third or fourth wave feminists that were more attentive to intersectionality and the possibilities of trans feminism. Through the ways that interviewees talked about this difference it is possible to see both the potential harmful effects of exclusionary feminist ideas on trans people and the potential to construct feminist discourse that creates new alliances among feminists. As I have previously illustrated (Abelson 2016), trans men often rejected exclusionary kinds of feminism, even if it was the framework that began their feminist consciousness, because they disagreed with its essentialist understandings of sex and gender and poor treatment of both transgender and masculine people. This also illustrates how common narratives about second wave and lesbian feminism reflect only the exclusion of trans people and not the lesbian feminists who called for inclusion.

Resisting Feminism

Trans men who were suspect of or rejected feminism represented about one third of the interviewees. Aaron said, "I think I'm a small minority, but I have a really negative reaction to feminism." Some of these men cited the explicitly transphobic positions of some feminists, but they also tended to distance themselves from feminism because of the way they defined feminism itself. The interviewees who resisted feminism were less likely to identify as feminists in the past, although some certainly had. This group was like many cisgender men who are not particularly interested in taking on a feminist identity for themselves.

I have shown (Abelson 2016) that these non- and anti-feminist men saw feminism as only representing the interests of the narrow subject position of women who were cisgender, white and class-privileged. In some ways, this echoes the many critiques of dominant feminism from women of color feminists that form the basis for intersectional feminist analyses (Combahee River Collective 1983; Crenshaw 1989). The women-centered nature of some feminist spaces also represented a conflict with their masculine identities. For example, Aaron said he resented that his feminist mother had taken him to women's meetings because being in those spaces conflicted with his male identity. He said, "I was pretty uncomfortable. There's a zillion women and then me." Not only did Aaron have a negative reaction to feminism in general but also being forced by his mother into spaces that were meant exclusively for women made him uncomfortable and deepened his anti-feminist sentiments. This illustrates both the limits of particular streams of feminism that focus on essentialist understandings of women, and the problems of excluding people who are not women. Though not the only experience that created Aaron's anti-feminist views, perhaps a more gender-inclusive space could have helped him shift to a more positive view of feminism. In contrast to the men who could identify as feminist through a conceptualization of feminisms, the experience of this group, including men like Aaron, illustrates both the limits of individuals with a narrow view of feminist possibilities, but also the limits of feminist movements that are accessible only to some people.

In line with common mainstream post-feminist discourses (McRobbie 2004), some men distanced themselves from feminism because they thought feminism was too strident or no longer necessary. For example, Silas described a character in his favorite novel, "I commend the author for having her get in touch with her feminine side and also making her a very strong character, but not to the point where she was stuck up like feminist characters that are off-putting." Like some other men, Silas appreciated strong women, but thought feminists went too far. Although some agreed with some basic feminist principles, they characterized feminists as man-hating, angry women who did not understand what it was like to be a man. A few of the men, particularly those who had formerly identified as feminists, said that feminists really did not understand men's lives or what it's like to deal with the demands of contemporary masculinity. David explained, "I feel a very limiting factor of feminism is that there really isn't room for men to tell their side of the story...and the gender box is just smaller." Though statements like these could have produced fruitful insights into the construction of masculinity in the contemporary United States, they more often resembled men's rights discourses, which argue that men as a group are the most truly oppressed in contemporary gender systems (Messner 1998).

While the majority of the men I interviewed identified as feminists, or at least believed gender inequality was a problem, there were a few whose views on gender and women conflicted with basic feminist principles. These men espoused both generally misogynist and specifically trans misogynist beliefs by questioning the existence of gender inequality along with joining in exclusionary feminists who question whether trans women belong in women's spaces. For example, several of these men described women in general as overly emotional or questioned whether trans women were authentically women if they did not meet normative standards for feminine appearance. While this was a relatively small group, the views of these trans men should be of particular concern for feminists. This is not to say that all trans men should be feminists or feminist politics are the only paths to social justice activism, but rather that it should be a concern for feminists when they are not. In the end, the onus is on men and other gendered people to examine their misogyny, but also on feminists to create broader movements that address the needs of an even wider swath of marginalized peoples, as both Sylvia Rivera and Pauli Murray asked for so long ago.

Transfeminist Possibilities

Emerging out of broader feminist work alongside early queer studies, transfeminism was first named as such in the early 1990s. One of the earliest articulations of transfeminism is credited to Emi Koyama's (2003) "Transfeminist Manifesto" (Stryker and Bettcher 2016). For Susan Stryker, transfeminism asks us to start with acknowledging that a person's sense of their own gender can be quite individual and does not necessarily reflect their political values and commitments—this is in line with what are commonly considered to be many third (and perhaps fourth) wave feminist generation understandings of the relationship between one's identities and their politics. Transgender and cisgender people alike often have a sense of themselves as being a man or a woman, but only transgender people are usually asked to defend their gender identity as a political choice.

Transfeminists offer new ideas through which to sharpen feminist analysis of gender, race, and other aspects of difference. Julia Serano (2007), for example, in her "Trans Woman Manifesto" coined the term "trans misogyny" to refer to specific discrimination against trans women and trans people who express femininity. She calls for a feminism that brings together people of all genders and sexualities to combat multiple forms of gender inequality. Elías Cosenza Krell finds that Serano's argument and focus on trans misogyny ignores any consideration of race, class, and nation. Thus, it might behoove transfeminists to also consider the term "transmisogynoir" to focus on the violence and discrimination experienced by black and potentially other trans women and trans feminine people of color. This concept builds on Moya Bailey's term "misogynoir," which specifically names the intersection of "racism, antiblackness, and misogyny that black women experience" (Krell 2017: 236). Several edited volumes and special journal issues have explored transfeminism in the academic realm. The 2016 "Trans/Feminism" issue of *TSQ: Trans Studies Quarterly* is a particularly significant contribution. The issue highlights both the variety of transfeminist thinking, cultural production, and activism in Anglophone contexts and the active work outside these dominant spaces, such as in Japan and Latin America, to explore transfeminist possibilities (Stryker and Bettcher 2016).

One promising stream in transfeminist work is activism and scholarship on trans political economy that centers trans and feminist concerns as linked to capitalism, especially in its neoliberal form. Dan Irving (2012) illustrates that the economy has "everything" to do with trans rights. This work makes connections between transgender people and issues including labor, consumption, and the distribution of material resources in local, transnational and global contexts, on topics varying from missing and murdered indigenous women to safe housing and migration (Irving et al. 2017). It can also speak to broader feminist concerns regarding care work and affective labor, such as in Aren Aizura's (2013) work on international medical tourism that shows that white and Asian trans women receive different standards of care in Thai gender clinics.

Recent articulations of transfeminist of color thinking in and out of academic spaces help to point us to the future of transfeminism by engaging with core feminist issues like gendered violence and reproductive justice for populations that are often left out of mainstream feminist thinking and organizing. micha cárdenas, in formulating a vision of reproductive futurity for trans women of color, defines trans of color feminism as, "a feminism that responds to the violence done to trans women of color, and the historical absence of trans women in both white and women of color feminism" (cárdenas 2016: 55). In contrast to images of trans women of color as only victims of violence, her feminist "bioart" project documents her effort to bank reproductive tissue. She finds that there are many obstacles to fulfilling her desire to have children, including financial barriers, insurers that do not cover these procedures and informational barriers, since most trans reproductive health information is geared to trans men's pregnancies. At the same time, new technologies allow her and other trans women to share information and support to make their reproductive goals possible. Reina Gossett (2011) names further, and often insurmountable, barriers to reproductive justice in the prison industrial complex for incarcerated trans people, who are disproportionately people of color and poor. Besides the isolation from family caused by incarceration when they are in the system, including being unable to raise their own children, incarcerated trans people are likely to lack of access to medical care which can lead to loss of reproductive capacity. Further, Gossett (2011: 335) cites attorney Gabriel Arkles, "The only way that trans people are put into facilities that match their gender is by having a type of surgery that may or may not be right for the them, that is nearly impossible to get, and results in sterilization." Using politics linked with art, poetry, theory and new technologies, transfeminists of color are expanding the scope of core feminist issues and creating new possibilities for coalition. Pauli Murray's work, that was both deeply intersectional and questioned fixed categories of gender, race, and class, foreshadowed the powerful potential of trans of color feminist organizing.

Through examining the complex relationships between historical and contemporary feminist movements and trans issues, it is clear that the fabric of feminist pasts and presents are interwoven with trans people and that there have always been trans feminists. Despite simplistic narratives, trans and cisgender feminists alike have fought for the place of trans people in feminist movements, even when those who advocate for exclusion have been the most forceful. This illustrates how cisgender feminists who want to meaningfully include trans people in feminist movements have often failed to have the loudest voices. For those that are interested in building broad-based intersectional feminist movements, this is a history that cannot continue to be repeated. Finally, transfeminism offers one model to meet the potential for more just futures for all who are willing to listen and imagine new possibilities.

Notes

1 I use "she" and "her" to refer to Murray, because those are the pronouns she used, but acknowledge that she might use different pronouns or identify otherwise if she were coming of age today.
2 For an example of similar controversies in San Francisco, see (Stryker 2017).
3 See also (Hollibaugh 2000).

References

Abelson, Miriam J. 2016. "Trans Men Engaging, Reforming, and Resisting Feminisms." *TSQ: Transgender Studies Quarterly* 3(1–2):15–21.

Ahmed, Sara. 2016. "An Affinity of Hammers." *TSQ: Transgender Studies Quarterly* 3 (1–2):22–34.

Aizura, Aren Z. 2013. "The Romance of the Amazing Scalpel: 'Race,' Labor, and Affect in Thai Gender Reassignment Clinics." Pp. 496–511 in *Transgender Studies Reader 2*, edited by S. Stryker and A. Z. Aizura. New York: Routledge.

Bettcher, Talia M. 2016. "A Conversation with Jeanne Córdova." *TSQ: Transgender Studies Quarterly* 3(1–2):285–293.

Butler, Judith. 2004. *Undoing Gender*. New York: Routledge.

cárdenas, micha. 2016. "Pregnancy: Reproductive Futures in Trans of Color Feminism." *TSQ: Transgender Studies Quarterly* 3(1–2):48–57.

Combahee River Collective. 1983. "Combahee River Collective Statement." in *Home girls: A Black feminist anthology*, edited by B. Smith. New York: Kitchen Table Women of Color Press.

Connell, Raewyn. 2012. "Transsexual Women and Feminist Thought: Toward New Understanding and New Politics." *Signs* 37(4):857–881.

Crenshaw, Kimberlé. 1989. "Demarginalizing the Intersection of Race and Sex: A Black Feminist Critique of Antidiscrimination Doctrine, Feminist Theory and Antiracist Politics." *University of Chicago Legal Forum* (1):139–167.

Echols, Alice. 1989. *Daring to Be Bad: Radical Feminism in America, 1967–1975.* Minneapolis, MN: University of Minnesota Press.

Feinberg, Leslie. 1993. *Stone Butch Blues: A Novel.* Ithaca, NY: Firebrand Books.

Fisher, Simon D.Elin. 2016. "Pauli Murray's Peter Panic: Perspectives from the Margins of Gender and Race in Jim Crow America." *TSQ: Transgender Studies Quarterly* 3(1–2):95–103.

Gabriel, Davina Anne. 1995. "Interview with the Transsexual Vampire: Sandy Stone's Dark Gift." *TransSisters* (8):15–27.

Gan, Jessi. 2013. "'Still at the Back of the Bus': Sylvia Rivera's Struggle." Pp. 291–301 in *The Transgender Studies Reader 2*, edited by S. Stryker and A. Z. Aizura. New York, NY: Routledge.

Gossett, Che. 2011. "Abolitionist Imaginings: A Conversation with Bo Brown, Reina Gossett, and Dylan Rodriguez." Pp. 323–343 in *Captive Genders: Trans embodiment and the prison industrial complex*, edited by E. A. Stanley and N. Smith. Oakland, CA: AK Press.

Hale, C. Jacob. 1998. "Tracing a Ghostly Memory in My Throat: Reflections on Ftm Feminist Voice and Agency." Pp. 99–129 in *Men Doing Feminism*, edited by T. Digby. New York, NY: Routledge.

Hartmann, Susan M. 2002. "Pauli Murray and the 'Juncture of Women's Liberation and Black Liberation.'" *Journal of Women's History* 14(2):74–77.

Hines, Sally. 2005. "'I Am a Feminist but…': Transgender Men and Women and Feminism." Pp. 57–77 in *Different Wavelengths: Studies of the Contemporary Women's Movement*, edited by J. Reger. New York, NY: Routledge.

Hines, Sally. 2017. "The Feminist Frontier: On Trans and Feminism." *Journal of Gender Studies*, 1–13.

Hollibaugh, Amber L. 2000. *My Dangerous Desires: A Queer Girl Dreaming Her Way Home.* Durham, NC: Duke University Press.

Irving, Dan. 2012. "Elusive Subject: Notes on the Relationship between Critical Political Economy and Trans Studies." Pp. 153–169 in *Transfeminist Perspectives in and beyond Transgender and Gender Studies*. Philadelphia, PA: Temple University Press.

Irving, Dan, Vek Lewis, Nael Bhanji, Raewyn Connell, Qwo-Li Driskill and Viviane Namaste. 2017. "Trans★ Political Economy Deconstructed: A Roundtable Discussion." *TSQ: Transgender Studies Quarterly* 4(1):16–27.

James, Sandy E., Jody L. Herman, Susan Rankin, Mara Keisling, Lisa Mottet, Ma'ayan Anafi. 2016. *The Report of the 2015 U.S. Transgender Survey.* Washington, DC: National Center for Transgender Equality.

Koyama, Emi. 2003. "The Transfeminist Manifesto." Pp. 244–259 in *Catching a Wave: Reclaiming Feminism for the 21st Century*," edited by R. Dicker and A. Piepmeir. Boston: Northeastern University Press.

Krell, Elías Cosenza. 2017. "Is Transmisogyny Killing Trans Women of Color?: Black Trans Feminisms and the Exigencies of White Femininity." *TSQ: Transgender Studies Quarterly* 4(2):226–242.

Lewis, Abram J. 2017. "Trans History in a Moment of Danger: Organizing Within and Beyond 'Visibility' in the 1970s." Pp. 57–89 in *Trap Door: Trans Cultural Production and the Politics of Visibility*, edited by R. Gossett, E. A. Stanley, and J. Burton. Cambridge, MA: MIT Press.

Mack, Kenneth W. 2012. *Representing the Race: The Creation of the Civil Rights Lawyer*. Cambridge, MA: Harvard University Press.

Marcus, Eric. 1992. *Making Gay History: The Half Century Fight for Lesbian and Gay Equal Rights*. New York: Harper Perennial.

McRobbie, Angela. 2004. "Post-Feminism and Popular Culture." *Feminist Media Studies* 4(3):255–264.

Messner, Michael A. 1998. "The Limits of 'The Male Sex Role' An Analysis of the Men's Liberation and Men's Rights Movements' Discourse." *Gender & Society* 12 (3):255–276.

Noble, Bobby. 2006. *Sons of the Movement: FtMs Risking Incoherence on a Post-Queer Cultural Landscape*. Toronto: Women's Press.

Phipps, Alison. 2016. "Whose Personal Is More Political? Experience in Contemporary Feminist Politics." *Feminist Theory* 17(3):303–321.

Riddell, Carol. 1980. "Divided Sisterhood a Critical Review of Janice Raymond's the Trans-Sexual Empire." *News from Nowhere*. Liverpool: Great Britain.

Risman, Barbara J., Judith Lorber, and Jessica Sherwood. 2012. "Toward a World beyond Gender: A Utopic Vision." Presentation at the American Sociological Association annual meetings, Denver, CO.

Rosenberg, Rosalind. 2002. "The Conjunction of Race and Gender." *Journal of Women's History* 14(2):68–73.

Schilt, Kristen and Danya Lagos. 2017. "The Development of Transgender Studies in Sociology." *Annual Review of Sociology* 43(1):425–443.

Serano, Julia. 2007. *Whipping Girl: A Transsexual Woman on Sexism and the Scapegoating of Femininity*. Emeryville, CA: Seal Press.

Shugar, Dana R. 1995. *Separatism and Women's Community*. Lincoln, NE: University of Nebraska Press.

Sides, Josh. 2009. *Erotic City: Sexual Revolutions and the Making of Modern San Francisco*. New York, NY: Oxford University Press.

Stryker, Susan. 2006. "(De)Subjugated Knowledges: An Introduction to Transgender Studies." Pp. 1–18 in *The Transgender Studies Reader*, edited by S. Stryker and S. Whittle. New York: Routledge.

Stryker, Susan. 2017. *Transgender History: The Roots of Todays Revolution*. New York: Seal Press.

Stryker, Susan and Talia M. Bettcher. 2016. "Introduction: Trans/Feminisms." *TSQ: Transgender Studies Quarterly* 3(1–2):5–14.

The Tide Collective. 2016. "A Collective Editorial." *TSQ: Transgender Studies Quarterly* 3(1–2):276–277.

Ware, Susan. 2002. "Pauli Murray's Notable Connections." *Journal of Women's History* 14(2):54–57.

Williams, Cristan. 2014. "Fact Checking Janice Raymond: The NCHCT Report." *The TransAdvocate*. Retrieved September 23, 2017.http://transadvocate.com.

Williams, Cristan. 2016. "Radical Inclusion: Recounting the Trans Inclusive History of Radical Feminism." *TSQ: Transgender Studies Quarterly* 3(1–2):254–258.

Zengin, Aslı. 2016. "Mortal Life of Trans/Feminism: Notes on 'Gender Killings' in Turkey." *TSQ: Transgender Studies Quarterly* 3(1–2):266–271.

4 Online Feminism is Just Feminism

Offline and Online Movement Persistence

Alison Dahl Crossley

#MeToo [Twitter campaign started by Tarana Burke for women to share experiences with sexual assault, sexual harassment, and other forms of gender-based violence.]

#SayHerName [Twitter campaign led by Kimberlé Crenshaw and the African American Policy Forum to draw attention to police violence against Black women.]

#EffYourBeautyStandards [Body positive Instagram campaign started by Tess Holliday, highlighting sizeist, sexist, racist, and classist beauty standards.]

#HobbyLobby [Twitter campaign against retailer Hobby Lobby, related to Supreme Court decision allowing companies like Hobby Lobby to deny women insurance coverage of some contraceptives.]

#BlackGirlMagic [Twitter, Instagram, and Facebook campaign started by CaShawn Thompson to celebrate and honor the strength of Black women and girls, now also a book (*Browne 2018*)].

#TimesUp [A movement against sexual harassment started by women in Hollywood, building upon the momentum of #MeToo.]

Whether you use Twitter or not, you are likely familiar with at least one of the above hashtags. These campaigns generate millions of Twitter, Instagram and Facebook posts. They also draw significant media attention to the campaigns, and catalyze offline organizing, policy change, and feminist community building. While these online campaigns are relatively new, their sentiments and aims are not. In fact, these hashtags draw attention to causes that feminists have been fighting for over the course of generations: centering and highlighting the experiences of women and girls; undoing racist, sexist, and heteronormative beauty norms; objecting to interpersonal and relation-based abuse and violence against women; working for reproductive justice; and drawing attention to intersectionality and the heterogeneity of women's experiences. These themes point to continuity in feminist grievances and mobilization, not to mention the durability of inequality. But what are the relationships between on- and offline feminism? Is online feminism important to the movement? To understand how the feminist movement persists, a wide lens is necessary.

In this chapter, I examine the ways in which online feminism sustains and advances the feminist movement. By situating online feminism in the scholarship about the feminist movement, I show how online and offline feminism have a symbiotic relationship. As the title suggests, I document how online feminism is really just feminism. Thinking of online and offline feminism separately is neither accurate nor analytically useful, and obscures significant continuity in the movement.

Online and Offline Feminism

A large body of research documents the shifting forms, tactics, and targets of offline U.S. women's and feminist movements (Crossley 2017; Hurtado 2003; Naples 1998; Reger 2005, 2012; Roth 2004; Rupp and Taylor 1987; Staggenborg 1996; Suarez, Chapter 2 this volume; Whittier 1995). The similarities between on- and offline feminism become evident when examining literature about offline women's movements—specifically the importance of interpersonal networks, feminist solidarity, and everyday feminism.

The social networks driving online feminism, such as Twitter, Instagram and Facebook, are sometimes thought of as relatively new phenomena closely linked with the rise of Silicon Valley. However, scholars have found that, for decades, interpersonal ties have been critical to the emergence and sustenance of offline feminist and women's movements (Freedman 1979; Rosenthal et al. 1997; Taylor 1989; Roth 2004; Rupp 1997). As feminism is one of the longest lasting social movements, it inevitably ebbs and flows over time as it responds to political opportunities and cultural reception to feminist claims. The theory of social movement abeyance (Taylor 1989; Crossley 2017) elucidates how social networks and communities of feminists are critical to the ongoing nature of the feminist movement. Communities and networks of feminists sustain each other over shifts in the movement, and are then poised to protest and galvanize others when mobilizing grievances demand. Social networks are undoubtedly essential to many movements. However, because feminists have historically possessed less access to dominant politics and power arenas than other activists, they rely more on community, solidarity and social networks to advance their movement (Blackwell 2010).

Networks of feminists sustain the feminist movement. Nancy Naples writes, "Women's social networks, in particular, are powerful resources for promoting resistance strategies, especially for those most marginalized in contemporary society" (2005: 231). Feminists' pre-existing networks in large part gave rise to the 1960s women's liberation movement (Freeman 1975). The strong connections among feminists were responsible for the rising tide of 1970s feminism. Although the communication networks that fostered the feminism of the 1970s were in the form of phone calls, letter writing and in-person community building, the connectivity function is similar to those that gave rise to #YesAllWomen and #Metoo: when the political opportunity demanded it, pre-existing networks of feminist activists were ready to mobilize. For example, in the aftermath of the University of California, Santa Barbara (UCSB) homicides, networks of feminist students were already in place, poised to respond to the sexist motivations of the shooter through street protest; the incident rapidly led to the massive online campaign #YesAllWomen (Crossley 2017). Scholars have also found that campus anti-rape movements were significant precursors to the emergence and sustenance of #MeToo (Heldman, Ackerman, and Breckenridge-Jackson 2018) (See Chapter 8 this volume). These social networks allow feminist individuals to learn about feminist grievances outside their own everyday spheres of influence, to understand how their own individual or community grievances are shared with others, and to organize campaigns to advance equality (Crossley 2015). The salience of off- and online social connections to the advancement of feminists encourages us to dig deeper into our investigation of the value of online feminism.

Over generations of feminism, scholars have found that offline communities have fuelled the movement through periods of flourishing and even decline (Staggenborg 1998; Taylor 1989). From women's clubs to women's circles (Ballakrishnen, Fielding-Singh, and Magliozzi forthcoming 2018), close-knit friendships have played a central role in the feminist movement (Nelson 2018). Rupp and Taylor (1987) found that in the 1950s, participants in the National Women's Party were bound together by their dedication to suffrage and feminist ideology, as well as by their close interpersonal relationships. Writing about Chicana feminism, Hurtado notes the importance of connections between women: "Respondents told countless other stories about women around them who showed them what it was like to live as a woman of Color in this society. My respondents used these women's lived experiences to define their feminisms" (2004: 206). Indeed, since the early 1900s, networks of women and consciousness-raising groups created interpersonal networks that fuelled the growth of the feminist movement, helped participants understand their individual experiences within a larger framework of sexism, racism, and homophobia, and propelled the movement between surges (Ferree and Hess 1995; Nelson 2018; Reger 2004; Roth 2004).

Although feminist networks have been uniformly central to the advancement of the movement, like the movement itself, feminist networks are heterogeneous. For example, Roth (2004) compares 1960s and 1970s Black, Chicana and White feminisms, and argues that they were largely separate movements. One major difference between their feminisms was their relationships with the male-dominated related movements, such as the organizing between Chicana feminists and the Chicano Movement, or White feminists and the New Left movement. Roth found that this heterogeneity between feminist organizing perpetuated different types of feminisms (see also Maätita 2005). Regardless of their racial, ethnic, or demographic compositions, what Hurwitz and Taylor (2012) call "women's cultures" are the foundations of feminism and social change more broadly.

Feminist networks need not be face-to-face to be impactful, as exhibited by the exchange of feminist zines, (i.e., handmade photocopied pamphlets distributed by mail in the 1990s) (Bates and McHugh 2005; Piepmeier 2009), and pen pal networks, which Taylor and Leitz (2010) found to be central to creating collective identity and emotional transformation among women experiencing postpartum depression and incarcerated for committing infanticide. Given the importance of the Internet in facilitating communities, gatherings, organizations, campaigns and circles, it is important examine its relevance to feminism.

During varying historical moments and movement contexts, scholars found that the incorporation of feminist principles in offline everyday life nourishes the movement (Reger 2012; Whittier 1995; Faupel and Werum 2011; Rupp and Taylor 1987; Taylor and Whittier 1992). Participants incorporate feminist values in their careers, relationships and other facets of everyday lives (Whittier 1995; Taylor and Raeburn 1995; Hasso 2001). While there is some debate about whether and how everyday and interactional activities propel social movements (Haenfler, Johnson, and Jones 2012), elsewhere I introduce a typology of everyday feminism, addressing how feminism shapes respondents' *perspectives, personalities, interactions, language, relationships, understanding of their own privilege* and *beauty norms* (Crossley 2017). Other feminist scholars (Whittier 1995; Mansbridge and Flaster 2007) illustrate how these taken-for-granted activities drive the movement. Without everyday feminism, during which feminists live out their ideals and create lives consistent with their feminist objectives, momentous and extraordinary feminism would not be able to thrive. Everyday feminism and collective feminist action are not mutually exclusive, nor does everyday feminism replace collective feminist organizing. Up until this point theorizations of everyday feminism have been based on offline feminism, although given the everyday nature of social media use, the question of how the Internet shapes the everyday nature of feminist organizing is also raised.

Research and commentary about online feminism points to its meaningful nature for community building, solidarity, and feminist transformation (Bowles Eagle 2015; Locke and Lawthom 2018; Martin and Valenti 2013; Rentschler 2015; Scarborough 2018). Hashtag activism about feminism and violence against women and girls is an opportunity for women and girls to "share their own experiences, and through doing so, challenge 'commonsense' understandings of this abuse and promote gendered solidarity" (Berridge and Portwood-Stacer 2015:341). Researching *Ms. Magazine*'s online discussion board, Duncan (2005: 162) found that it fostered strong community ties. She writes "Online networking…provides feminists with a home place, a protected space to return to and build a community after working toward activist goals" (see also Ayers 2003). Nip (2004) found that participation in an online forum created solidarity and an oppositional culture among participants. I found that online feminism, specifically Facebook and blogs, enlarges feminist networks and deepens communities (Crossley 2015). Other research has focused specifically on feminist bloggers. Keller (2012) found that teenage girl bloggers challenged conventional forms of feminism and activism in their online writing. A study of an Australian feminist blog network (Shaw 2012: 42) found that it "functions to critique the ideology of mainstream discourses at least partly in order to change them and participation in this community can be understood as discursive activism." Precisely because the feminist movement has relied on friendship networks for such a long period of time, it makes a valuable case for examining whether the online nature of these networks contributes to feminist organizing. Research has predominately focused on the implications of online feminism only, without consideration of the larger relationships between offline and online feminism and the continuity of the movement. In general, the blind spots to online feminism come at great cost. Scholars have stated that young feminists are not as visible in their organizing as were previous generations of feminists (Siegel 1996; see Peltola et al. 2004). This perceived invisibility exists in large part because young feminists are online, and our understandings of movement activity and protest typically based on offline action.

Attention towards online mobilization has sparked debates in social movement research, including if and how online technologies alter mobilization. Discussions include whether online activism is similar to or different from traditional offline activism—and whether we need new theories of social movements to more accurately reflect the influence of online mobilization (Earl and Kimport 2011). In research about online posts of white nationalists, a much different context than the women's movement, Caren, Jowers, and Gaby found that *social movement online communities* "use the Internet not only for activism, but more importantly to create an identity and a distinct community within their virtual space" (2012: 167; see also Earl and Kimport 2011). While social media studies find that it aids in street protest, social media campaigns based upon online friendship networks have found to be largely unsuccessful (Lewis, Gray, and Meierhenrich 2014). Polletta and her collaborators ask whether the Internet "creates new terrains of contention" (2013: 17) and argue that online activism allows mobilized individuals to "engage in political action with much less risk, even less inconvenience" (2013: 32). It is important to note, however, that much of the research about online movements is about the Internet and its facilitation of street protest, not about community building and solidarity, central tactics of feminists (Earl and Schussman 2003; Earl et al. 2010). The case of online feminism presented in this chapter sheds light on these debates.

The Case for Online Feminism

To understand the meaning and uses of online feminism to feminists today, and to analyze the connections between on and offline feminism, I gathered data at three institutions of higher education. Feminist scholars frequently look to college students and young women to understand whether feminist mobilizations continue. In the introduction to the first volume of *Different Wavelengths: Studies of the Contemporary Women's Movement*, Jo Reger (2005) paraphrased a famous Gloria Steinem quote: If we would like to understand what is happening to feminism in the 21st century, we should ask young feminists. This chapter is based on an analysis of college students' feminist mobilization. Using interviews, participant observation, and a survey, I gathered individual and organizational level data in 2011 at UCSB, the University of Minnesota, Twin Cities and Smith College. I chose these three institutions because they differ in respect to type of institution, geographic region, student demographics, and in student activist/feminist culture. Through 75 in-depth interviews with a racially diverse group of participants, participant observation in feminist and social justice student organizations at each campus and a survey of 1,400 students, I learned about their feminist organizing and identities, as well as the role of online feminism in their feminist activism.

Interview respondents were currently enrolled, undergraduate college students, primarily between the ages of 18–21. Participants self-identified as white (n=42), Latina/o (n=8), mixed race/other (n=13), Asian American (n=6), African American (n=5), American Indian (n=1); heterosexual (n=46), queer (n=9), bisexual (n=9) gay/lesbian (n=7), queer and bisexual (n=1) and non-specified sexuality (n=3); women (n=68), men (n=7), including a transgender male. Many were first generation college students. Twenty-seven students self-identified as poor, working or lower-middle class and 48 in the middle-class range. The respondents shared a degree of educational privilege. However, this sample diverges from a number of studies that focus on the experiences of white feminists: 33 of the 75 respondents identified as Latina/o, mixed race, Asian American, African American or Native American. UCSB specifically has attracted a diverse undergraduate student body. Approximately a third of the interview participants belonged to feminist organizations and served as key informants about their communities. The remaining participants were involved in social justice-oriented organizations or expressed interest in feminist, gender and/or social justice issues.

The semi-structured, in-depth interviews lasted between 60 and 90 minutes. The interview included general questions about the respondents' backgrounds, hopes for their future and experiences with social inequalities. Interview participants were asked about their perceptions of feminism, if they identify as feminist, and their processes of coming to feminist consciousness or resistance. For those students who belonged to feminist organizations, I asked them details about their organizations, including successes and challenges, and strategies and tactics of the organization. The interview schedule included a section on the media and Internet use, probing deeper into their engagement with online feminism. All interviews were digitally recorded, transcribed, and coded to capture emerging themes related to feminist identities, tactics and grievances.

Drawing on offline feminism research and the interview data, I identify three primary themes related to the benefits of online feminism. First, *the creation and sustenance of feminist solidarity and the dissemination of feminist information* (i.e., histories, ideologies, campaigns); second, the *diversification of media narratives about feminism and women;* and finally *offline impact.* My focus is on how feminists employ Twitter, blogs and Facebook on behalf of the feminist movement.

Dissemination of Feminist Information and Creation of Solidarity

Young women have been (erroneously) generalized as being unfamiliar with and unaware of the mobilization of previous generations of feminists and of the continued need for the feminist movement (Rivers and Barnett 2013). While this belies the realities of young women's continued involvement in feminism and relatively stable levels of feminist identification in the U.S. population (Ferree and Hess 1995), it is relevant to our understanding of the ways in which individuals use the Internet to learn about feminism. Indeed, educating and spreading the word about feminism, its ideologies, histories, and campaigns are critical in the continuation of the feminist movement and the creation of feminist community. As I heard someone say, "Feminism isn't like an indie band you hope nobody else hears about." In fact, I found the Internet critically used as a means to learn about feminist history, ideologies, and perspectives on current events.

When I asked my interview participants where they learned about the feminist movement and its history, many listed the Internet as the place in which they first understood feminism and why it might be a useful identity for them. In spite of a cacophony of voices online, feminist blogs were crucial for their understanding of the feminist movement. Popular blogs of import to respondents included: "Planned Parenthood's Possible Defunding and Black Women" (Racialicious), "The Struggle for Transgender and Genderqueer Legitimacy" (Feministing), "The Girl's Guide to Having An Abortion" (Jezebel). Online articles such as these allowed participants to view their personal experiences through a feminist lens, including understanding the personal and structural ramifications of our binary gender system, our underinvestment in women's health and reproductive healthcare, and how the intersections between race and class shape and drive inequality.

To illustrate the impact of feminist blogs in particular, I present brief accounts from interview participants who shared in detail their reliance on

feminist blogs. The first, a white lesbian undergraduate student I interviewed, who had many feminist friends, was in a feminist organization, and
had read feminist material from the library from a young age. She also read
feminist blogs every day. She said, "I think in general, reading feminist blogs
is a good way to get your feminism on, to be up to date and informed,
being educated is the best way to have weapons on your side." She had a
sophisticated understanding of feminism and the complexities and contradictions in the movement, due in part to the fact that the feminist blogs she
read presented a host of approaches to feminism and incorporated consideration of feminism's past. A heterosexual African American woman
undergraduate spoke at length about what she learned from her frequent
reading of the blog Racialicious, which she told me helped her understand
"imperialism, and how racism, classism, and sexism is part of imperialism."
Later she said that reading feminist blogs regularly is "seeking a community
who thinks like me, but who doesn't look like me." In particular, she
learned online about the intersections between race, gender, and sexuality,
as well as the commonalities among women of color.

A white, queer, male undergraduate respondent, who also spoke carefully
about the nuances and complexities within the feminist movement, said.
feminist blogs "help me grapple with feminism; they help me address feminist topics more effectively." When I asked a different white, straight, male
undergraduate student about how he came to embrace feminism, he said he
recently began to understand his male privilege because of what he read
online. He shared a story of recently getting off the city bus near his apartment at the same time a woman passenger disembarked. Because of what he
read in a feminist blog, he understood that he could be perceived as threatening in a public space, especially at night. As a result, even though he and
the woman passenger were headed in the same direction, he waited at the
bus stop for a bit so she could continue on her way without worry. Prior to
reading online feminist content, he had not previously considered how he
could feel comfortable in public in a way many women do not. These
examples show how online feminism provided information and perspectives
that respondents did not fully acquire in their offline lives, in particular,
personal accounts of gender inequality and feminism, and a sense of how to
live out feminist ideals in one's everyday life. Mobilized participants used
blogs as an educational tool and mode of connection with other feminists
online, as well as in conjunction with offline movement expression.

While my participants' examples explain the nuances of online feminism,
larger campaigns draw attention to feminist issues and create solidarity of
women and feminists online. These public displays of solidarity often
happen on Twitter. Anita Hill noted that there were no hashtags when she
experienced workplace harassment. She said, "Some people think it's about
the hashtag and it's about social media; I think those are just platforms…I
think the real goal of the MeToo movement is to build empathy and
community, and they're doing an excellent job at that" (Campisi and

Ahmed 2018). In another example, on January 19, 2016 musician Bethany Cosentino of rock bank Best Coast joined a chorus of other women musicians on Twitter to point to music publicist Heathcliff Berru who sexually harassed a number of women with whom he worked. One of these harassed women, Amber, initially tweeted about her experiences. Cosentino responded:

> When I saw these tweets, I knew I had to speak up, because Heathcliff has sexually harassed me too. I had never shared my story publicly because: I was afraid of the backlash that I might receive or that I would come across like some kind of wrathful bitch. After I read Amber's tweets, I decided it was time to tweet in support of her. I wasn't just one of his victims—I knew plenty of other women who had their own "Heathcliff stories." After I supported Amber, the floodgates opened. Women started writing how they had felt person-ally victimized by his actions. By the following morning, Heathcliff had stepped down as the CEO of his PR company, which has since become defunct....I am so glad that this situation was finally brought to light and that *these victims now have a supportive bond and can provide strength to others who may want to come forward.*
>
> (Cosentino 2016) [emphasis added]

The tweets collectively demonstrated a critical mass discussing issues of great import to women now, as well as historically feminist issues. While Cosentino's experiences were pre- #MeToo, they paved the way for the massive cultural shift driven by the hashtag, in particular millions of women sharing their common experiences with sexual harassment, sexual assault, and violence perpetrated by men. What Cosentino described in her tweet, as well as the outcomes of #MeToo, are similar to the desired outcomes of offline circles or consciousness-raising group (Nelson 2018). When women realize that their own individual experiences are the same as those of other women, they find support and community. This closely ties to the broader traditions in feminism that uplift the experiences and voices of women, protect their communities and each other, and bring attention to painful topics that disproportionately affect women.

The Diversification of Media Narratives about Feminism and Women

The media is an important avenue through which individuals learn about feminism and feminists—including their goals, tactics, communities and campaigns (Farrell 1995). Participants shared the ways in which both inter-personal discussions of feminism and media depictions of the movement taught them about feminism. At the Clayman Institute for Gender Research's Online Feminism Conference in 2014, we convened activists and scholars from across the country to speak about the challenges and opportunities of online feminism. One of the recurring themes during the conference was how online feminism diversifies and expands media narratives of feminism and women. In other words, online feminism provides a large stage for feminism and for heterogeneous feminist voices.

Feminist hashtags on Twitter offer a way to learn about other women's experiences and to contribute to feminist campaigns about feminist topics. But because of Twitter's wide reach, it also diversifies media narratives about feminism and women more broadly and is accessible to a wider audience. For example, #youokaysis was started by Feminista Jones, an author and writer with a large social media following, and is a campaign to support other women as they are experiencing street harassment—encouraging women, when witnessing other women being harassed on the street, to approach them and ask if they are okay or need support. In another example, #YesAllWomen affords an opportunity for women across the world to recount experiences of sexism and harassment. It was started by @gildedspine in direct response to the Isla Vista massacre in May 2014 in which the gunman targeted women students. A third example is #whyIstayed, started by Beverly Gooden, which provides opportunities for women to share the complex reasons for staying with or leaving an abusive partner, and to learn about other's experiences with relationship violence, a topic not easily spoken about in public but of particular importance to feminists (Clark 2016). Writing about #YesAll-Women, and relevant to each of these feminist hashtags, Thrift writes that they "assert a critical, feminist intervention in how we conceptualize and choose to narrate misogynist aggression and gender violence in American culture" (2014: 1091).

These hashtags have generated millions of tweets, fostering online and offline conversations about timely feminist issues. The conversations on Twitter and beyond draw attention to the endurance of sexism and interrelated inequalities, and the need for feminism in the face of competing narratives. During the aforementioned conference, Jones said Twitter gives a broad variety of feminists "access to the podium." She said that Twitter allows individuals with differing backgrounds to make known their perspectives on feminism and amplifies their voices, regardless of their background or credentials. Social media can provide the opportunities to draw attention to the voices and experiences of individuals who would not otherwise be in public discourse. For example, a woman with sharp and insightful comments on gender, race, and current events, but who may not have an advanced degree, be seen as an expert, or traditionally have access to reporters, may now be quoted in a legacy or prestigious media outlet because she has created a voice online. A similar shift was exhibited in the evolution of #MeToo. African American woman Tarana Burke started using the term eleven years prior to its resurgence. White actor Alyssa Milano tweeted Burke's sentiment in 2017, giving rise to the massive online campaign. The origins of #MeToo had the potential to be whitewashed, although there was a successful campaign to give Burke the credit she deserved.

Enlarging the podium is critical and especially valuable to the feminist movement. Part of the reason that feminism has been seen by some as monolithic, or as dominated by particular groups of white women, is in part because journalists historically have gone to the same individuals as spokes-women for the movement. As a result, similar ideologies are consistently published in the media, making feminism more monolithic than it actually is (Jonsson 2014). This has specifically been a problem because historically feminists of color are not sought as representatives of the movement (Suarez, Chapter 2 this volume; Springer 2005). Although feminism has proliferated across a variety of racial and ethnic communities, white women have been held up as the historical bearers of feminism, causing the "whitewashing" (Roth 2004) of a very diverse and complex movement (Jonsson 2014; Reger 2012). In addition to the broadening the podium to individual voices, campaigns like #BlackGirlMagic not only propel Black feminism but also educate others on Twitter. Twitter perpetuates the long tradition of feminists promulgating an alternative worldview (Whittier 1995), one that is different from those views that are covered in many mainstream and legacy media outlets.

Offline Impact

It is often questioned whether online feminism advances the movement in important ways, or whether online activism is feckless "slactivism" (Lewis, Gray and Meierhenrich 2014). Online feminism, as I have shown, is mean-ingful in several ways that are consistent with tactics of previous generations of feminist activists. There are also signs of the offline impact of online fem-inism, some of which highlight the gray areas between on- and offline fem-inism. For example, the Women's Marches across the world on January 21, 2017 were some of the largest in-person protest gatherings in history. The idea for the march first emerged on Facebook, and Instagram, Facebook, Twitter, and an app were used for logistics. The subsequent Women's Con-vention in Detroit, in which thousands of feminists gathered to plan for the next year of activism, also followed a similar pattern. To provide another example, the Time's Up Movement has been impactful online and offline (see Chapter 1 this volume). Women have been empowered to share their experiences with sexual harassment online, and women who need funding to support legal and public relations bills in the aftermath of sexual harassment can apply to the Time's Up Legal Defense Fund.

When my research participants spoke about feminism and how it shaped their lives, they often spoke about online and offline feminism as a single form of feminism. At the beginning of one interview, I had to smile at the response to my question about how feminism influences everyday life. A white lesbian undergraduate student said she "put on her feminism when she woke up in the morning" and that it shaped most aspects of her life, including her relationship with her transgender man partner, her activism, and everyday minutiae. She also read feminist blogs every day, shared copious links on Facebook regarding feminism, and spoke face to face with friends about the content she posted online—the Internet drove in-person conversations about feminism and feminist perspective on current events. Many participants spoke about the porous boundaries between their off- and online movement expression. They reported that they spoke face-to-face with friends about what they read on feminist blogs, often a seamless conversation because many of them read the same blogs. One participant said that she tries to read feminist blogs as much as she can, but more often learns about feminist news from her fellow feminist group members who do read blogs regularly. The impact of blogs surpassed the boundaries of the virtual world, and respondents' use of online content facilitated offline relationships.

Facebook was an important venue for members of offline feminist organizations—participants disseminated the word about issues in their networks, about upcoming rallies and protests, and about offline meetings and campaigns. They said more people attended when they made an event page, showing how feminist organizations used their Facebook networks as a free organizational resource and as a tactic to expand the reach of their campaigns. Respondents spoke about their dependence on Facebook in the age of budget cuts and lack of institutional support for their feminist organizations. By using the Internet to make up for limited resources and support, they circulated Facebook event pages to their friendship networks.

Examples of the success of online campaigns also highlight the offline impact of online activism. For example, #MeToo has led to the arrest of Harvey Weinstein, and to the public outings of serial sexual harassers. Although the successful outcomes of #MeToo were certainly not in isolation, the hashtag galvanized and allowed women to feel that they are not alone in their experiences. In addition, the 2013 campaign by feminists, which included the feminist organizations Women, Action and the Media and the Everyday Sexism Project effectively, campaigned Facebook to change its posting policy due to rampant sexism on its site. Other online campaigns include #notbuyingit, when the Representation Project successfully petitioned the Disney Store to remove its sexist children's shirts from the market (Siddiquee 2013). Shirts aimed towards boys read "Be A Hero" and the related girls' shirts read "I Need a Hero." As these examples illustrate, online feminism includes targeted campaigns for immediate change as well as the solidarity building highlighted throughout the chapter. All of these components of online feminism are intertwined and advance the feminist movement.

Conclusion

Feminism is propelled by online mobilization. An examination of the persistence of feminism through online activity informs us about the current status of the feminist movement and makes visible the online mobilization that is often invisible (Siegel 1996; Stacey 1987; see Peltola et al. 2004). As I have shown, in many ways online feminism replicates offline feminism. Feminists sustain their movements during times of abeyance and flourishing through social networks and communities, as they have in previous generations of organizing (Taylor 1989; Crossley 2017). I show how online feminism replicates this, through both online social networks, and communities, as well as how online feminism informs and shapes participants offline interactions. What participants learned online about feminism was critical to their connection with the movement as well as to their creation and nourishment of feminist community and solidarity.

Like women's clubs, consciousness-raising groups, and letter-writing campaigns, feminist Tweeters, bloggers, and Facebook users spread feminist ideologies, create solidarity and community, challenge dominant media perspectives, and nourish oppositional culture. As feminists have been known to highlight the everyday in terms of its importance to feminist movements and culture, it is clear that the frequency with which participants were engaging with online feminism means that it is an important component of the ongoing and everyday nature of feminism. This everyday nature of online feminism is perhaps the clearest example of the blurriness of the borders between on and offline feminism.

In contrast to previous forms of feminism, however, the Internet allows for interaction with other activists and adversaries at unparalleled speed and frequency. Whereas past generations relied on snail mail, newspapers, zines, and face-to-face gatherings to expand movement networks or engage with adversaries, technological advancements have changed the communication patterns and information flow that are critical to mobilizing and perpetuating a movement. This speed and technological advancement result in more and more people online—busily gathering and disseminating information, and connecting with individuals known and unknown.

While this has many benefits, it is important to note, "digital spaces are not a utopia for online campaigning" (Turley and Fisher 2018:129). A disturbing downside of online feminism is increased opportunity for harassers to target and silence the women who benefit so much from Internet technologies and social media (Lumsden and Morgan 2016). Online harassment is a form of sexism and inequality that is entirely produced by the emergence and growth of Internet technologies (Thompson 2018). While feminists have always faced adversaries in their efforts to create social change, they experience unprecedented levels of hostility and sexism online, shedding light on how online activism has created new forms of inequality. Online harassment has been identified as a serious social problem—a Pew study found that "2/3 of Americans have witnessed abusive or harassing behavior against others online" (Duggan 2017:10) and that women, and especially young women, experience "sexualized forms of abuse at much higher rates than men" (Duggan 2017:7; Citron 2011). Online harassment causes the Internet to be less accessible to women than men. Given the online qualities of our lives, and that our professional and social lives are intimately intertwined with online technologies, we cannot underestimate the cost of harassment to women generally and feminists specifically. In this sense, it is clear that online activity has created "new terrains of contention" (Polletta 2013) and challenges arguments that describe online activism as low-cost and low-risk. There is a dearth of research about the connections between feminism and online harassment, an area of needed research.

While there are lingering questions about the importance and significance of online activism to social movement mobilization (Lewis, Gray, and Meierhenrich 2014), in some ways online feminism is a separate discussion from broader movement analysis. Feminists rely on culture, community, and solidarity, creating new worldviews and validating the experiences of women and girls. In many ways, unlike many other social movements, the forming of strong feminist cultures is a movement goal in and of itself. Separate from the mainstream media and the institutions, organizations, and relationships that center white men and consistently devalue women and women of color specifically, feminists have sustained themselves and their families and communities through normalizing an oppositional worldview. I argue that in many ways online feminism stands on its own due to the movement's historic reliance on culture, community and solidarity, and that many of the theories of understanding offline feminism are applicable to online feminism. While there may be some interesting differences between online and offline feminism that can be informed by analysis of online social movements more broadly (Earl and Schussman 2003; Earl et al. 2010), this chapter demonstrates how online feminism replicates and perpetuates forms of feminism that are familiar from pre-Internet organizing periods. Indeed, it may be that social movement scholarship about online movements could benefit from considering the case of online feminism. Very few explorations of online social movements consider the importance of community, solidarity, and culture (but see Caren, Jowers and Gaby 2012). The ways in which feminists online perpetuate the movement, and use the Internet as an effective tool to perpetuate its central ideologies, is perhaps an invitation for a broad examination of the varieties of manners by which the Internet advances social movements and how online and offline mobilization cannot be separated.

In many respects, this research demands consideration of the similarities between on- and offline mobilization. Because Internet technology shapes our offline as well as online lives, it is difficult to distinguish the boundaries between online and offline movement activity. Feminists use the Internet to understand the feminist movement, to connect with other feminists online and offline, and to aid in their offline communities and organizations, thus blurring the boundaries of online and offline organizing. I suggest that analyzing the boundaries or creating categories of online and offline movement activity may not be a fruitful endeavor given the depth of the connections between the two. This research encourages us to abandon distinctions between online feminism and offline feminism, because it is all feminism. It is crucial to make online feminism part of our narratives about the continuity of feminism and persistence of gender inequality, so that we clearly understand the variation in and breadth of how activists create feminist change.

Acknowledgements

I wish to thank Jo Reger, Fátima Suarez, and Heather Hurwitz for their comments.

References

Ayers, Michael. D. 2003. "Comparing Collective Identity in Online and Offline Feminist Activists." Pp. 145–164 in *Cyberactivism: Online Activism in Theory and Practice*, edited by Martha McCaughey and Michael D. Ayers. New York: Routledge.

Ballakrishnen, Swethaa, Priya Fielding-Singh and Devon Magliozzi. Forthcoming 2018. "Intentional Invisibility: Professional Women and the Navigation of Workplace Constraints. *"Sociological Perspectives*.

Bates, Dawn and Maureen C. McHugh. 2005. "Zines: Voices of Third Wave Feminists." Pp. 179–194 in *Different Wavelengths: Studies of the Contemporary Women's Movement*, edited by Jo Reger. NewYork: Routledge.

Berridge, Susan and Laura Portwood-Stacer. 2015. "Introduction: Feminism, Hashtags and Violence Against Women and Girls." *Feminist Media Studies* 15 (2):341–358.

Blackwell, Maylei. 2010. "Líderes Campesinas: Nepantla Startegies and Grassroots Organizing at the Intersection of Gender and Globalization." *Aztlán: A Journal of Chicano Studies* 35(1):13–47.

Bowles Eagle, Ryan. 2015. "Loitering, Lingering, Hashtagging: Women Reclaiming Public Space Via #BoardtheBus, #StopStreetHarassment and the #EverydaySexism Project." *Feminist Media Studies* 15(2):350–353.

Browne, Mahogany L. 2018. *Black Girl Magic*. New York: Roaring Brook Press.

Campisi, Jessica and Saeed Ahmed. 2018. "Anita Hill on #MeToo: I Didn't Have a Hashtag." *CNN*. Retrieved June 11, 2018. https://www.cnn.com/2018/06/11/us/anita-hill-hashtag-metoo-trnd/index.html.

Caren, Neal, Kay Jowers and Sarah Gaby. 2012. "A Social Movement Online Community: Stormfront and the White Nationalist Movement." Pp. 163–193 in *Media, Movements, and Political Change, Research in Social Movements, Conflicts and Change Volume 33*, edited by Jennifer Earl and Deana A. Rohlinger. Bingley, UK: Emerald Publishing.

Citron, Danielle. 2011 "Civil Rights in Our Information Age." Pp. 31–49 in *Offensive Internet: Speech, Privacy, and Reputation*, edited by Saul Levmore and Martha C. Nussbaum. Cambridge: Harvard University Press.

Clark, Rosemary. 2016. "'Hope in a hashtag:' the discursive activism of #WhyIStayed." *Feminist Media Studies* 16(5):788–804.

Cosentino, Bethany. 2016. "Burgers, Bitches, and Bullshit: Best Coast's Front Woman on Battling the Patriarchy." *Lenny Letter*, Feb. 2. Retrieved Feb. 3, 2016. http://www.lennyletter.com/life/a248/burgers-bitches-and-bullshit-bethany-consentino/.

Crossley, Alison Dahl. 2015. "Facebook Feminism: Social Media, Blogs, and New Technologies of Contemporary Feminism." *Mobilization* 20(2): 253–268.

Crossley, Alison Dahl. 2017. *Finding Feminism: Millennial Activists and the Unfinished Gender Revolution*. New York: New York University Press.

Duggan, Maeve. 2017. "Online Harassment 2017." Pew Research. Retrieved July 20, 2017. http://www.pewinternet.org/2017/07/11/online-harassment-2017/.

Duncan, Barbara. 2005. "Searching for a Home Place: Online in the Third Wave." Pp. 161–178 in *Different Wavelengths*, edited by Jo Reger. New York: Routledge.

Earl, Jennifer and Katrina Kimport. 2011. *Digitally Enabled Social Change: Activism in the Internet Age*. Cambridge, MA: MIT Press.

Earl, Jennifer and Alan Schussman. 2003. "The New Site of Activism: On-Line Organizations, Movement Entrepreneurs, and the Changing Location of Social Movement Decision-Making." *Research in Social Movements, Conflicts, and Change* (24):155–187.

Earl, Jennifer, Katrina Kimport, Greg Prieto, Carly Rush and Kimberly Reynoso. 2010. "Changing the World One Webpage at a Time: Conceptualizing and Explaining Internet Activism." *Mobilization* 15(4):425–446.

Farrell, Amy Erdman. 1995. "Feminism and the Media: Introduction," *Signs: Journal of Womenin Culture and Society* 20(3):642–645.

Faupel, Alison and Regina Werum. 2011. "Making Her Own Way: The Individualization of First-Wave Feminism, 1910–1930." *Mobilization* 16(2):181–200.

Ferree, Myra Marx. 2007. "On-line Identities and Organizational Connections: Networks of Transnational Feminist Websites." Pp. 141–166 in *Gender Orders Unbound? Globalization, Restructuring and Reciprocity*, edited by Ilse Lenz, Charlotte Ullrich, and Barbara Fersch. Opladen, Germany: Barbara Budrich Publishers.

Ferree, Myra Marx and Beth B. Hess. 1995. *Controversy and Coalition: The New Feminist Movement Across Four Decades of Change*. New York: Routledge.

Freedman, Estelle. 1979. "Separatism as Strategy: Female Institution Building and American Feminism, 1870–1930." *Feminist Studies* 5(3):512–529.

Freeman, Jo. 1975. *The Politics of Women's Liberation*. New York: David McKay.

Haenfler, Ross, Brett Johnson,and Ellis Jones. 2012. "Lifestyle Movements: Exploring the Intersection of Lifestyle and Social Movements." *Social Movement Studies* 11(1):1–20.

Hasso, Frances S. 2001. "Feminist Generations? The Long-Term Impact Of Social Movement Involvement on Palestinian Women's Lives."*American Journal of Sociology* 107 (3):586–611.

Heldman, Caroline, Alissa R. Ackerman and Ian Breckenridge-Jackson. 2018. *The New Campus Anti-Rape Movement: Internet Activism and Social Justice*. New York: Rowman & Littlefield.

Hurtado, Aida. 2003. *Voicing Chicana Feminisms: Young Women Speak Out on Sexuality and Identity*. New York: New York University Press.

Hurwitz, Heather McKee and Verta Taylor. 2012. "Women's Cultures and Social Movements in Global Contexts." *Sociology Compass* 6(10):808–822.

Jonsson, Terese. 2014. "White Feminist Stories: Locating Race in Representations of Feminism in The Guardian." *Feminist Media Studies* 14(6):1012–1027.

Keller, Jessalynn Marie. 2012. "Virtual Feminisms: Girls' Blogging Communities, Feminist Activism and Participatory Politics." *Information, Communication & Society* 15(3):429–447.

Lewis, Kevin, Kurt Gray and Jens Meierhenrich. 2014. "The Structure of Online Activism." *Sociological Science* 1:1–9. doi:10.15195/v1.a1.

Locke, Abigail and Rebecca Lawthom. 2018. "Social Media Platform as Complex and Contradictory Spaces for Feminisms: Visibility, Opportunity, Power, Resistance, and Activism." *Feminism and Psychology* 28(1):3–10.

Lumsden, Karen and Heather Morgan. 2017. "Media framing of trolling and online abuse: silencing strategies, symbolic violence, and victim blaming." *Feminist Media Studies* 17(6):926–990.

Martin, Courtney E. and Vanessa Valenti. 2013. "#Femfuture: Online Revolution." Barnard Center for Research on Women. http://bcrw.barnard.edu/publications/femfuture-online-revolution/.

Maätita, Florence. 2005. "Que Viva La Mujer: Negotiating Chicana Feminist Identities." Pp. 23-39 in *Different Wavelengths: Studies of the Contemporary Women's Movement*, edited by Jo Reger. New York: Routledge.

Mansbridge, Jane and Katherine Flaster. 2007. "The Cultural Politics of Everyday Discourse: The Case of 'Male Chauvinist Pig'." *Critical Sociology* 33(4):627–660.

Naples, Nancy, ed. 1998. *Community Activism and Feminist Politics*. New York: Routledge.

Naples, Nancy. 2005. "Confronting the Future, Learning from the Past." Pp. 215–235 in *Different Wavelengths: Studies of the Contemporary Women's Movement*, edited by Jo Reger. New York: Routledge.

Nelson, Laura. 2018. "Feminism Means More than a Changed World…It means the creation of a new consciousness in women: Feminism, Consciousness-Raising, and Continuity between the Waves." Pp. 175–197 in *100 Years of the Nineteenth Amendment: An Appraisal of Women's Political Activism*, edited by Holly J. McCammon and Lee Ann Banaszak. New York: Oxford University Press.

Nip, Joyce Y. M. 2004. "The Queer Sisters and Its Electronic Bulletin Board: A Study of the Internet for Social Movement Mobilization." *Information, Communication and Society* 7:23–49.

Nussbaum, Martha C. 2011. "Objectification and Internet Misogyny." Pp. 68–87 in *Offensive Internet: Speech, Privacy, and Reputation*, edited by Saul Levmore and Martha C. Nussbaum. Cambridge: Harvard University Press.

Peltola, Pia, Melissa A. Milkie and Stanley Presser. 2004. "The 'Feminist' Mystique: Feminist Identity in Three Generations of Women." *Gender and Society* 18 (1):122–144.

Piepmeier, Alison. 2009. *Girl Zines: Making Media, Doing Feminism*. New York: New York University Press.

Polletta, Francesca, Pang Ching Bobby Chen, BethGharrity Gardner and Alice Motes. 2013. "Is the Internet Creating New Reasons to Protest?" Pp. 17–36 in *The Future of Social Movement Research: Dynamics, Mechanisms and Processes*, edited by Jacquelien van Stekelenburg, Conny Roggeband, and Bert Klandermans. Minneapolis, MN: University of Minnesota Press.

Rainie, Lee, Sara Kiesler, Ruogu Kang and Mary Madden. 2013. "Anonymity, Privacy, and Security Online," *Pew Research Center*. Retrieved June 26, 2014. http://www.pewinternet.org/files/oldmedia//Files/Reports/2013/PIP_AnonymityOnline_090513.pdf.

Reger, Jo. 2004. "Organizational 'Emotion Work' Through Consciousness-Raising: An Analysis of a Feminist Organization." *Qualitative Sociology* 27(2):205–222.

Reger, Jo, ed. 2005. *Different Wavelengths: Studies of the Contemporary Women's Movement.* New York: Routledge, 2005.

Reger, Jo. 2012. *Everywhere and Nowhere: Contemporary Feminism in the United States.* Oxford: Oxford University Press.

Rentschler, Carrie. 2015. "#Safetytipsforladies: Feminist Twitter Takedowns of Victim Blaming." *Feminist Media Studies* 15(2):353–356.

Rivers, Caryl and Rosalind C. Barnett. 2013. *The New Soft War on Women: How the Myth of Female Ascendance Is Hurting Women, Men—and Our Economy.* New York: Penguin Books.

Rosenthal, Naomi, Meryl Fingrutd, Michele Ethier, Roberta Karant and David McDonald. 1985. "Social Movements and Network Analysis." *American Journal of Sociology* 90:1022–1054.

Rosenthal, Naomi, David McDonald, Michele Ethier, Meryl Fingrutd and Roberta Karant. 1997. "Structural Tensions in the Nineteenth Century Women's Movement." *Mobilization* 2(1):21–46.

Roth, Benita. 2004. *Separate Roads to Feminism: Black, Chicana, and White Feminist Movements in America's Second Wave.* Cambridge, UK: Cambridge University Press.

Rupp, Leila J. 1997. *Worlds of Women: The Making of an International Women's Movement.* Princeton, NJ: Princeton University Press.

Rupp, Leila J. and Verta Taylor. 1987. *Survival in the Doldrums: The American Women's Rights Movement, 1945 to the 1960s.* New York: Oxford University Press.

Scarborough, William J. 2018. "Feminist Twitter and Gender Attitudes: Opportunities and Limitations to Using Twitter in the Study of Public Opinion." *Socius* 4:1–16.

Shaw, Frances. 2012 "'HOTTEST 100 WOMEN' Cross-platform Discursive Activism in Feminist Blogging Networks." *Australian Feminist Studies* 27(74):373–387.

Siddiquee, Imran. 2013. "Disney Store Removes 'I Need a Hero' Shirt in Response to #NotBuyingIt Petition." The Representation Project. Retrieved June 1, 2018. http://therepresentationproject.org/disney-store-removes-i-need-a-her o-shirt-in-response-to-notbuyingit-petition/.

Siegel, Roberta. 1996. *Ambition and Accommodation: How Women View Gender Relations.* Chicago: University of Chicago Press.

Springer, Kimberley. 2005. "Strongblackwomen and Black Feminism: A Next Generation?" Pp. 3–21 in *Different Wavelengths: Studies of the Contemporary Women's Movement*, edited by Jo Reger. NewYork: Routledge.

Staggenborg, Suzanne. 1996. "The Survival of the Women's Movement: Turnover and Continuity in Indiana." *Mobilization* 1(3):143–158.

Staggenborg, Suzanne. 1998. "Social Movement Communities and Cycles of Protest: The Emergence and Maintenance of a Local Women's Movement." *Social Problems* 45(2):180–204.

Taylor, Verta. 1989. "Social Movement Continuity: The Women's Movement in Abeyance." *American Sociological Review* 54(5):761–775.

Taylor, Verta and Lisa Leitz. 2010. "From Infanticide to Activism: Emotions and Identity in Self-Help Movements." Pp. 446–475 in *Social Movements and the Transformation of American Health Care*, edited by Jane Banaszak-Holl, Sandra Levitsky, and Mayer N. Zald. New York: Oxford University Press.

Taylor, Verta and Nikki Raeburn. 1995. "Identity Politics as High Risk Activism: Career Consequences for Lesbian, Gay, and Bisexual Sociologists." *Social Forces* 42 (2):252–273.

Taylor, Verta and Nancy Whittier. 1992. "Collective Identity in Social Movement Communities: Lesbian Feminist Mobilization." Pp. 104–129 in *Frontiers in Social Movement Theory*, edited by Aldon D. Morris and Carole McClurg Mueller. New Haven: Yale University Press.

Thompson, Laura. 2018. "'I can be your Tinder nightmare:' Harassment and misogyny in the online sexual marketplace." *Feminism and Psychology* 28(1):69–89.

Turley, Emma and Kenny Fisher. 2018. "Tweeting Back While Shouting Back: Social Media and Feminist Activism." *Feminism & Psychology* 28(1):128–132.

Thrift, Samantha C. 2014. "#YesAllWomen as Feminist Meme Event." *Feminist Media Studies* 14(6):1090–1092. doi:10.1080/14680777.2014.975421.

Whittier, Nancy. 1995. *Feminist Generations: The Persistence of the Radical Women's Movement.* Philadelphia, PA: Temple University Press.

5 The "Man Question" in Feminism

Kelsy Kretschmer and Kristen Barber

In October of 2017, nine months after organizing the largest single-day protest event in history, Women's March leaders planned the first annual Women's Convention. Held in Detroit, organizers included a broad range of topics, with a common thread of resistance to the Trump administration and mobilizing for future elections (Davey 2017). Bernie Sanders, a U.S. senator from Vermont who had run against Hilary Clinton in the caustic 2016 Democratic primaries, was announced as the convention's opening night speaker. Sanders proved to be an immediately controversial choice. Feminists hotly debated whether or not Sanders could be considered a movement ally. Even if he was, should he be taking up space at the convention? On a Facebook page devoted to the Portland Women's March, one commenter lamented that by agreeing to speak he was preventing women from opportunities to "be heard, make connections and advance [themselves] and others." Another group member quickly pointed out that Sanders had recently urged Democrats to bend on reproductive rights issues if it meant more votes. In her petition to have Sanders removed from the opening night lineup, Amanda Hambrick Ashcraft (2017) noted that "Having a man's face [as a convention speaker] only continues the invisible presence, work and voices of women." Women's March co-president Tamika Mallory defended the choice to include Sanders, calling him a "fierce champion of women's rights" who had promoted "female voices throughout his career" (Hamedy 2017). Perhaps in response to the controversy, Sanders ended up backing out of the convention, opting instead to travel to hurricane-ravaged Puerto Rico (Williams 2017).

While Sanders's inclusion in the 2017 Women's Convention was contested for historically specific reasons, this saga highlights dilemmas feminists have long faced when deciding to include men in movement events. Many feminists welcome men, arguing that their support is critical for ending women's inequality. But because feminism's primary goal has been to bring women's marginalized experiences and interests to the center of public conversation, scholars and activists have struggled with how much space should be yielded to men. The most severe critics have responded to "male feminism" with incredulity, because for men "fighting patriarchy means fighting themselves" (Kahane 1998: 213; also see Digby 1998 and Heath 1987). Women in the movement sometimes fear that men may end up appropriating it for their own purposes because they systematically benefit from the same gendered power relationships feminism is meant to stem (Ashe 2007).

Despite these fears around men's inclusion, they have always played a part in feminist movements. Many activists have welcomed their participation and support, arguing that if men are blocked from feminist projects, then feminists are forced to settle for convincing only half of society that women's equality is necessary (e.g., Alilunas 2011). This perspective is boosted by empirical research, which found that it is men's support for gender equality rather than women's that improves wives' status in households (Cunningham 2005; Yavorksy 2017). But *how* men engage feminism matters. Scholars and activists endorsing this perspective advocate for a kind of consciousness-raising among men, where men are included in ways that ask them to confront their role in women's subordination, as well as their stake in rectifying gender inequality.

Beginning with the first stirrings of feminism in the United States through the current era of activism, we pay attention to men's diverse motivations for supporting feminism. After all, not all men benefit equally from gender equality. Black men, for example, do not ride the glass escalator (Williams 1992) to positions of management like white men. Race intersects with masculinity to position some men closer to what cultural anthropologist Gayle Rubin (1984) refers to as the "charmed circle," by which men reap the rewards of patriarchy. Some men indeed feel an ethical obligation to mitigate the unearned advantages they are given for being men (Brod 1998; Pease 2002), while others find patriarchy also works against them because of their race or sexual identity. We close this chapter by discussing the newest forms of feminist organizing, including the costs and benefits of how men have been included.

Abolition and Feminism

Dating at least back to the abolition movements in the United States and in Europe, men's groups such as The National Men's League for Woman Suffrage organized in support of women's rights to speak publicly and to vote in elections. Debates about women's place in public life bubbled to the surface in anti-slavery spaces. This is because women were part of the conversation, with both white and Black women among the most ardent and active opponents of slavery. Maria W. Stewart, for example—a Black women's rights advocate and abolitionist—fought for especially Black girls to realize a life beyond servitude. Yet women were kept from participating as full members in abolition organizations, which frequently blocked them from leadership positions and from speaking at events. White men who supported the protection and extension of slavery frequently compared the "natural" inferiority of women to that of slaves. Sociologist Patricia Hill Collins (1986: S17) is careful to distinguish between Black and white women's oppression, though, noting that while white (middle- and upper-middle-class) women have lived as "house dogs," Black women have toiled as "mules."[1] The popular argument of women's inferiority forced abolitionist organizations to grapple with women's membership head-on, sometimes resulting in the schism between abolitionists who supported women's rights and those who opposed women's equality altogether.

There were abolitionist men who chafed at the poor treatment women members received in abolition organizations. William Lloyd Garrison, organizer of the 1832 New-England Anti-Slavery Sociology, which later became the American Anti-Slavery Society, insisted organizations give women full voting rights and create space for then to speak at meetings.[2] Women's abolition work helped them develop political acumen, and their humiliation at the hands of some abolitionist men inspired them to mobilize their new organizing skills (Douglass and Foner 1992). Having met in the anti-slavery movement, Lucretia Mott and Elizabeth Cady Stanton organized the 1848 Seneca Falls Convention. The meeting, including almost 200 women and a few dozen prominent men, was the first to lay out a clear agenda for a U.S. feminist movement.

Black men played important roles in the initial era of U.S. feminism. For them, the joint dehumanization of all women and of Black people as a group highlighted the necessity for universal suffrage. As one of 37 men attending the Seneca Falls Convention, Frederick Douglass served as a critical ally to Stanton in convincing attendees to include suffrage as a central goal. This was difficult since, for many white women, claiming the right to vote was too radical and would only alienate elites who might be convinced to support a statement denouncing women's generally poor treatment (Walker 1973). Before the convention, Douglass (1848) wrote forcefully, in *The North Star*, that if the government was to be considered just, it must rely on the free consent of *all* those governed, including women. Women, he wrote, "were justly entitled to all we claim for men." For the rest of his life, Douglass took great pride in being "sufficiently enlightened" to have supported feminism in its earliest era (Douglas and Foner 1992: 14).

The alliance between Black men and white female suffragists cracked when the proposed 14th amendment extended the protection of citizenship only to freed men, explicitly excluding women from the constitution for the first time. Black men and women who had been united with white women behind universal suffrage were forced to choose among their priorities. In a speech to the suffragist Equal Rights Association, Douglass expressed the desperation of many Black men and women in choosing to support the amendment, explaining that the worst treatment Black women faced was because of their race, not their sex. For them, enfranchised Black men would be able to protect and improve their circumstances. He feared that including women in the amendment might provoke a stronger public backlash, resulting in defeat for all of them, and a devastating outcome for the uniquely vulnerable Black population.

Furious at their exclusion, white women toured the country arguing against the amendment. Stanton and well-known feminist Susan B. Anthony, consequently abandoned the universal suffrage organizations, which included Black men's rights, in favor of more militant women's suffrage organizations (Walker 1973). Stanton was particularly vitriolic toward her former allies, claiming that she would cut off her own arm before she would "demand the ballot for the Negro [man] and not the woman" (Davis 2011: 76). White women wove in other racist rhetoric, arguing that white female voters would be able to help protect white men's interests over those of newly enfranchised Black men's. Black women were left in the lurch, whereby they faced pressure to align with either a Black civil-rights agenda that was sexist or a feminist movement prioritizing white women's interests. This original tension around Black women's intersecting experiences with discrimination resurfaced in the 1960s era women's movement and continues to be a major source of conflict in contemporary feminism.

While alliances between abolitionist men and suffragist women hit a low point in this period, the animosity between them did not characterize all relationships. Black abolitionist Robert Purvis refused to support the cause of Black men if it meant leaving women behind, arguing that he would demand for "his daughter all that he asked for his son and himself" (Walker 1973: 29–30). Julia Ward Howe, a respected white suffragist leader, announced she would support Black male suffrage, even if it excluded women's access to the ballot. And after the turn of the century, WEB DuBois, in his widely read newspaper, *The Crisis,* used his influence to make the case for women's suffrage. Women's suffrage was important, he noted, because it was the morally right choice and because "votes for women means votes for Black women" (Kroeger 2017: 91). If white women would vote to preserve their racial privileges, then Black women's voting power was an important hedge protecting Black's civil rights.

In the early 20th century, a variety of men's organizations working for women's right to vote emerged across the country. The National American Women's Suffrage Association (NAWSA)—the largest and best-known suffrage association—courted powerful men for support, including men in "publishing, industry, finance, science, medicine, and academia," among others (Kroeger 2017: 1). Just as feminists urge now, suffragists cajoled progressive men in the early 20th century to use their privilege to help achieve movement aims. The National Men's League for Women's Suffrage, for example, argued that "it ought to hurt any man's pride to let it be said that the women of Americ[a] have to beg and implore and campaign and make so many sacrifices to gain a thing that belongs to them as a matter of right" (111).

Women in the suffrage movement polarized over accepting these partnerships with men's groups. Leaders of the NAWSA worried that bringing men into the movement would simply mean more work for female leaders charged with organizing men's participation. Despite their early reluctance, these suffragists eventually made room for men. The benefits of associating with powerful men were clear. Groups like The National Men's League for Women's Suffrage—which originated in 1907 London and emerged three years later in New York—prioritized the authority of the women's groups, claiming center stage only when called upon by the movement's female leaders (Kroeger 2017). They lobbied other powerful men, wrote editorials and pamphlets, marched, and donated their resources to the cause. While credit for the Nineteenth Amendment certainly belongs to the women who spent decades dedicated to its passage, men in the movement provided an important boost by marshalling their considerable resources and privileges.

Insider Men and Government Allies

The 19th Amendment, adopted in 1920, was a watershed moment for feminists. It also created a juncture for feminists to choose where to focus next. The U.S. feminist movement entered what historians and sociologists call "the doldrums," a period in which mobilization waned and leaders sharply divided over their preferred goals and tactics. Many rank-and-file activists drifted back to their regular lives, at least temporarily satisfied with the suffrage victory. Leaders created smaller organizations—abeyance structures—that continued to work, albeit in more limited ways, on feminist goals, including jury representation and labor protections for women (McCammon 2012; Rupp and Taylor 1987; Taylor 1989).

Despite the diminished prominence of the feminist movement in the years following suffrage, women's lives were changing in important ways. More middle-class white women were joining the workforce, and they increasingly demanded fairer treatment in their jobs. The employment sector was rife with gender and racial discrimination. Black women, poor white women and immigrant women had long been in the workforce, ghettoized into mostly low-skilled, low-paying jobs. Employers routinely refused to hire women, paid them less than their male colleagues, barred them from better-paid positions and fired them when got married, became pregnant, or were deemed "too old." Women's frustration with institutional inequalities created demand for a new wave of feminism, which would erupt in 1966 with the founding of the National Organization for Women (NOW). The seeds of a new movement were planted with the inclusion of sex discrimination, known as Title VII, in the Civil Rights Act of 1964. Segregationist Congressman Howard Smith, added sex as an amendment to kill the larger bill. He believed that Northern Democrats would vote to support racial equality legislation, but they would balk if forced to also support gender equality. To nearly everyone's surprise, the bill and the amendment passed into law, and women's Title VII claims were to be lodged with the newly created Equal Employment Opportunity

Commission (EEOC). For the first time, women could pursue employment discrimination grievances through the federal government.

The EEOC staff was deeply committed to pursuing racial justice, but far less interested in sex discrimination. Only one of the four male commissioners at the time, Richard Graham, took seriously women's claims. Graham would say later in interviews that he became a feminist "on the job," under the tutelage of the only female EEOC commissioner, Aileen Hernandez (Bernstein 2007). Graham became an outspoken advocate for women's equality, traveling to investigate women's working conditions and promoting the EEOC guidelines for gender equality. He also became a member of the underground feminist movement in Washington D.C., filled with mainly women who kept low profiles while using government channels to advance women's interests (Rosen 2000).

Graham played a critical role in getting the EEOC to seriously consider women's claims of discrimination, and ultimately in facilitating the birth of NOW. When it became clear existing women's clubs and professional organizations were unwilling or unable to pressure the EEOC on women's issues, it was, by some accounts, Graham's idea that feminists should create a new, explicitly political organization to serve this function (e.g. Banaszak 2009). Catherine East and Mary Eastwood, two members of the feminist network in Washington D.C., pursued this idea with Betty Friedan, author of *The Feminine Mystique* and already a prominent voice for women's equality. At the 1966 meeting of the states' Commissions on the Status of Women, Friedan led a contingent of women in pressing the Commissions to demand that the EEOC do a better job pursuing women's discrimination claims and that it reappoint Graham at the end of his one-year term. After their proposals were rejected, the group used the rest of the meeting to sketch the details for their new advocacy organization. With Friedan serving as NOW's first president, Graham agreed to serve as the co-vice president of the new organization, alongside Aileen Hernandez, his former EEOC colleague. NOW grew to be the largest feminist organization in the United States, representing hundreds of thousands of men and women.

Men's Place in the Contemporary Movement

As the movement grew, more men were exposed to feminist ideas and there was greater space for them to participate in the movement. Most feminists welcomed them into movement spaces. Other feminists argued for men's total and purposeful exclusion from the movement and its events. As feminist philosopher Sandra Bartky (1998: xi) notes, "the discoveries we [women] made about the nature and extent of our sometimes blatant but often disguised oppression could not and would not have been made 'in the presence of the oppressor.'" These separatist spaces were important for women to identify common struggles amongst themselves, and thus to identify the mechanisms of systematic sexism. Focusing solely on sexism, though, often meant focusing on the problems of white women. Black feminist thought and multicultural feminism arose to counter a feminism that ignored how race distinguished women's experiences of oppression within a *racialized* patriarchy.

While some women felt they could only express themselves authentically in the absence of men, most feminists believed that the movement could only be successful by changing men's attitudes toward women—and increasingly changing men's attitudes toward masculinity as a narrow and damaging set of expectations. This necessitated men's inclusion in feminist organizing and education outreach. Research indicates that bringing men into anti-violence mobilization, for example, is an effective strategy for reducing violence against women (World Health Organization 2009). Social movement programming provides such concrete opportunities for men's deeper commitment to feminist principles (Carlson et al. 2015).

Since the 1990s, feminists have proven more willing to include men in their events and organizations. It is telling that news reports of Take Back the Night marches and later-occurring SlutWalks increasingly included mentions of male participants (Kretschmer and Barber 2016). During early reporting of Take Back the Night, feminist leaders grappled with whether these events were about ending violence more generally, or if they should narrowly focus on women's safety from men. Leaders have made different decisions about this balance, with some now including men as full partici-pants and expanding the events' themes to include a discussion of men's experiences as victims. Other organizers block men's participation com-pletely to keep the focus on women, and some strike a middle ground of allowing men to participate in limited and controlled ways. In contrast to the dilemmas revealed in Take Back the Night coverage, reporting on the more recent SlutWalks shows no distinctions between men and women as participants. SlutWalk coverage was also much more likely to include dis-cussions of violence against gender and sexual minorities.

Despite the growing acceptance of men as equal participants, scholars have pointed to the problematic ways men sometimes participate in feminist movements and events. Even at events designed specifically for men sym-pathetic to feminist aims, participants often end up reproducing gender inequalities. For example, in his study of "Walk a Mile in Her Shoes," a march during which men demonstrate against violence toward women by marching in women's shoes and clothing, sociologist Tristan Bridges casts doubt on how effective the event is in transforming participants into fem-inists. While drag performances can be political—and are important to queer communities (e.g. Han 2015; Rupp and Taylor 2003)—the men in Bridge's study used drag to highlight their supposed differences from women as a group, and to police each other's masculinity. Men could wear a pair of heels, but only in jest. This leaves gender divides intact and sexual violence against women played a noticeably small role in these events, despite being the stated purpose.

Shifts to include men as full participants reflects feminism's growing emphasis on the problems men face because of patriarchy, as well as expanding discussions of transwomen and genderqueer. While conservative men reject feminism in defense of their "rightful," dominant place in the gender order (Lingard and Douglas 1999), other men support greater gender equality and see the "costs" they suffer in patriarchal systems. Many men do not want to be implicated in the oppression of women and are eager to support gender-equalizing policies (see also Digby 1998). And some men have embraced the notion that "hegemonic masculinity" (Connell and Messerschmidt 2005)—or valorized definitions of manhood—constrict possibilities for what it means to be a man, as well as subordinate men whose racial and sexual locations do not allow them to fit white, hetero-sexual masculine ideals. In response to evolving ideas around men's role in both the reproduction and deconstruction of gender inequality, activists have been increasingly opening feminist organizations, events, and pro-grams for men's participation (Connell 1997; Esplen 2006; Flood 2007; Pease 2002).

Yet, including men as partners in feminist movements continues to be tricky business for feminist leaders. When men are full participants, they might "take over" feminist campaigns and revel in the attention they receive for participating in the events (Ashe 2007). Men may receive an unequal (and unearned) amount of credence for very little feminist work. These men face scrutiny over whether they are "real" feminists or instead trade on their masculine privilege to become leaders and earn a dispropor-tionate amount of applause as "good guys."

Because an inclusive feminist logic underscores the ways all people are disadvantaged by conventional gender expectations, men also sometimes emphasize their own victimhood while downplaying their privileged posi-tion relative to women. One key example is the growth of "men's rights" and "father's rights" movements, which focus on *feelings* of unfairness while ignoring oppression as a structural phenomenon. They overlook the fact that costs to men often come at the hands of other men, not women (Messner 2000). And scholars have argued that men's willingness to see themselves as victims reflects the extent to which they are used to their interests being at the center of public conversation (Crowe 2011). Focusing on the costs of patriarchy might be helpful in motivating men to show up for feminism (Pease 2002), but it also risks dislodging women's experiences as the focus of the movement. And men risk conflating *costs* with *oppression*.[3] For men to begin understanding gender oppression, they need to ground feminism firmly in women's and gender-nonconformists' experiences and grapple with just how these experiences result from *structural* inequalities.

Despite these critiques, other scholars argue men will only buy into feminist ideology when movement leaders articulate men's stakes in its success, rather than relying on altruism alone (Brod 1998). And many men's groups indeed have instituted policies for their groups that keep women's interests, experiences, and needs in the foreground of their work. This approach has been prevalent in Take Back the Night events, in which community groups host concurrent but separate men's discussion groups focused on their roles in dismantling patriarchy. Other times, men have been asked to participate in the event by providing childcare or refreshments for women marchers, or by lining the march route with candles. These modes of participation included men, thwarting complaints of their exclusion, while still maintaining women's central position (Kretschmer and Barber 2016).

Men are brought into the movement in other ways, as well. College campuses have proven to be a core institution for carrying feminism forward. Title IX of the 1972 Higher Education Act mandated that educational institutions receiving federal funding had to ensure equal access for women. The most well known outcome of this legislation is the expansion of sports and recreational opportunities for women. But after years of feminist legal work, courts have interpreted Title IX to include a focus on students' vulnerability to sexual harassment and violence on college campuses. In 2011, the Department of Education produced a set of guidelines requiring colleges and universities to promptly investigate accusations of sexual harassment and violence, stop such behavior, prevent it from reoccurring, and provide remedies to victim-survivors (Silbaugh 2015). Because roughly half of the U.S. population enrolls in a college or university, and because these institutions are designed to change the way people think about the world, they are practical settings to introduce men to feminist ideas and practices. Campus men have access to a variety of venues that might expose them to feminist models for "healthy masculinity", including women and gender studies courses, women's centers and student groups devoted to men's stakes in feminism and anti-racism.

Feminists fought to establish Women and Gender Studies (WGS) on college campuses. WGS has served as the academic arm of the feminist movement; and because men have access to these courses, they provide a promising avenue for bringing men into the movement. A wide swath of research has indicated that participating in WGS courses increases students' awareness of sexism and decreases their investment in conventional gender norms and hostile misogyny (Bryant 2003; Stake and Hoffman 2001; Katz et al. 2004). In addition to changed attitudes, WGS courses also appear to increase student participation in feminist activism (Stake and Hoffmann 2001; Stake and Rose 1994). Beyond simply intending to do more, both men and women reported that after having taken a WGS course, they confronted others about sexism and attended feminist events and meetings (Stake 2007).

While feminist college courses seem like a promising way to reach young men, there may be significant limitations to the approach. One potential barrier is low enrollment of men in these types of courses. It might help to require specific core university courses in gender studies *and* racial/ethnic studies instead of a general diversity requirement. Some scholars also worry these classes produce more "workshop" activism, limiting men's engagement in the outside world (Carlson et al. 2015). Such critics argue that engaging men in feminist work requires changing their mindset from passive consumers of feminist knowledge to "change agents who could affect policy and practice in their communities and places of work" (p. 1418). Men may see WGS courses as an easy way to gain college credit without deeper engagement in equality outside the classroom.

Other scholars have expressed concerns about how men react to WGS curriculum, especially when it raises negative emotions. Robert K. Pleasants (2011), who works in education and WGS, found that even when male students elected to take gender courses, they often resisted the curriculum and experienced a variety of unhelpful emotions, including guilt, offense, victimization, and hopelessness. But women's studies courses may have different effects for men and women students. Among students enrolled in WGS courses, for example, feminist attitudes increased for women but decreased for the small number of men (Thomsen et al. 1995). Some of these attitudes might be shaped by the resistance men experience from those in their peer group when explaining their choice to study gender and feminism (see Schmitz and Haltom 2016). They often face skepticism for why they enroll in or what they learn in WGS courses. Their allegiance to masculinity comes under suspicion, leading men to explain their studies in non-feminist terms. While these studies cast some doubt on the effectiveness of WGS as an entry point for men into feminist movements, it is important to remember that men are not a monolithic group and their varying social locations are likely to create different reactions to WGS curriculum. Queer men, for example, may feel more comfortable and confident than straight men when discussing gender inequality in the classroom, especially when they are also politically active on LGBTQ issues (Schmitz and Kazyak 2017).

There are roughly 500 women's centers currently operating across the United States. They are typically the "hub of campus activism related to the pursuit of gender equity" and serve as advocate institutions for victims of domestic and sexual violence (Marine, Helfrich and Randhawa 2017: 46). Since the 1970s, women's centers have become more gender inclusive, welcoming trans women and genderqueer people with specialized programing. These centers have also expanded their programing to include men for a variety of reasons, including organizational survival. By reaching out to men, centers increase the number of students they serve, justifying their presence on campuses. Staff at these centers also see reaching men as central to their feminist mission. By bringing men to the center, problems of gender inequality and violence become problems all students have a role in addressing. College women's centers are already structured to focus on problems of gender inequality, but they have been particularly important for generating and housing men's student groups devoted to developing healthy masculinities. In a 2004 survey study of 75 college women's centers in the United States, 33 percent of the centers reported including programs devoted to men, including a focus on creating male feminist allies, ending sexual violence, and supporting student-fathers (Kasper 2004).

Bringing men into women's centers is not without drawbacks. Staff, founders, and alumni can struggle with balancing the benefits of including men with the loss of specialized space for women only (Marine, Helfrich and Randhawa 2017). Some staff of gender-inclusive women's centers even report they "like[d] it better when it's just women" (p. 53). While younger women have shown greater openness to the idea that men can be feminists, older feminists are sometimes disappointed when women's centers begin to include men in their programming. The centers also struggle with staffing and space constraints needed to accommodate new constituents, and resistance to changing names when moving from women's centers to more gender inclusive organizations. These problems highlight the tension between what individual feminists might prefer and the organizational realities of running fiscally dependent centers on co-ed campuses.

In the last decade, colleges and universities have seen an increase in independent student groups devoted to developing healthy masculinities on campuses. Many emerged from campus women's centers but became independent to better attract men to the programs. These groups often aim to help young men outgrow "toxic masculinity"—the gender attitudes most men are raised with that demean women while embracing dominance, violence, and homophobia (Connell and Messerschmidt 2005; Banet-Weiser and Miltner 2016). Group mentors teach men to communicate respectfully with women and negotiate consent with sexual partners. These organizations also train men to be good "bystanders" who will intervene when they see other men committing harm (Messner, Greenberg and Peretz 2015; Messner 2016).

Men's student groups often carry feminist aims by helping men see women as autonomous and equal full humans. Yet, they also sometimes drift in their purposes. College administrators sometimes use them to boost retention rates for men of color. Others use the groups to focus on community service and developing men's leadership skills. These are worthy goals, but it is a stretch to see their connection to feminism's overarching goals toward gender equality. Some men's groups are created to demonstrate compliance to the new guidelines around sexual assault reporting under Title IX. For example, at the University of Redlands, a small private liberal arts school in California, a men's student group ran workshops that would educate students "to be active bystanders in sexual assault situations, how to practice affirmative consent, and how to abide by new Title IX regulations" (University of Redlands 2018). While important, this effort ultimately serves institutional concerns of image and litigation.

Conclusion

In 1993, political scientist Kathy E. Ferguson, wrote, *The Man Question: Visions of Subjectivity in Feminist Theory*. Her focus was on moving beyond the limits of science focused on men as de facto experts and "subjects," and beyond men's studies of the 1980s, which reinforced gender essentialism. Instead, Ferguson argued that masculinity as a concept and an expectation is a problem that needs explaining, and early masculinities scholars such as Michael A. Messner, Raewyn Connell, Tom Digby and Bob Pease, have been integral to pushing forward the "man question" in scholarship. And Jackson Katz shows us what it can look like to do feminist activism for audiences of men. This work is important, but complicated, especially as it remains unclear what men's helpful involvement looks like.

Many feminist organizers, scholars and activists contend with the question of what to do with men, whether they are apathetic, hostile, or allies. After all, men arrive to feminism with the privileges they've accrued in the world; and the struggle for movement leaders is how to welcome men while not bolstering the privileges they are used to. This is particularly difficult for white, middle- and upper-middle-class straight men who adhere to the idea of meritocracy; whereby they believe they have earned their opportunities rather than occupying the center of the charmed circle. For men who identify as or want to be feminist allies, the struggle is to demonstrate support without assuming ownership of a movement that's not for them; and sometimes this means acknowledging they are not welcome in all movement spaces.

Bernie Sanders did not address the controversy over his invitation to the Women's March Convention. Removing himself from the program was an opportunity to dialogue about men's place in feminism and to demonstrate what it means to be a feminist ally focused on women's voices. Instead, he explained that his attention was needed in Puerto Rico to help cope with the aftermath of Hurricane Maria, leaving unresolved the questions about his specific claims to the new wave of feminism, and more generally, fights over how much space men should be afforded in the movement. Versions of this dilemma have played out in many movements and across multiple generations, including with whites in the resurgent civil rights movement and heterosexual people in the LGBTQ movement. Men's role in feminism has grown only more complicated over time, as new movement generations grapple with how to include men suffering under stifling patriarchal limitations while continuing to center women's perspectives.

Notes

1 This insight was originally offered by Nancy White, who was paraphrasing her mother, while being interviewed by John Gwaltney (1980: 148).
2 William Lloyd Garrison argued slavery was an evil institution in part because it failed to distinguish between men's and women's roles in work and family. This

argument legitimized Garrison's group at a time when their acceptance of women as equal members was scandalous. It also undermined the feminist messages his group projected by reinforcing the idea women's place was in the home as mothers and domestics (Hoganson 1993).

3 "Costs" of masculinity are not the same as oppression—although men often interpret it as such (Messner 2000). Oppression is an institutionalized and structural reality that results in unequal and unfair evaluation and treatment. Costs, on the other hand, come with men trying to live up to hegemonic definitions of masculinity as aggressive, heterosexually promiscuous, or emotionally removed. These are costs are harmful but do not impede white, straight men's abilities to trade on patriarchal dividends.

References

Alilunas, Peter. 2011. "'The (In)Visible People in the Room: Men in Women's Studies.' Men and Masculinities." *Men and Masculinities* 14(2):210–229.

Ashcraft, Amanda Hambrick. 2017. "Remove Bernie Sanders from Opening the Women's Convention." Change.Org. Retrieved November 28, 2017. https://www.change.org/p/women-s-march-organizers-remove-bernie-sanders-from-opening-the-women-s-convention.

Ashe, Fidelma. 2007. *The New Politics of Masculinity: Men, Power and Resistance.* London: Routledge.

Banaszak, Lee Ann. 2009. *The Women's Movement Inside and Outside the State.* New York, NY: Cambridge University Press.

Banet-Weiser, Sarah and Kate M. Miltner. 2016. "#MasculinitySoFragile: Culture, Structure, and Networked Misogyny." *Feminist Media Studies* 16(1):171–174. https://doi.org/10.1080/. doi:14680777.2016.1120490.

Bartkey, Sandra. 1998. "Foreward." In *Men Doing Feminism*, edited by Tom Digby. London: Routledge.

Bernstein, Adam. 2007. "Richard Graham, Early EEOC, Teacher Corps Leader," September 29. Retrieved August 20, 2018. http://www.washingtonpost.com/wp-dyn/content/article/2007/09/28/AR2007092801922.html.

Bridges, Tristan S. 2010. "Men Just Weren't Made To Do This: Performances of Drag at 'Walk a Mile in Her Shoes' Marches." *Gender & Society* 24(1):5–30. https://doi.org/10.1177/0891243209356924.

Brod, Harry. 1998. "To Be a Man, or Not to Be a Man—that Is the Feminist Question." Pp. 197–212 in *Men Doing Feminism*. New York, NY: Routledge.

Bryant, Alyssa N. 2003. "Changes in Attitudes Toward Women's Roles: Predicting Gender-Role Traditionalism Among College Students." *Sex Roles* 48(3):131–142. https://doi.org/10.1023/A:1022451205292.

Carlson, Juliana and Erin Casey, Jeffrey L. Edleson, Richard M. Tolman, Tova B. Neugut, Ericka Kimball. 2015. "Strategies to Engage Men and Boys in Violence Prevention: A Global Organizational Perspective." *Violence against Women*, 21(11), 1406–1425. http://doi.org/10.1177/1077801215594888.

Collins, Patricia Hill. 1986. "Learning from the Outsider Within: The Sociological Significance of Black Feminist Thought." *Social Problems* 33(6): 14–32.

Connell, R. W. 1997. "Men, Masculinities and Feminism." *Social Alternatives* 16 (3):7–10.

Connell, R. W. 2005. *Masculinities.* Cambridge: Polity.

Connell, R. W. and James W. Messerschmidt. 2005. "Hegemonic Masculinity: Rethinking the Concept." *Gender & Society* 19(6):829–859. https://doi.org/10. 1177/0891243205278639.

Crowe, Jonathan. 2011. "Men and Feminism: Some Challenges and a Partial Response." *Social Alternatives* 30(1):49–53.

Cunningham, Mick. 2005. "Gender in Cohabitation and Marriage: The Influence of Gender Ideology on Housework Allocation Over the Life Course." *Journal of Family Issues* 26(8):1037–1061. https://doi.org/10.1177/0192513X04273592.

Davey, Monica. 2017. "At Women's Convention in Detroit, a Test of Momentum and Focus." *The New York Times*, October 28, 2017. Retrieved August 20, 2018. https:// www.nytimes.com/2017/10/28/us/women-convention-detroit-march.html.

Davis, Angela Y. 2011. *Women, Race, & Class*. New York, NY: Vintage Books.

Digby, Tom. 1998. *Men Doing Feminism*. New York, NY: Routledge.

Douglass, Frederick. 1848. "The Rights of Women." *The North Star*, July 28, 1948.

Douglass, Frederick and Philip S. Foner. 1992. *Frederick Douglass On Women's Rights*. New York, NY: Da Capo Press.

Esplen, Emily. 2006. *Engaging Men in Gender Equality: Positive Strategies and Approaches: Overview and Annotated Bibliography*. Brighton: Institute of Development Studies.

Ferguson, Kathy E. 1993. *The Man Question: Visions of Subjectivity in Feminist Theory*. Berkeley: University of California Press.

Flood, Michael. 2007. "Involving Men in Gender Practice and Policy." *Critical Half* 5(1):9–14.

Gwaltney, John Langston. 1980. *Drylongso, a Self-portrait of Black America*. New York, NY: Vintage.

Hamedy, Saba. 2017. "Bernie Sanders Speech at Women's Convention Prompts Backlash." *CNN*, October 12. Retrieved August 20, 2018. www.cnn.com/2017/ 10/12/politics/bernie-sanders-womens-convention/index.html.

Han, C.Winter. 2015. *Geisha of a Different Kind: Race and Sexuality in Gaysian America*. New York, NY: New York University Press.

Heath, Stephen. 1987. "Male Feminism." Pp. 1–32 in *Men in Feminism*, edited by Alice Jardine and Paul Smith. New York, NY: Methuen.

Hoganson, Kristin. 1993. "Garrisonian Abolitionists and the Rhetoric of Gender, 1850–1860." *American Quarterly* 45(4):558–595. https://doi.org/10.2307/2713309.

Kahane, David J. 1998. "Male Feminism as Oxymoron." Pp. 213–235 in *Men Doing Feminism*, edited by Tom Digby. New York, NY: Routledge.

Kasper, Barbara. 2004. "Campus-Based Women's Centers: A Review of Problems and Practices." *Affilia* 19(2):185–198. https://doi.org/10.1177/0886109903262755.

Katz, Jennifer, Samantha Swindell, and Sherry Farrow. 2004. "Effects of Participation in a First Women's Studies Course on Collective Self-Esteem, Gender-Related Attitudes, and Emotional Well-Being1." *Journal of Applied Social Psychology* 34(10):2179–2199. https://doi.org/10.1111/j.1559-1816.2004.tb02696.x.

Kretschmer, Kelsy and Kristen Barber. 2016. "Men at the March: Feminist Movement Boundaries and Men's Participation in Take Back the Night and Slutwalk." *Mobilization: An International Quarterly* 21(3):283–300. https://doi.org/10.17813/ 1086-671X-20-3-283.

Kroeger, Brooke. 2017. *The Suffragents: How Women Used Men to Get the Vote*. Albany, NY: SUNY Press.

Lingard, Bob and Peter Douglas. 1999. *Men Engaging Feminisms: Pro-Feminism, Backlashes and Schooling*. Buckingham, UK: Open University Press.

Marine, Susan B., Gina Helfrich and Liam Randhawa. 2017. "Gender-Inclusive Practices in Campus Women's and Gender Centers: Benefits, Challenges, and Future Prospects." *NASPA Journal About Women in Higher Education* 10(1):45–63. https://doi.org/10.1080/19407882.2017.1280054.

McCammon, Holly J. 2012. *The U.S. Women's Jury Movements and Strategic Adaptation: A More Just Verdict.* New York, NY: Cambridge University Press.

Messner, Michael A. 1993. "'Changing Men' and Feminist Politics in the United States." *Theory and Society* 22(5):723–737. https://doi.org/10.1007/BF00993545.

Messner, Michael A. 1997. *Politics of Masculinities: Men in Movements.* Thousand Oaks, CA: Sage Publications.

Messner, Michael A. 2000. "White Guy Habitus in the Classroom: Confronting the Reproduction of Privilege," *Men and Masculinities* 2:457–469.

Messner, Michael A. 2016. "Forks in the road of men's gender politics: Men's rights vs. feminist allies." *International Journal for Crime, Justice and Social Democracy* 5:6–20.

Messner, Michael A., Max A. Greenberg and Tal Peretz. 2015. *Some Men: Feminist Allies and the Movement to End Violence Against Women.* New York, NY: Oxford University Press.

Pease, Bob. 2002. "(Re)Constructing Men's Interests." *Men and Masculinities* 5 (2):165–177. https://doi.org/10.1177/1097184X02005002003.

Pleasants, Robert K. 2011. "Men Learning Feminism: Protecting Privileges Through Discourses of Resistance." *Men and Masculinities* 14(2):230–250. https://doi.org/10.1177/1097184X11407048.

Rosen, Ruth. 2000. *The World Split Open: How the Modern Women's Movement Changed America.* New York, NY: Viking.

Rubin, Gayle. 1984. "Thinking Sex: Notes for a radical theory of the politics of sexuality." Pp. 100–133 in *Social Perspectives in Lesbian and Gay Studies: A Reader,* edited by P.M. Nardi and B.E. Schneider. London: Routledge.

Rupp, Leila J. and Verta Taylor. 1987. *Survival in the Doldrums: The American Women's Rights Movement, 1945 to the 1960s.* New York: Oxford University Press.

Rupp, Leila J. and Verta Taylor. 2001. *Drag Queens at the 801 Cabaret.* Chicago: University of Chicago Press.

Schmitz, Rachel M. and Trenton M. Haltom. 2016. "'I Wanted to Raise My Hand and Say I'm Not a Feminist': College Men's Use of Hybrid Masculinities to Negotiate Attachments to Feminism and Gender Studies." *The Journal of Men's Studies,* 25(3):278–297. https://doi.org/10.1177/1060826516676841.

Schmitz, Rachel M. and Emily Kazyak. 2017. "Checking Privilege at the Door: Men's Reflections on Masculinity in Women's and Gender Studies Courses." *Gender Issues* 34(2):129–148. https://doi.org/10.1007/s12147-016-9178-1.

Silbaugh, Katherine. 2015. "Reactive to Proactive: Title IX's Unrealized Capacity to Prevent Campus Sexual Assault." *Boston University Law Review* 95:1049–1076.

Stake, Jayne E. 2007. "Predictors of Change in Feminist Activism Through Women's and Gender Studies." *Sex Roles* 57(1–2):43–54. https://doi.org/10.1007/s11199-007-9227-z.

Stake, Jayne E. and Frances L. Hoffmann. 2001. "Changes in Student Social Attitudes, Activism, and Personal Confidence in Higher Education: The Role of Women's Studies." *American Educational Research Journal* 38(2):411–436.

Stake, Jayne E. and Suzanna Rose. 1994. "The Long-Term Impact of Women's Studies on Students'personal Lives and Political Activism." *Psychology of Women Quarterly* 18(3):403–412. https://doi.org/10.1111/j.1471-6402.1994.tb00463.x.

Taylor, Verta. 1989. "Social Movement Continuity: The Women's Movement in Abeyance." *American Sociological Review* 54(5): 761–775.

Thomsen, Cynthia J., Andra M. Basu and Mark Tippens Reinitz. 1995. "Effects of Women's Studies Courses on Gender-Related Attitudes of Women and Men." *Psychology of Women Quarterly* 19(3):419–425. https://doi.org/10.1111/j. 1471-6402.1995.tb00084.x.

University of Redlands. 2018. "D.U.D.E.S. Resource Center." Retrieved August 20, 2018. http://www.redlands.edu/student-affairs/campus-diversity-and-inclu sion/programs/gender-programs/d.u.d.e.s/.

Walker, S.Jay. 1973. "Frederick Douglass and Woman Suffrage." *The Black Scholar* 4 (6–7):24–31. https://doi.org/10.1080/00064246.1973.11760855.

Williams, Christine L. 1992. "The Glass Escalator: Hidden Advantages for Men in the 'Female' Professions." *Social Problems* 39(3): 253–267.

Williams, Vanessa. 2017. "Bernie Sanders Will Not Attend the Women's Convention, but Instead Will Travel to Hurricane-Ravaged Puerto Rico." *Washington Post*, October 19, 2017. Retrieved August 20, 2018. https://www.washingtonp ost.com/news/post-nation/wp/2017/10/19/bernie-sanders-will-not-attend-the-womens-convention-but-instead-will-travel-to-hurricane-ravaged-puerto-rico/.

World Health Organization. 2009. "Promoting Gender Equality to Prevent Violence against Women." Retrieved August 20, 2018. http://www.who.int/vio lence_injury_prevention/violence/gender.pdf.

Yavorsky, Jill. 2017. "Searching for an Equal Co-Parent: Six Factors That Influence Whether Dad Pulls His Weight at Home." *Slate*, October 11. Retrieved August 20, 2018. http://www.slate.com/blogs/better_life_lab/2017/10/11/searching_ for_an_equal_co_parent.html.

6 Anti-Trafficking and Feminism

Survivors are Movement Activists

Lillian Taylor Jungleib

> Survivors need to be at the forefront of the movement, prized for their
> expertise and input and not just for their stories.
>
> Jada, anti-sex trafficking activist and survivor

Feminist activists working to end sex trafficking in the 21st century have
succeeded in bringing unprecedented public concern and resources to rescuing women from commercial sex.[1] Doing so involved the reframing of
forced prostitution, and sometimes all prostitution, as a form of violence
against women that must be eradicated. Research on the contemporary
anti-sex trafficking movement posits it is run largely by feminist allies
working on behalf of trafficking victims. Scholars, sex worker rights activists, and survivors of sex trafficking themselves note the absence of survivors able to participate as activists.[2] Survivors are generally included only in
the limited role of bringing authenticity to the movement through providing stories of their victimization that help legitimate the movement's claims
and goals.

Based on ethnographic fieldwork and interviews with survivor activists, I
argue that while survivor participation in the contemporary anti-sex trafficking movement is heavily restricted by movement structure and ideology,
survivors nonetheless make important activist contributions. Survivors co-opt
the roles provided for them to assert their humanity beyond the role of
victim, come out and build solidarity with other survivors, and use their
experiences to demand legitimacy as qualified experts to challenge the
dominant strategies and goals of the anti-sex trafficking movement. I find that
the substantive contributions of survivor activism are essential to building an
inclusive and effective feminist movement against sex trafficking.

The Movement Against Sex Trafficking

Anti-sex trafficking movement organizations frequently cite a 2017 International Labour Organization report that estimates there are 4.8 million
persons in forced sexual exploitation worldwide, 2 million of whom are
children. However, data regarding the actual rates of the problem are highly

disputed and prostitution researchers claim these estimates are grossly infla-ted (Jahic and Finckenauer 2005; Laczko and Gramegna 2003; Weitzer and Ditmore 2010). While the exact scale of the problem remains unclear, sex trafficking is certainly real and demands public concern and appropriate intervention, both domestically and transnationally.

The Trafficking Victims Protection Act of 2000 defines "severe" sex trafficking as compelling an adult into a commercial sex act through "force, fraud or coercion" or a child into a commercial sex act under any circum-stances (22 U.S.C. § 7101 2000). The anti-sex trafficking movement reg-ularly highlights experiences in commercial sex that fall under this definition, such as having a pimp, or migrating for the purposes of other employment and being tricked into prostitution. However, the vast major-ity of commercial sex does not fit this legal definition of severe trafficking. These experiences can include everything from working voluntarily as an escort to engaging in survival sex without coercion by a third party, neither of which fall under the legal definition of trafficking. A growing body of literature clearly establishes that commercial sex can better be understood as encompassing a wide range of worker experiences and degrees of agency (see Weitzer 2014; Agustín 2007; Zhang et al. 2014; Brennan 2014; Brents, Jackson and Hausbeck 2009). As in other service industries, degrees of safety and exploitation vary for workers based on their structural working condi-tions, both domestically and transnationally (Weitzer 2009). However, the mainstream anti-sex trafficking movement frames all prostitution as com-mercial sexual exploitation, conflating the substantial variation of experi-ences in prostitution into one universal experience of victimhood from which women must be rescued (Musto 2009; Weitzer 2010). This has led some scholars to argue the anti-sex trafficking movement may be best understood as a moral crusade (Weitzer 2007; Weitzer and Ditmore 2010). By highlighting the most extreme stories of traumatized victims, the movement is able to mobilize public anger, fear, and sympathy to victims and advance its agenda: the abolition of all commercial sex (Weitzer 2007).

Feminist Activism

Throughout its history, the U.S. women's movement has framed and reframed our public understanding of commercial sex, including sex traf-ficking. While prostitution had been constructed as sin or deviance, com-peting feminisms have sought to re-frame prostitution as either labor or violence against women. These oppositional understandings of prostitution create disparate movement goals. Feminists working to classify prostitution as a form of labor call for the decriminalization or regulation of voluntary prostitution to make sex work safer for those who perform it and for the eradication only of forced prostitution. In contrasts, feminists working to define all prostitution as violence against women seek to abolish all forms of prostitution. The contemporary anti-sex trafficking movement's framing of all prostitution as commercial sexual exploitation emerges out of the latter feminist perspective.

The contemporary movement against sex trafficking has roots going as far back as the turn of the 20th century during which women's groups organized against what contemporaries referred to as the epidemic of "white slavery." Cultural fears over "white slavery" were explicitly about the fears of the trafficking of white women into prostitution (Doezema 1999). However, scholars overwhelmingly agree that concerns over "white slavery" in the United States and Europe around the turn of the 20th century were unsubstantiated and that the abduction of women (both white women and women of color) into forced prostitution was extremely rare (see: Connelly 1980; Doezema 1999; Rubin 2011; Walkowitz 1980). Both the movement against white slavery and the contemporary anti-sex trafficking movement use similar rhetoric surrounding slavery, female innocence, and victimization. Both movements also have the same ultimate goal: the abolition of all prostitution (Doezema 1999; Rubin 2011).

Although the worldwide moral panic over white slavery was largely unfounded— most women in prostitution were at the time (as today) neither white nor forced—claims-makers were responding to an expansion of migration across national borders by women in commercial sex around the turn of the 20th century. Women's temperance groups in London, such as the British Women's Temperance Association, and then eventually across Western nations brought public attention and concern to this expansion of migratory prostitution. Initially there was tension in movement leadership between those who supported the regulation of prostitution in the name of public health and abolitionists who fought for an end to all prostitution. However, as the rise of women's purity and temperance movements overtook public discourse and policy throughout Europe and the United States, the mainstream movement increasingly rejected regulation-based strategies in favor of abolitionist approaches to managing prostitution and trafficking. In the United States, the movement to eradicate "white slavery" culminated in the passage of The Mann Act in 1910. This federal legislation attempted to target traffickers through making it illegal to transport women and girls across state lines for the purposes of prostitution (Pliley 2014). However, like many contemporary legal approaches to abate trafficking, the unintended impact of this legislation was harmful to women performing commercial sex as it drove the industry further underground (Beckman 1984).

Widespread public concern over trafficking re-emerged following World War II in response to the rise of transnational migratory prostitution and trafficking during the war. However, efforts to combat prostitution and trafficking around that time were largely unsuccessful in part due to the continued friction between regulationist and abolitionist activist approaches (Scully 2001). A United Nations 1949 convention solidified

the conflation of prostitution and sex trafficking by referring to "prostitution and the accompanying evil of the traffic in persons" and declaring
both to be "incompatible with the dignity and worth of the human person
and endanger the welfare of the individual, family, and the community"
(UN General Assembly 1949: Preamble). The convention was a major
victory for abolitionist feminists, setting the frame with which the international community understood commercial sex, but had little practical
import to curbing prostitution or trafficking on a global scale.

Between World War II and the 1960s, the women's movement entered
a period of abeyance (Taylor 1989). While the women's movement re-
emerged on a large scale in the 1960s it wasn't until the feminist sex wars[3]
of the 1980s that anti-prostitution feminist activists were able to bring
widespread concern back to the issue of prostitution and trafficking.
Throughout the 1980s and 1990s, combating violence against women,
including sex trafficking and prostitution, emerged as one of the central
goals of the international women's movement (Bertone 2004).

While a "pro sex" feminist perspective characterized by support of
"overt sexuality" and an emphasis on freedom for women's sexual decision
making has gained momentum and broader popular appeal in the contemporary United States overall (Reger 2017:117), the anti-prostitution
feminist position has come to dominate global feminist politics framing
commercial sex as a form of violence against women (Bertone 2004). Just
as with the tension between regulationists and abolitionists at the turn of
the century, and the feminist sex wars of the 1980s, competing contemporary feminisms call for vastly different framings and responses to
commercial sex in the 21st century. Andrea Bertone argues the divide
between these camps is more pronounced today than ever before as
transnational anti-sex trafficking activism has reached unprecedented success on a global scale (2004).

The power of the anti-sex trafficking movement in the 21st century is
bolstered by the turn towards what Elizabeth Bernstein (2012) terms *carceral feminism*, referring to the collaboration between feminist activists,
religious organizations, and the state under neoliberalism. Bernstein argues
these separate actors come together under a commitment to "carceral
paradigms of justice and the militarized humanitarianism as the preeminent
mode of engagement by the state" (2012: 45). This approach is especially
powerful because actors reinforce the legitimacy of the other agencies—
policing systems can report to be working in line with feminist aims
(ending violence against women) and the social movement benefits from
the resources, funding, and authority of the state. Activists working on
behalf of competing feminisms have managed to shift cultural understandings surrounding prostitution. In the 21st century the movement
against sex trafficking which frames of all prostitution as commercial sexual
exploitation has come to dominate the transnational conversation surrounding women in prostitution.

Survivor Exclusion

The anti-sex trafficking movement's framing of all women in commercial sex as victims makes relevant the rescue of women from, and abolition of, all forms of commercial sex. This logic, along with the carceral feminist structure of the movement, forms a protectionist orientation towards women in commercial sex and leaves little space for survivors to make decisions about their own lives. Research finds survivors left out of or even strategically excluded from anti-sex trafficking movement participation and leadership (Brennan 2005; Musto 2008). Due in part to the increasing professionalization of the movement, the mainstream anti-sex trafficking movement is comprised almost entirely of conscience adherents[4] (Harrington 1969; McCarthy and Zald 1977) who have no personal background in commercial sex. As such, the supposed movement beneficiaries—women who have been trafficked or involved in any type of commercial sex— are afforded limited avenues for participation as activists.

Shortly after the passage of the Trafficking Victims Protection Act in 2000, while the contemporary anti-sex trafficking movement was just starting to reach widespread success, Denise Brennan (2005) noted the absence of survivor voices in anti-sex trafficking social movement organizations overall, and particularly in leadership positions. She suggested movement organizations limited survivor participation out of an interest in protecting the most vulnerable victims and attributed the exclusion in part to the movement's newness. She called for more active inclusion of survivor voices within the movement over time. However, as the movement has grown, survivor participation has become even more restricted. Jennifer Musto (2008) attributes the absence of survivor participation and leadership to the increasing NGO-ification[5] of the movement and argues that, as a result, survivor participation is unlikely to improve without significant changes to movement structure.

While earlier feminist movements framed trafficking as violence against women and brought the issue to the international spotlight, today the anti-sex trafficking movement is primarily run by professional members of the criminal justice social service alliance (Dewey and Germain 2017) as a collaboration between social service agencies and the carceral state (Musto 2016). In the private sector, social movement organizations involve a collaboration between the religious right as well as abolitionist feminist organizations working specifically to end sex trafficking (Weitzer and Ditmore 2010). The movement's orientation to victims of trafficking remains overwhelmingly protectionist and leaves little opportunity for survivors to make decisions regarding their own lives, let alone influence anti-sex trafficking policy and goals (Musto 2016).

Not only does the formal structure of the social movement exclude survivors, but also the movement's framing of the issue is such that a very limited subsection of women in commercial sex identify with the anti-sex trafficking movement and its claims regarding victimhood and exploitation. Only women who felt that their experience in commercial sex was fundamentally victimizing can see their experiences reflected in the mainstream movement's ideology. Because the anti-sex trafficking movement's framing of the issue is based on such a small subset of overall worker experience, only those with the most egregious experiences in commercial sex are aligned with movement claims and goals. Further, only after rescue and reformation do women come to identify as survivors, leaving those women still engaged in commercial sex excluded from the movement.

Joan Kleinman and Arthur Kleinman point to the way victims are encouraged to share *trauma stories* as a form of "symbolic capital" they can use to gain access to resources and status (1996: 10). The trauma story is used as a "core cultural image of victimization" and transforms the person who has had the experience into "an image of innocence and passivity, someone who cannot represent himself, who must be represented" (Kleinman and Kleinman 1996:10). Similarly, Joel Best (1993) finds victims' *atrocity tales* are used by moral crusades to highlight the most extreme stories of victimization to garner sympathy and outrage and support for the cause.

Survivors and their stories also bring authenticity to a movement. Zakiya Luna (2017) argues social movements engage in *proximity practices* to claim their perspective is most in line with the "marginal community" being represented, and these authenticity claims are especially critical in cases where oppositional movements are competing to frame an issue around which the broader public has limited knowledge, as in the case of sex trafficking. Luna finds that "marginal movement actors [survivor activists] must simultaneously engage and challenge the structure" shaped by the dominant group (2017: 435). As a result, survivors are often invited to share their stories of victimization at anti-sex trafficking movement events but are excluded from participation as activists or leaders.

The analysis that follows is based on ethnographic fieldwork in the anti-sex trafficking movement and interviews conducted with survivors and activists in a major U.S. city over an 18-month period during 2015 and 2016. During this time, I regularly attended anti-sex trafficking movement events including meetings, conferences, fundraisers and informal gatherings of activists, as a participant observer. I also conducted approximately 30 semi-structured interviews with survivors most of whom are activists, as well as approximately 10 "expert" interviews with conscience adherent members of the movement including members of law enforcement, district attorneys and directors of non-profit organizations.[6] This research was conducted as part of a larger ethnographic research project about the impact of prostitution policies on women in commercial sex. All survivor participants in this study identify as women and are currently over the age of 18. Most are between 18 and 35. About half were involved in commercial sex as minors, and about half became involved only as adults.

Destiny is white, all other survivors identify as women of color, the vast majority of whom identify as black.

All survivor participants in this study present themselves publicly as no longer working in commercial sex. All identify publicly with the term *survivor* in their activist work in line with the terminology of the broader social movement. Most use this term to identify specifically as a survivor of sex trafficking, signaling involvement with a pimp or trafficker during all or part of their time prostitution. Several use this term more broadly to identify as a survivor of commercial sexual exploitation, defining their experience in prostitution as inherently exploitative and traumatic, though they may or may not have been forced by an individual person. In less formal settings, many participants also use other language to talk about their background, often terms that refer to their experiences rather than to an identity, such as "in the life," "in the game," or "getting money." Without exception, all survivors in this study fight to be seen for their activist contributions to the anti-sex trafficking movement, rather than defined by their experiences in commercial sex. In keeping with this commitment, throughout this chapter I do not emphasize the specific traumatic experiences of any individual participant.

Surivior Activist Participation

Movement leaders and organizers actively seek out survivors to tell their trauma stories at movement events and for public display to bring authenticity to the anti-sex trafficking movement and legitimacy to movement claims and goals. Despite the essential role of survivors, participation opportunities are typically limited to storytelling. And yet, survivors co-opt the roles to assert their humanity beyond the role of victim, build solidarity with other survivors, demand legitimacy as qualified experts, and challenge the dominant strategies and goals of the anti-sex trafficking movement. Survivor activists against trafficking must negotiate working within the movement's structure while simultaneously resisting the movement from the inside.

Asserting Humanity

To resist the victim designation by asserting personhood is a powerful form of resistance by survivors. The one formal way survivors are typically included in movement events is through being asked to speak about their experiences of victimization. Testimony by victims at movement events is frequently the highlight of the program and movement leaders rely on these events to further the movement's claims making and inspire other conscience adherents to participate in, and fund, the movement. While some survivors decline these speaking engagements to avoid being cast as a victim, others use the podium in a range of ways to assert their activist commitments and goals. One way survivors can resist the trauma story is by focusing their stories not on their experiences in commercial sex but on the things that make them most ordinary. This includes resisting the victim frame on a fundamental level through asserting their basic personhood.

Jada was trafficked throughout Western Europe as a teenager and moved to the United States to rebuild her life where she founded a leading non-profit organization serving girls and women who have engaged in commercial sex. She said, "People try to pigeonhole us into a survivor box but I refuse to let them. My experiences in the commercial sex industry are a part of who I am, but they don't define me or limit me." Jada understands that she and other activists must overcome the stigma of being trafficking victims, even within the anti-sex trafficking movement.

At an activist event showcasing art made by victims of sex trafficking, as at most movement events, attendees were primarily non-survivor activists including law enforcement, social service providers, and members of the general public. Survivors present frequently highlighted aspects of their life other than their experiences in commercial sex. Ashley described herself as someone who "love[s] to grow and take care of my plants." Kiara shared "I am a great mother to my children. I am an artist. I love to read and write. I absolutely love to do hair and makeup." Jada talked about how "I really love anything related to interior design, especially renovating furniture which I do to unwind most weekends." Jada also states her point more explicitly, "Like anyone else I'm a multi-faceted complex human being." These survivors resist highlighting their victim status by doing the exact opposite— sharing what makes them like everyone else. In doing so, many invoke positive gendered categories such as "good mother" or feminine skills such as "hair and makeup" or "interior design," contrasting their potential status as fallen women with a positive femininity. Because the category of "prostitute" or even "trafficking victim" is so stigmatized as to be completely dehumanizing, survivors reject victim status through asserting their basic humanity to an audience of non-survivor movement participants, resisting the stigma survivors experience even within the mainstream anti-sex trafficking movement.

Dehumanization is often central to survivor's experience in relation to the anti-sex trafficking movement overall, not just to their presence as activists. Most survivors' first contact with the movement is through being arrested for prostitution, the primary mechanism through which the movement attempts to rescue women. For many survivors, the feelings of stigmatization and dehumanization extend back to this first point of contact. Dominique is an anti-sex trafficking activist who works at a criminal diversion program for women arrested for prostitution-related offenses. She leads group therapy sessions, runs sex trafficking prevention trainings in the greater community, and speaks at conferences and public events. In an interview, she explains that she has been trying to assert her humanity since first getting arrested in an undercover sting while being trafficked by a man she considered her boyfriend, who she now refers to as her pimp. She recalls the first time she was booked into jail:

> I just was so in over my head and the police obviously didn't really have any regards for anything that was going on. And I remember walking past some of the cells where the guys were, and no bra or anything and me trying to yell out, "I'm a master's student," and hoping that meant anything. I was like, let them know that I'm a good person. For them to understand that I have a family, that I have a father. I think that I wanted them to understand that, first, I'm human.

While Dominique often shares publicly about being trafficked, she consistently contextualizes this experience within her identity as a graduate student. She consciously uses these public engagements as opportunities to emphasize how ordinary her life is except for this one experience. Many survivors cite their supposed rescue from commercial sex, the very solution advanced by the anti-sex trafficking movement, to be the most dehumanizing and stigmatizing part of their experience in commercial sex.

In a setting where survivors are asked to recount their experiences to bring authenticity to the movement against trafficking, survivors resist the victim designation by frequently drawing upon other parts of their life to highlight their humanity. Through focusing on aspects of their lives that make them clearly like anyone else, or demonstrating a reputable form of femininity, survivors resist telling stories which would focus on their traumatic experiences and reinforce their victim status. To have to proclaim oneself as a "human being" and "like anyone else" speaks to the way survivors experience the victim designation as fundamentally erasing their humanity.

Building Collective Identity

Survivor activists also resist the victim role by invoking their status as survivors in line with coming out as a social movement tactic (Whittier 2012). By doing so, they build collective identity with other survivors (Taylor and Whittier 1992). The term "survivor" itself is a politicized social movement identity. Survivors use the term not only to mean they have exited sex trafficking or commercial sexual exploitation, but also as a collective identity tied to the anti-sex trafficking movement.

Tasha is a well-respected survivor activist in the movement who runs a leadership organization helping survivors rebuild their lives after exiting commercial sex. She also offers trainings on sex trafficking to law enforcement and service providers. She explains, "Survivor leadership means openly identifying as a survivor, for the benefit of other survivors in need of a role model, and to break negative stereotypes about individuals in the commercial sex industry." In coming out and openly identifying as a survivor, Tasha seeks to connect with other survivors and to challenge the stigma surrounding women in commercial sex. She identifies as a survivor of sex trafficking publicly but does not dwell on the details of her traumatic experiences. Rather, she highlights the work she does to build community with other women who have been through similar experiences. Tasha was asked to speak about her victimization at an anti-sex trafficking awareness event comprised almost entirely of non-survivor activists. Despite the makeup of the audience, Tasha still addressed her remarks to any other survivors possibly present. In doing so she emphasized to survivor and non-survivor audience members alike the importance of building survivor community. She said, "The road to healing and discovery is a very long one. Be kind and patient with yourself while you are on the journey. Surround yourself with people who make you feel loved, accepted and who remind you of how wonderful you truly are." Her approach de-centers the non-survivor participants and emphasizes the degree to which her coming out is about building connections with other survivors rather than characterizing herself as a victim.

At a community human trafficking awareness event, Joanne also reaches out directly to other survivors. She said:

> To every survivor, I want you to know it doesn't stop here. Being free doesn't mean you must always wear the hat of your past. None of us are required to become stagnant with the title of survivor. And though being a survivor is part of who I am, it's not all that I am.

At the same event, Huong advises:

> It is possible to do more than just overcome your trauma. It is possible to reclaim your identity, to find purpose and meaning, and to feel love and joy. It's ok to explore and try new things and it's ok to break out of the ideas of who you, and others, think you should be.

Although in all of these cases the primary audience is non-survivors, survivor activists nonetheless take space to make direct appeals to reach out and build a survivor identity with each other. These appeals build connections between, and spaces for, survivors in the movement by strategically delivering their message at events designed for the general public and non-survivor activists.

Survivors also build a shared identity with other survivors and with women still involved in commercial sex through doing the on-the-ground activist work of building coalitions and organizations, networking with one another, and reaching out directly to those still in commercial sex. In contrast to conscience adherents, survivors who work or volunteer in anti-sex trafficking organizations frequently do so in a capacity that involves providing direct services to other survivors or women in commercial sex.

Unlike most of the self-identified survivors speaking at events, Tiana does not identify as having been sex trafficked. Rather, she uses the term "survivor" to refer to her experience working for decades as an independent prostitute in service of a drug addiction. Now in her 50s, Tiana is employed by an organization serving and works to counsel other black women from her neighborhood out of commercial sex (Oselin 2014). Despite her activist work, because her story falls outside of the desired victim story, Tiana is rarely asked to speak at movement events. Instead, Tiana emphasizes the importance of sharing her story with other women in commercial sex to whom she is offering help. She talks about the way coming out around her own experience helps her to connect to the young women who come for help. She explains clients "Be like, 'oh, you don't understand what I'm going through'" but she responds "'Yes I do baby. I've been there.'"

Imani works at an organization serving prostitutes, primarily doing community prevention outreach, and is also involved in mentoring young women in juvenile halls who have been involved in the sex industry. She talks about the importance of giving girls "somebody to talk to [...] even as far as being able to bring them a bag of Hot Cheetos to the Juvenile Hall, that just really means a lot to them." She explains, "Being able to support them where they're at and meeting them at their needs is just something that I really support and I feel like it's a big part of the movement." While survivor activists place a value on the importance of mentoring and building solidarity with other women in the life, this is a perspective rarely shared by non-survivor activists. For Imani, offering connection and support is "part of the movement," r an important activist contribution. However, her approach—giving support to women still in commercial sex and trying to meet their needs—is in direct contradiction to the approach of the mainstream movement that champions only the rescue of women.

Survivor activists network and build friendships, alliances, and professional relationships with one another through informal networks within the broader anti-sex trafficking movement. By sharing their histories on their own terms and using these disclosures to build connections with others, survivor activists can transform the sharing of their experience from a trauma story into a coming out, whether on stage or behind the scenes.

Demanding Recognition as Qualified Experts

Survivors come out not only to build collective identity with other survivors but to position themselves as qualified experts within the movement. While the expertise of survivors may in some ways constitute a form of "dirty knowledge" (Douglas 1966), survivors are able to use their unique insider status to demand to be taken seriously. Survivors even use their experiences to directly challenge strategies and goals of the mainstream anti-sex trafficking movement.

The contrasting orientation of activists emerged starkly at a sex trafficking awareness event in a packed church. Destiny was invited on the panel to share her history, which she did during her speech. But she also asserted that she was the true panel expert, as the only survivor featured among "experts" including members of local government and law enforcement as well as leaders of rescue organizations. When an audience member asked a police captain what he would say to someone currently being trafficked, he responded strongly that the hypothetical victim should immediately "get out of this lifestyle because it's a dead end" and that "we [the police department] are here to help you." The panel moderator took this further, asking the panel at-large to agree that "there is no reason for [victims] to be afraid" and any victim should "get help today." While all the professional "experts" nodded and softly clapped confirming the captain's sentiments, Destiny disagreed with a visible grimace. Her marked disagreement prompted the moderator to comment, "Destiny, I don't like the look you're giving." As the moderator's comment makes clear, Destiny's contributions beyond her personal story of victimhood were not only unsolicited but were expressly unwelcome. Still, Destiny insisted that there may be a lot of good reasons for someone in commercial sex to choose not to "get out right now" including basic safety concerns and lack of resources and alternatives. "I don't want to just be like 'Oh, you'll be fine,'" she explains, "I don't want to downplay the risk that they might actually be experiencing." In speaking out, she affirmed her expertise and knowledge of the many complex barriers women face when attempting to exit commercial sex. Destiny's explanation prompted other panel members to agree that there are legitimate reasons why people involved in commercial sex might not want or be able to exit immediately, changing the course of the conversation to include an analysis of structural barriers. In sum, Destiny's objection undermined a fundamental claim of the movement: women in commercial sex just need to be saved.

Some survivors claim expertise during their first coming out. Tiffany worked in grassroots community organizing for almost 20 years, successfully winning campaigns advocating for the rights of low-wage workers in the United States and Mexico. Throughout her activist career she never shared her experience of having been "trafficked by a gang" until she became involved in fight over prostitution-free zones[7] in her city. She recalls listening to a police officer testify about local prostitution, "He described these women as dirty drug addicts making millions off of walking in their neighborhoods. So I shared my experience and the experiences of others I know." For Tiffany, coming out and sharing her story was part of her activist commitment to campaigning for the rights of workers. As she explains, "We carry a knowledge that no one else has, and that voice needs to be heard if we are going to make a substantial change in human trafficking." Similarly, Melissa makes a direct claim to her authority grounded in her experience, saying, "I will never be ashamed of what God has brought me out of. Without that, I would not be able to train law enforcement, community advocates, medical professionals and faith based communities on how to help others like me."

Other survivors develop a sense of themselves as experts over the course of years. Morgan first became involved in activism and public speaking as a young teenager when she was sent to an intervention program for minors in the sex trade. Through the organization she was encouraged to share her story of victimization publicly and at the time she obliged. Having spent her teen years and early adulthood in and out of the commercial sex industry, she says, "I still really love public speaking and am proud to be on panels at colleges and events... not to tell my story, but to share ideas and recommendations, particularly around prevention."

Positioning themselves as experts often means survivors are the only voices demanding structural change or posing survivor-informed care at a given event. While speaking on a panel at an event dedicated to celebrating the success of a new countywide human trafficking task force, Dominique called for the focus to shift away from women in the life. While the rest of the day had been focused on psychological individual-level intervention strategies, Dominique spoke up for the need for large-scale structural reform. "I think we should focus on community development," she explained. She talked about just having been in a nearby neighborhood well-known for street prostitution and seeing "motels and the girls in the hot shorts and you see the guys out there with the dogs and stuff [and] if we could develop these communities [or put] a community center in these places!" Her suggestions located the "problem" of trafficking not within individual actors, but as a larger issue calling for structural and economic reform. In this auditorium filled with high-ranking members of law enforcement, district attorneys, and judges she directly confronted the celebrated policies that claim to help victims of trafficking through carceral protection. "I was trafficked," Dominique says, "I graduated with a degree in communications [and] all of my work and all of that schooling and that $20,000 worth of student loans is going down the drain because I have a criminal record." After the event, several members of the task force politely thanked Dominique for coming to speak, though none appeared to take her concerns or suggestions seriously.

Destiny, the founder and executive director of an organization dedicated to outreach and support for women in commercial sex, recommends a specific "trauma-informed" approach when conducting outreach that she calls "listening to the invitation." Destiny explains this means "we're listening to what are we being invited to by her [the outreach recipient]. This sets it up so that we're empowering her and letting her lead the mentoring relationship." As she described, this practice "empowers the person that we're working with and shows them a measure of respect." Her organization also trains others to replicate this model of outreach in their own communities. This orientation of providing support and service differs dramatically from the protectionist rescue efforts typically adopted by anti-sex trafficking rescue organizations.

Often the very rescue efforts heralded by the movement can represent the largest barriers to exit commercial sex. Dominique, who works at the prostitution diversion program, sees first hand how current policies put forth by the anti-sex trafficking movement advocating increased policing in the name of rescuing women can harm the very women they purport to serve. Anti-sex trafficking organizations overwhelmingly advocate for a system in which increased law enforcement efforts target traffickers and buyers of commercial sex and treat women as victims. However, Dominique finds that often pimps face no consequences even though "the reality [is that] these girls' jaws are being broken open, and they're being thrown out of cars, and they're being starved to death." At the same time, overwhelmingly her clients are arrested for prostitution-related offenses and are put in "a situation where they get records and they have to get back on the street" even when they want to leave commercial sex. Further, she explains that her clients regularly express "that if they didn't have a record, if they could just find a job, and just have an apartment, and have their [kids] living at home with them, [...] that they wouldn't be doing this. But that's not a reality because we're criminalizing these girls." From her experience as a survivor and her professional experience which regularly brings her into contact with women who have been arrested for prostitution, Dominique has a sophisticated understanding of the ways the policies advocated for by the anti-sex trafficking movement affect women on the ground. When speaking at movement events and conferences, which she does regularly, Dominique shares her personal experiences but also strongly advocates for policies which give women who want to leave "the life" realistic opportunities to find other work and avoid criminal sanctions.

At the celebration of a new county-level human trafficking task force, survivors focused their stories on their activist work as leaders in the community. The questions from the audience illustrated the survivors' success in shifting the focus away from victimhood. A social worker asked the survivors for advice when working with parents whose children have been trafficked. Another asked about racial disparities and the reason for the overrepresentation of black girls as victims of trafficking. A police officer asked about the place of men in the anti-sex trafficking movement. All of the audience's questions oriented the survivors as experts on trafficking, and not at all to their specific personal traumas. At least at this community level, survivor activists were able to transcend the opportunities available to them as victims and demand to be taken seriously as experts and activists. While survivors may often be invited to events to share their stories of victimhood, they refuse to be reduced to their trauma stories or atrocity tales to blindly advance of the movement's agenda. Instead, survivors manage to assert their authority as the true experts, at times even challenging the strategies and goals of the anti-sex trafficking movement.

Conclusion

Overall, I find that survivor activists are demanding a seat at the table. Currently valued for their victim stories rather than their activism or expertise, survivors face stigma and exclusion even within the anti-sex trafficking movement. Survivors are forced to navigate working within restricted opportunities to participate as activists in the movement while also attempting to create change in the movement from within.

Survivor activists, as with many others who believe in or advocate for feminist positions, do not necessarily identify as feminists (Crossley 2010). Jo Reger (2012) finds contemporary feminism is "everywhere and nowhere." Feminism can be a "set of ideas and identities diffused into the culture and structure of society" which "informs, sometimes unconsciously" the activism of contemporary feminists (2012: 5). She also finds contemporary feminism can "maintain its relevance but is submerged into other movements, issues, and groups" (p. 5). The survivor activists who work on the front lines of the movement are part of a long history of feminist activism working to redefine trafficking and prostitution as violence against women and to end that violence. As such, I argue that the survivor activist identity *is* a feminist identity.

Survivors already can and do make essential movement contributions. Survivors are able to offer unparalleled support to peers in commercial sex. It is survivors who are bringing a feminist structural analysis to the movement against sex trafficking and demanding massive structural reforms. Survivors call for not only an end to trafficking and commercial sexual exploitation but to systems of oppression that keep women, especially working class women and women of color, particularly vulnerable to circumstances which make entering or staying in prostitution a rational choice. All of these contributions are essential to the success of a feminist social movement against trafficking.

Questions remain regarding the overall impact and future of survivor activism. As the anti-sex trafficking movement grows in success and comes to increasingly dominate our cultural understanding of commercial sex and legal responses, opportunities for survivors to impact the movement's strategies and goals become increasingly restricted. There is little room for disparate narratives that are antithetical to the claims of the mounting moral crusade. In the face of this growing momentum, a shift to center anti-sex trafficking movement beneficiaries will require a fundamental transformation of the movement. It is the responsibility of feminist activists working on behalf of trafficking victims and women in commercial sex to fight alongside survivors to put the contemporary anti-sex trafficking movement back in line with fundamental feminist principles.

Notes

1 Throughout this chapter I use "commercial sex" as an umbrella term to refer to all forms of prostitution including that performed by victims of trafficking, chosen freely by sex workers, and all of the many experiences in between. The anti-sex

trafficking movement uses the term "commercial sexual exploitation" to describe all forms of prostitution and frame all forms as exploitation. I choose to use "commercial sex" in an attempt to balance both staying consistent with the language of the anti-sex trafficking movement while also recognizing all those who engage in prostitution and do not experience exploitation. I use the term "trafficking" specifically to refer to commercial sex that involves force, fraud, or coercion.

2 See Brennan (2005) and Musto (2008) and Grant (2014), respectively.
3 For more information on the feminist sex wars and their relationship to anti-sex trafficking activism see Miriam (2005).
4 McCarthy and Zald (1977: 1222) define conscience adherents as "individuals and groups who are part of the appropriate SM [social movement] but do not stand to benefit directly from SMO [social movement organization] goal accomplishment."
5 NGO-ification refers to the increased professionalization of the movement based in non-governmental organizations and their relationship to the Federal government (Musto 2008).
6 All names of participants are pseudonyms.
7 Prostitution-free zones are a designation for urban areas known for prostitution that expands law enforcement's authority to disperse and arrest people suspected to be congregating for the purposes of engaging in commercial sex. The designation gives the appearance of a "tough on crime" approach but typically only contributes to temporary displacement of street-based prostitution.

References

Agustín, Laura. 2007. *Sex at the Margins: Migration, Labour Markets and the Rescue Industry*. First edition. London: Zed Books.

UN General Assembly. 1949. *Convention for the Suppression of the Traffic in Persons and of the Exploitation of the Prostitution of Others*. Resolution 317(IV).

Beckman, Marlene D. 1984. "The White Slave Traffic Act: Historical Impact of a Federal Crime Policy on Women." *Women & Politics* 4(3):85–101.

Bernstein, Elizabeth. 2012. "Carceral Politics as Gender Justice? The 'Traffic in Women' and Neoliberal Circuits of Crime, Sex, and Rights." *Theory and Society* 41(3):233–259.

Bertone, Andrea M. 2004. "Transnational Activism to Combat Trafficking in Persons." *The Brown Journal of World Affairs* 10(2):9–22.

Best, Joel. 1993. *Threatened Children: Rhetoric and Concern about Child-Victims*. Chicago: University of Chicago Press.

Brennan, Denise. 2005. "Methodological Challenges in Research with Trafficked Persons: Tales from the Field." *International Migration* 43(1–2):35–54.

Brennan, Denise. 2014. "Trafficking, Scandal, and Abuse of Migrant Workers in Argentina and the United States." *The ANNALS of the American Academy of Political and Social Science* 653(1):107–123.

Brents, Barbara, Crystal Jackson, and Kathryn Hausbeck. 2009. *The State of Sex: Tourism, Sex and Sin in the New American Heartland*. New York, NY: Routledge, 2009.

Connelly, Mark Thomas. 1980. *The Response to Prostitution in the Progressive Era*. Vol. 2. Chapel Hill, NC: University of North Carolina Press.

Crossley, Alison Dahl. 2010. "'When It Suits Me, I'm a Feminist:' International Students Negotiating Feminist Representations." *Women's Studies International Forum* 33(2): 125–133.

Dewey, Susan and Tonia St Germain. 2017. *Women of the Street: How the Criminal Justice-Social Services Alliance Fails Women in Prostitution.* Reprint edition. New York: NYU Press.

Doezema, Jo. 1999. "Loose Women or Lost Women? The Re-Emergence of the Myth of White Slavery in Contemporary Discourses of Trafficking in Women." *Gender Issues* 18(1):23–50.

Douglas, Mary. 1966. *Purity and Danger: An Analysis of the Concepts of Purity and Danger.* New York, NY: Routledge.

Grant, Melissa Gira. 2014. *Playing the Whore: The Work of Sex Work.* New York, NY:Verso Books.

Harrington, Michael. 1969. *Toward a Democratic Left: A Radical Program for a New Majority.* London, UK: Penguin Books.

Jahic, Galma and James O. Finckenauer. 2005. "Representations and Mis-representations of Human Trafficking." *Trends in Organized Crime* 8(3):24–40.

Kleinman, Arthur, and Joan Kleinman. 1996. "The Appeal of Experience; The Dismay of Images: Cultural Appropriations of Suffering in Our Times." *Daedalus* 125(1):1–23.

Laczko, Frank and Marco A. Gramegna. 2003. "Developing Better Indicators of Human Trafficking." *The Brown Journal of World Affairs* 10(1):179–194.

Luna, Zakiya. 2017. "Who Speaks for Whom? (Mis) Representation and Authenti-city in Social Movements." *Mobilization: An International Quarterly* 22(4):435–450.

McCarthy, John D. and Mayer N. Zald. 1977. "Resource Mobilization and Social Movements: A Partial Theory." *American Journal of Sociology* 82(6):1212–1241.

Miriam, Kathy. 2005. "Stopping the Traffic in Women: Power, Agency and Abo-lition in Feminist Debates over Sex-Trafficking." *Journal of Social Philosophy* 36 (1):1–17.

Musto, Jennifer. 2008. "The NGO-Ification of the Anti-Trafficking Movement in the United States: A Case Study of the Coalition to Abolish Slavery and Traf-ficking." *Wagadu: A Journal of Transnational Women's and Gender Studies* 5:15–27.

Musto, Jennifer. 2009. "What's in a Name?: Conflations and Contradictions in Contemporary U.S. Discourses of Human Trafficking." *Women's Studies International Forum* 32(4):281–287.

Musto, Jennifer. 2016. *Control and Protect: Collaboration, Carceral Protection, and Domestic Sex Trafficking in the United States.* Oakland, CA: University of California Press.

Oselin, Sharon S. 2014. *Leaving Prostitution: Getting Out and Staying Out of Sex Work.* New York, NY: NYU Press.

Pliley, Jessica R. 2014. *Policing Sexuality: The Mann Act and the Making of the FBI.* Cambridge, MA: Harvard University Press.

Reger, Jo. 2012. *Everywhere and Nowhere: Contemporary Feminism in the United States.* New York, NY: Oxford University Press.

Reger, Jo. 2017. "Contemporary Feminism and Beyond." Pp. 109–128 in *The Oxford Handbook of U.S. Women's Social Movement Activism* edited by Holly J. McCammon, Verta Taylor, Jo Reger and Rachel L. Einwohner. New York, NY: Oxford University Press.

Rubin, Gayle. 2011. "The Trouble with Trafficking." Pp. 66–86 in *Deviations: A Gayle Rubin Reader.* Durham, NC: Duke University Press.

Scully, E. 2001. "Pre–Cold War Traffic in Sexual Labor and Its Foes." Pp. 74–106 in *Global Human Smuggling: Comparative Perspectives* edited by David Kyle and Rey Koslowski. Baltimore, MD: The Johns Hopkins University Press.

Snyder, R.Claire. 2008. "What Is Third-Wave Feminism? A New Directions Essay." *Signs: Journal of Women in Culture and Society* 34(1):175–196.

Taylor, Verta. 1989. "Social Movement Continuity: The Women's Movement in Abeyance." *American Sociological Review* 54(5):761–775.

Taylor, Verta and Nancy E. Whittier. 1992. "Collective Identity in Social Movement Communities: Lesbian Feminist Mobilization." Pp. 104–129 in *Frontiers in Social Movement Theory* edited by Aldon D. Morris and Carole McClurg Mueller. New Haven, CT: Yale University Press.

Trafficking Victims Protection Act of 2000. Pub. L. No. 106–386.114 Stat. 1464.

Walkowitz, Judith R. 1980. *Prostitution and Victorian Society: Women, Class, and the State.* Cambridge, UK: Cambridge University Press.

Weitzer, Ronald. 2007. "The Social Construction of Sex Trafficking: Ideology and Institutionalization of a Moral Crusade." *Politics & Society* 35(3):447–475. https://doi.org/10.1177/0032329207304319.

Weitzer, Ronald. 2009. "Sociology of Sex Work." *Annual Review of Sociology* 35(1):213–234.

Weitzer, Ronald. 2010. "The Movement to Criminalize Sex Work in the United States." *Journal of Law and Society* 37(1):61–84.

Weitzer, Ronald. 2014. "New Directions in Research on Human Trafficking." *The ANNALS of the American Academy of Political and Social Science,* 653(1):6–24.

Weitzer, Ronald and Melissa Ditmore. 2010. "Sex Trafficking: Facts and Fictions." Pp. 325–351 in *Sex for Sale: Prostitution, Pornography and the Sex Industry.* New York, NY: Routledge.

Whittier, Nancy. 2012. *The Politics of Child Sexual Abuse: Emotion, Social Movements, and the State.* New York, NY: Oxford University Press.

Zhang, Sheldon, Michael Spiller, Brian Finch, and Yang Qin. 2014. "Estimating Labor Trafficking among Unauthorized Migrant Workers in San Diego." *The ANNALS of the American Academy of Political and Social Science* 653(1):65–86.

Part II

Issues

7 #FemGA #SayHerName #NotHereForBoys

Feminist Spillover in U.S. Social Movements 2011–2016

Heather McKee Hurwitz

The relationship between feminist movements and other social movements is complex. Scholars argue that feminist movements influence other social movements, and other movements shape feminism. For example, feminist movements spun off from the New Left, civil rights movement, and Chicano movements (Roth 2004). Feminist tactics and framings contributed to the anti-nuclear and peace movements (Meyer and Whittier 1994) and environmental movements (Shiva and Mies 2014). On first glance, the Occupy Wall Street Movement (e.g., Occupy), Black Lives Matter (BLM), and protests in support of Bernie Sanders' Presidential Campaign (e.g., Bernie activism) may appear to have little to do with feminism. However, in this chapter, I trace how feminists participated in these movements to illustrate the continued salience of feminist activism in contemporary movements. I find that these movements developed feminist tactics and strategies, contributing to mass mobilizations. I also find that the goals and framings of the mass mobilizations influenced feminist activism. Feminism in these "other" not-explicitly-feminist spaces formed through the processes of "social movement spillover" (Meyer and Whittier 1994), a concept I expand by identifying several new "feminist spillover mechanisms" that infuse feminism into contemporary mixed-gender movements.

The hashtags of #FemGA #SayHerName #NotHereForBoys are examples of feminist activism within three "other" not-explicitly-feminist spaces. Starting in 2011, participants in the Occupy movement advocated for democracy and against economic inequality. They set up more than 1,000 protest encampments and held general assemblies, or town hall meetings, to demand tighter regulations of the banking industry, housing justice, and campaign finance reform. Feminists within Occupy created Feminist General Assemblies or #FemGA. These protests were separate feminist events modeled off the Occupy-style general assemblies. Instead of only focusing on economic justice like much of the main Occupy movement, participants in #FemGA advocated ending sexism within Occupy and in society broadly.

Moving forward to 2013, in response to the murder of Trayvon Martin, three queer Black women, Alicia Garza, Patrisse Cullors, and Opal Tometi, coined the phrase and hashtag #blacklivesmatter, a demand for civil rights and justice, and an end to police violence. In early 2015, BLM feminist and academic Kimberlé Crenshaw with her staff at the African American Policy Forum and the Center for Intersectionality and Social Policy Studies at Columbia University Law School developed the #SayHerName Media Guide. The online guide reports on police brutality and murder endured by Black women and advocates for an end to the violence. While mainly the killings of Black men sparked BLM, the authors of the #SayHerName media guide, "push back on the myth that Black women are not also at risk."

Late 2015 and early 2016, competition in the U.S. presidential election heated up. Many activists shifted their activism into support for one or more candidates. In 2016, on the television show, *Real Time with Bill Maher*, feminist leader Gloria Steinem promoted Hillary Clinton's campaign and also criticized millennial women who were supporting candidates other than Hillary. She reasoned that they participated in Bernie Sanders' activism because, "when you're young, you're thinking, where are the boys? The boys are with Bernie." Her surprisingly sexist comment sparked #NotHereForBoys, hashtag activism symbolizing women's and feminists' legitimate support for Bernie Sanders' platform.

As these short vignettes suggest, feminism intermingled with Occupy, BLM and Bernie activism online and offline. Feminists participated in and contributed resources to support the mass mobilizations. Also, feminists harnessed the excitement of the mass actions to further develop feminism. David Meyer and Nancy Whittier (1994) have encapsulated this process, one social movement influencing another and vice-versa, as social movement spillover. Meyer and Whittier find that feminists influence other social movements using "mechanisms of transmission." When activists build coalitions and/or when feminist personnel work in other movements, leaders and members meet and collaborate and they share tactics, strategies, and framings with each other. Also, activists influence each other when activists meet in progressive movement spaces such as activist community centers or bookstores, share activist art and publications, and maintain friendships with activists from other movements. In addition, when feminists partner with politicians to change legislation or transform workplace cultures, they may transform the entire political or cultural context for other activists, creating new or different political opportunities for future activism.

To influence Occupy, BLM and Bernie activism, feminists within each movement use the established spillover "mechanisms of transmission" (Meyer and Whittier 1994). For example, in Occupy, feminist peace activists participated in the working groups or committees. Also, local feminist groups participated in Occupy by camping in their town squares in solidarity. In BLM, past and continuing activism by women of color reproductive justice organizations influenced the movement's frames and strategies. Nationally known feminist activists and organizations contributed leadership to BLM. Also, many local feminist groups and individuals have created actions online and offline as a part of #SayHerName. Also, online and offline, the progressive social movement community buzzed about #NotHereForBoys, stirring feminist dialogue and action. Enlivened by #NotHereForBoys and Bernie activism in general, the Global Women's Strike created a coalition of feminist groups to hold an event focused on women's rights and aspects of Bernie Sanders' platform during the 2016 Democratic National Convention. Due to their participation across porous social movement communities, some feminists have participated in many or all of these movements during this cycle of protest. Feminist personnel, coalitions, and social movement communities facilitated the spread of feminism to these new mobilizations.

Examining these movements, I draw on the "mechanisms of transmission" identified by Meyer and Whittier (1994) and three additional feminist spillover mechanisms: gender conflict, online activism and social media, and the feminist social movement community. A variety of forms of *gender conflict* spark feminist involvement in other movements (Evans 1979; Hurwitz and Taylor forthcoming; Robnett 1997). I reveal how the mechanism of gender inequality led feminists to respond to gender inequalities, sexual harassment, and the marginalization of women, and become active in these "other" movements. Also, activists use *online activism and social media* as a mechanism to address gender conflict and advocate feminist politics in general. While riding the momentum of the new mobilizations, feminists use social media to call for protests and spin-off groups that both support feminism and the new movements. Also, feminists today utilize resources from the *feminist social movement community* as a mechanism to spread feminism within new mobilizations. While Meyer and Whittier (1994) recognized social movement communities as a spillover mechanism, social movement communities change over time. In this study, I reveal how feminist social movement communities' contemporary organizational structures facilitate spillover. Feminist social movement communities are broader than just activist organizations. Feminist social movement communities encompass feminists in social movement organizations and cultural spaces such as feminist bookstores, as well as myriad adherents to feminism who are unofficially affiliated with feminist organizations through friendship or ally networks (Buechler 1990; Staggenborg 1998; Taylor and Whittier 1992). Since the 1960s and 1970s, feminists have fought against gender inequalities in their families, workplaces, schools, religious institutions, and other contexts. As feminists achieved social changes in these not-explicitly-activist contexts, the feminist social movement community expanded into a range of additional institutions. Increasingly, feminist social movement communities include feminists from a variety of institutional contexts such as the music industry, educational and medical institutions, the government and military, and more (McCammon et. al. 2017[1]; Staggenborg 2013; Katzenstein 1999; Staggenborg and Taylor 2005). Feminists maintain their movements by working within an array of organizational structures (Staggenborg and Taylor 2005), and I argue that this institutionally diverse community provides unique opportunities for spillover. Beyond activist organizations or feminist cultures, the contemporary feminist social movement community fuels spillover by providing legitimacy and resources to new mobilizations from a particularly wide range of institutional contexts. I conclude that feminist spillover mechanisms account for new and changing forms of feminism, new tactics and strategies due to internet technologies, and the problems and opportunities present in the latest cycle of protest.

Drawing on in-depth interviews, participant observation, and movement documents from Occupy, BLM, and Bernie activism, the remainder of this chapter explores the questions, what are the features of feminist activism within the most recent movements in the United States since 2011? And, how do feminists spread feminism within "other" spaces? I compare and contrast the variety of means that feminists use to influence other movements and offer suggestions for future research about how feminism persists in not–explicitly–feminist spaces.

The "Other Spaces"

My research on feminist and women's participation in not–explicitly–feminist movements or "other spaces" began in 2011 with the Occupy movement. I studied how women and feminists contributed to the movement and the gender conflict within the movement. Gender conflict is an umbrella term for conflicts within social movements that threaten or harm women, genderqueer or transgender persons, and sexual minorities (Hurwitz and Taylor forthcoming). Reports of sexual harassment and the formation of separate feminist organizations within Occupy motivated me to spend 150 hours with activists in New York City, San Francisco/Oakland and at a national conference of Occupiers called the Occupy National Gathering in Philadelphia in the summer of 2012. I interviewed 73 Occupy participants and collected an archive of more than 500 movement documents such as flyers, zines, conference call minutes and movement newspapers.

Then, in 2016, I began to wonder, "What happened to Occupy?" I went back to New York, San Francisco, and Oakland. Meeting with activists, I learned about their involvement in Occupy spin-off groups such as the Alternative Banking Working Group and Occupy the Farm, BLM and Bernie activism. In addition to my main field sites, I also studied the Democratic and Republican National Conventions because many Occupy, BLM and Bernie activism participants protested around the conventions. I spent 200 hours participating in and observing protests, events and meetings and interviewed 33 additional people. Nine undergraduate research assistants and I collected and catalogued nearly 800 electronic and paper documents about the movements.

By immersing myself in the ethnographic data about feminism within each movement, I identified several patterns of feminist spillover. Because many of the participants in this study remain active in a variety of social movements and many shared critiques about the movements, I use pseudonyms to identify quotes from interviewees. For activists I describe or quote from a publicly available record (a flyer, website, news article, etc.) I have used the participant's published name. In the following sections, I describe feminist spillover in each movement individually and then compare and contrast the different ways that feminism is both submerged and essential within each of these recent mobilizations.

Occupy

Occupy began in New York City's Zuccotti Park on September 17, 2011 and spread to more than 1,000 cities and towns across the United States and globally by mid-October (Gould-Wartofsky 2015). The movement's signature tactic was protest encampments: camping and demonstrating overnight in town squares. In addition, they rallied and marched, held town hall meetings or "general assemblies," shared free food with other protesters and homeless persons, developed extensive social media networks and more (see for example, Gould-Wartofsky 2015; Maharawal 2016). "We are the 99%" became the key slogan of the movement. The 99 percent symbolized mass solidarity on the basis of class in opposition to the most wealthy 1 percent, the government, corporations and banks.

Feminist Community Shapes Occupy

To help develop Occupy, established feminist organizations contributed personnel, spread the word online and through word-of-mouth about protests, and contributed funds, food, signs and other resources. Feminists participated in the planning meetings and first weeks of the encampments. Local feminist collectives and non-governmental organizations joined with national organizations, such as Feminist Peace Network and CODEPINK, to recruit feminists to support Occupy. For example, the Raging Grannies, a group of progressive grandmothers, created and distributed songbooks and led crowds in singalongs. Per their signature shtick, they changed popular song lyrics to convey progressive and feminist messages, such their revamped "Occupy Wall Street Maids" to the tune of "Union Maid" with the lyrics, "We're Occupy Wall Street maids, We've never been afraid, to speak our minds for human kind, and wage the fight for women's rights." Feminists brought strategies, tactics, and their ability to frame protests to appeal to women and other feminists into Occupy (Maharawal 2016).

Beyond social movement organizations, other feminist leaders from a variety of fields influenced Occupy. Feminists used resources from a range of institutions to legitimate the movement as they participated in it. They furthered Occupy and feminism by bringing together feminist analysis and activism with the goal for economic justice. Wielding their influence in the music industry, Yoko Ono, Patti Smith, Debbie Harry, Ani DiFranco, Jill Sobule and Joan Baez contributed to *Occupy this Album*. Influential feminists such as Eve Ensler, Angela Davis, Alice Walker, Gloria Steinem, Judith Butler and many more blogged, wrote articles, spoke at protests and encouraged their fans and followers to support the movement. For example, in *Occupy! An OWS-Inspired Gazette* published December 14, 2011, feminist professor Silvia Federici advocated for a feminist reframing of Occupy:

> Clearly a broad coalition of social forces must come together ... but what is also needed is a new feminist initiative on the terrain of social reproduction ... we need to revalue the work involved in our reproduction, as the foundation for finding new revolutionary alternatives to the capitalist failure to produce a life worth living.

Federici's article is a key example of feminist spillover. She argues that economic justice movements such as Occupy will be successful if women's invisible reproductive labor is valued. She advocates feminist activists join with Occupy. In addition to feminist social movement organizations and personnel, feminists leveraged their authority in the arts, academia, and other contexts to spread Occupy's message.

Gender Conflict Sparks Feminist Participation

Despite the contributions of feminists from the movement's beginning, some women, genderqueer and transgender persons, and sexual minorities reported conflicts, inequalities and even racialized gender and sexual violence within Occupy meetings and protests. Addressing sexism within Occupy became another route for feminist influence. For example, in the progressive Berkeley, California-based newspaper, *Slingshot*, in the *Hella Occupy Extra Edition 2011*, enola d! writes, "At one general assembly, some people spoke out about not feeling comfortable in the camp because they were being hit on by older men or because they were being insulted by homophobes. A proposal to section off a wimmin/queer/trans safer space for camping passed overwhelmingly." Also representative of sexism, harassment and violence in the movement is an open letter from an anonymous activist from Occupy Tucson published in *The Post Script* zine. The letter exposes a male leader for attacking a woman in the encampment and refusing to reconcile the situation. Later, a group of white men backed up the man and blamed the woman victim for causing the violence. The author of the letter laments, "The fact that Occupy Tucson is a space in which violence and silencing can occur with no consequences makes me feel extremely unsafe." While the story of gender conflict in Oakland appears productive because it led to a separate zone for gender and sexual minorities and encouraged their participation, the story of gender conflict in Tucson sparked the feminist-inspired open letter but harmed and discouraged women in the movement. Longtime feminist organizer, Jade, summarizes the pressures women endured within Occupy's culture of male-dominance:

I think about the times that I was around women and how women were surprised that the culture of Occupy reflected the culture that we lived in, and just overnight everybody didn't become different. And I would say what was cool was how many women got radicalized by it - to really see we do have a culture still that is dominated by male voices.

Gender conflict and the culture of male dominance was a source of infighting for Occupy that both hampered the participation of women and provided a political opportunity for feminist mobilization.

A variety of groups emerged from within Occupy to respond to gender conflict. Usually experienced feminist activists led the groups. The organizations infused feminist politics into Occupy. Participants in Oakland Occupy Patriarchy, Women Occupying Wall Street, the Speakeasy Caucus and Safer Spaces groups responded to harassment, violence and the unease of women and gender and sexual minorities at the encampments. For example, the Safer Spaces group in New York created an "Occupy Wall Street Community Agreement" and recruited Occupiers to take the feminism-inspired pledge.

Feminist Online Activism and Occupy

In addition to protests in the streets and encampments, feminists influenced Occupy online using Facebook event pages, blogging, google groups, crowdfunding, live streaming, Twitter, Tumblr, by emailing each other individually, using group text messaging "Celly" software and the "Maestro" online conference call system. For example, in advance of their People of Color (POC) focused Feminist General Assembly, Women Occupying Wall Street (WOWS) initiated a whiteboard campaign on their Tumblr because "we decided that it would be great to get pictures of POC showing their feminism." Participants submitted selfies holding signs saying, "I am a feminist" or "Yo soy feminista." The campaign broadened participation in #FemGA to Occupiers and feminists online. The tactic allowed feminist organizations to participate in Occupy through individuals such as Cary, a sales manager at The Feminist Press, Jaime-Jin, the executive director of Border Crossers, and Joanne N. Smith, founder and executive director of Girls for Gender Equity. From the whiteboard campaign to Facebook groups created to support feminist activism to #FemGA activism, social media was a major tool activists used to spread feminism within Occupy. Social media allowed Occupiers to create feminist solidarity despite gender conflict. Also, online activism became a vehicle to involve feminist communities beyond Occupy in the movement.

Black Lives Matter

The BLM movement has unified protests against Black people killed and harassed by the police such as Mike Brown, Eric Garner, Sandra Bland,

Tamir Rice and many more. Since 2013, activists have utilized a range of tactics to protest the police killings. The movement's tactical repertoire includes hashtag activism, marches, conferences, and mass actions such as the "Weekend of Resistance" in Ferguson, Missouri in 2014.

Feminist Social Movement Community Supports BLM

From its inception, BLM benefited from feminist spillover. Feminist personnel and organizations have shaped BLM. Also, feminists working in a range of other institutions and mingling with other activists in social movement communities have influenced the development of the movement. Garza, Cullors, and Tometi, the creators of #blacklivesmatter, have contributed key feminist leadership to the movement. Garza works for the National Domestic Workers Alliance. Tometi leads the Black Alliance for Just Immigration. And Cullors has led a variety of criminal justice and prison reform organizations in Los Angeles including Dignity and Power Now. Garza, Cullors, and Tometi are experienced activists and they draw on their own individual experiences fighting for the rights of women and people of color to benefit BLM. Also, they have brought their dense ties to social movement communities into the movement.

Beyond the three founders, the feminist social movement community, particularly feminists in the fields of academia, health, and entertainment, legitimated BLM by explaining how and why Black lives matter. A few of the many Black feminist scholars who have shaped BLM include Cathy Cohen, Kimberlé Crenshaw, Kellie Jones, Andrea Ritchie, Priscilla Ocen and Angela Davis. The Trust Black Women partnership, spearheaded by reproductive justice organization Sister Song, issued a formal statement of solidarity with BLM. Feminist celebrities who have joined protests and tweeted to support the movement include Rosario Dawson, Gloria Steinem, Susan Sarandon, and electrifyingly, Beyoncé, arguably the main contributor of feminist art to the movement. For example, the music and videos of Beyoncé's *Lemonade* album celebrate Black womanhood, oppose police brutality, and expose the maltreatment of Black people during Hurricane Katrina. Exemplary is Beyoncé's 2014 Super Bowl half-time show performance of the hit song, "Formation," which she performed alongside a team of Black women dancers wearing outfits inspired by the uniforms of the Black Panthers: black leather jackets and hotpants and black berets. While commemorating the 1960s Black Power movement, the concert asserted powerful Black femininity and symbolized a call to action for BLM. Bringing their varied expertise to the movement, feminists across the feminist social community shifted resources and public opinion to promote BLM.

Gender Conflict Transforms BLM

Despite the leadership and activism of many strong women, several forms of gender conflict have threatened BLM and simultaneously have opened routes for feminists to influence the movement. In an article first posted in *The Feminist Wire* in 2014, Garza explains how groups have ignored her leadership and misused the phrase "Black Lives Matter." She explains that groups who modify the phrase to "Our Lives Matter" or other variations have, "completely erased the origins of their work–rooted in the labor and love of queer Black women." When spin-off actions fail to center the experiences of Black people and undermine Garza, Cullors and Tometi's queer Black feminist leadership, the actions reproduce the invisibility of Black people and women leaders.

Feminist activism in BLM has sought to include Black women's experiences in the movement and disrupt gender conflict when it has taken the form of male-dominated or gender-blind activism. In an interview on black-youthproject.com, Garza argues for the importance of feminism in BLM:

> We're not here just fighting for Black men. We acknowledge for us to get free as Black people, we can't leave anybody behind and that has to be the innovation in terms of this generation's movement. We have to learn from movements prior to us that, quite frankly, could not be sustained because of the question of the disenfranchisement of women, because of the question of patriarchy.

Garza argues that feminists must confront gender conflict by including women in the movement and using intersectional analyses. In alluding to the marginalization of women in social movements historically, Garza suggests that feminist spillover within BLM is crucial for the survival of the movement today. Similarly, Cathy Cohen argues that Black feminism in BLM informs how activists strategically target state violence and broaden the movement to be inclusive of all Black people: "[Feminism] makes us stop and ask about the role that women, and here I mean both cis and trans women, are playing at this particular time in the multiple movements that are emerging" (Cohen and Jackson 2016: 776). BLM benefits from feminist activists and scholars who acknowledge and challenge gender inequalities that disadvantage, threaten, or harm women, genderqueer persons and sexual minorities.

Feminists have spilled over into BLM to nurture diversity and inclusivity within the movement. Exemplary was a conflict over transgender persons' participation in the 2015 BLM national conference. In a September 23, 2015 article in the *Washington Post*, Brittney Cooper, assistant professor at Rutgers University and co-founder of Crunk Feminist Collective, describes how the incident transformed the movement:

> At the opening night party, held at a local club, a man of trans experience was forcibly removed from a men's bathroom by club security. The act catalyzed a series of conversations throughout the weekend about the deep and necessary work of challenging our own

transphobia and creating a space that is trans inclusive. Among the suggestions were an active marking of gender-neutral bathrooms, long considered the ground zero for whether spaces are trans inclusive, and visible designation of people's preferred gender pronouns (he, she or they, for instance.) A new proposal was the request that we more frequently refer to each other not only as brothers and sisters, but also as "siblings" or "sibs" — gender-neutral terms that retain the loving kinship we attempt to signal by using brother or sister, but don't traffic in gender binaries.

Drawing on feminist framing and transgender rights movements, women and transgender participants in BLM sparked debates and led actions to make BLM more inclusive of Black people of all gender, sexual, class, and other identities. Gender conflict within BLM became an opportunity to strengthen Black and intersectional feminisms and recruit new participants to feminist consciousness and action.

BLM and Feminist Social Media

Feminists supported BLM through a variety of social media campaigns. Initially, Garza, Cullors, and Tometi diffused #blacklivesmatter rapidly online using Twitter. Activist, blogger, and mother Feminista Jones sparked #nmos14 (National Moment of Silence in 2014), a nationwide vigil in 35 states to protest the police shooting of Mike Brown in Ferguson, Missouri. In addition, on Mother's Day 2017, women and feminist BLM activists created the spin-off campaign, National Mama's Bail Out Day. Fueled by a viral campaign video and "crowd-funding" or social media-driven online fundraising, 25 groups raised $400,000 to allow Black mothers in prison to spend Mothers' Day at home with their children. Feminists in each of these campaigns used both online social media tools and offline activism to advocate for BLM.

Images of women's activism have diffused rapidly through Facebook, Twitter and other social media platforms to raise awareness and solidarity for BLM. For example, Ieshia L. Evans refused to leave the middle of the street in protests in Baton Rouge on July 9, 2016 against the police killings of Philando Castile and Alton Sterling. In a now iconic photograph of Evans' civil disobedience, she stands calmly, her sundress billowing around her, while two white police officers in riot gear rush to arrest her. The viral image captures the dignity of Black femininity in opposition to police brutality. Another example is the image of Ashley Williams, a Black queer organizer, who unfurled a sign reading "We have to bring them to heel" in front of Hillary Clinton during a campaign fundraiser. The phrase was excerpted from a speech Clinton gave in 1996 that supported expanding the prison system. The viral image and video of Ashley captured a sentiment among a sector of BLM activists who questioned Clinton's support for racial justice. When women and feminist activists capture video and photos of their acts of civil disobedience and spread them around the world over social media, they garner support for BLM and women's activism. Unlike the marginalization of Black women activists in the 1950s to 1960s civil rights movement (Robnett 1997), women activists in BLM embody the phrase Black Lives Matter by taking center stage in the media spotlight.

The social media campaign to most directly respond to the lack of public awareness about Black women who are harassed, harmed, and killed by the police is #SayHerName. Kimberlé Crenshaw and her team of activists and scholars at Columbia University Law School developed the #SayHerName report and social media guide. In an interview on National Public Radio's Morning Edition on October 12, 2015, Crenshaw elaborated on the need for #SayHerName: "We're not used to demanding justice for black women's families. This is just a habit of marginalizing what happens to the women in our community." The online guide includes stories of women who have been murdered and abused by the police, their pictures, and details about the harm they faced at the hands of police. For example, page 29 details the story of Tajai Rice, sister of Tamir Rice:

> The police killed [Tamir] as he played with a toy gun in the park. This case has understandably caused a national outcry. Less well known is the fact that Rice's 14-year-old sister also endured a violent confrontation... As she ran toward his side after he was shot, the police tackled the distraught girl, handcuffed her and forced her into the back seat of the police car... [this] reflect[s] a profound devaluing of Black life and of the loving bonds that exist between Black people.

By sharing the stories of Black women who experience police violence, #SayHerName asserts that Black women's lives matter. Groups around the United States have performed street protests and media campaigns united under the #SayHerName hashtag. To educate the public and recruit feminists to participate in BLM, #SayHerName activists have held conferences at Columbia University Law School in 2016 and Barnard College in 2017. Activists conducted major presentations on #SayHerName at the Women's March Convention in October 2017 and the entire National Women's Studies Association National Conference in November 2017 was dedicated to "40 Years After Combahee: Feminist Scholars and Activists Engage the Movement for Black Lives." BLM and feminist activists together galvanize online and offline feminist mobilization against police brutality and for civil rights.

Bernie Sanders' Presidential Campaign

Activists formed a variety of spin-off organizations beyond the official Bernie Sanders campaign. People for Bernie, Veterans for Bernie, Millennials for Bernie, and The Bushwick Berners were mixed-gender grassroots groups that recruited members according to a particular identity or location. In addition to typical electoral campaign actions such as phone banking, canvassing, and registering people to vote, Bernie activists also used tactics atypical of electoral campaigns. They created massive marches, rallies, activist art such as banners and screen-printing, and social media/online activism including Facebook groups and events.

Bernie Sanders-Inspired Feminist Communities and Coalitions

Although feminist activism in support of Hillary Clinton's historic run for the U.S. presidency received wider media attention, women and feminist personnel, organizations and feminists within the wider social movement community contributed to Bernie activism. Women and feminists participated in the official campaign, ran the field offices, trained volunteers, protested and some became Democratic Party delegates to advocate for Sanders' platform. For example, Nina Turner, Susan Sarandon and Rosario Dawson gave speeches and interviews to encourage their fans to support the platform spearheaded by Sanders. The National Nurses United, one of the largest women-dominated unions and professional associations in the country, endorsed Sanders' campaign. Nurses participated in activism for Sanders in local rallies and the Democratic National Convention. Feminists in the peace movement supported Sanders because of his record for voting for peace and against wars in Congress while many rejected Clinton because she voted to attack Iraq in 2003. Lesbian and queer feminists valued Sanders' initial and consistent support for gay marriage. Socialist feminist activists especially embraced Sanders' democratic socialist politics such as his pro-choice stance on abortion, advocacy for universal single payer health care, and refusal to accept corporate campaign contributions. As feminists built solidarity around Sanders' political platform, Bernie activism became a political opportunity to benefit feminism.

Representative of the coalitions of women's and feminist organizations that came together within Bernie activism was the "Women's Speak Out for Peace" during the Democratic National Convention. The Global Women's Strike & Women of Color/GWS, coordinated the event. Nine other groups endorsed the event and the planning group consisted of thirteen organizations including Queer Strike and the U.S. PROStitutes Collective San Francisco Bay Area. Illustrative of the event's focus on recruiting women and feminist participants, organizers provided childcare and refreshments. Also, Pacifica Radio's nationally syndicated show *Sojourner Truth* broadcast the event. The family of Berta Cáceres, a celebrated Honduran environmental activist murdered in 2016, opened the program with a call for justice for Berta. Next, a woman spoke from Michigan's Flint Lives Matter group. She discussed how the catastrophic lead poisoning of Flint's water system threatens the environment and democracy with developers and politicians capitalizing on the disaster for their own gain. Additional ecofeminists critiqued Clinton's plan to expand the fracking industry. A contingent of #blacklivesmatter mothers and other family members of people who have been killed by the police demanded a stop to police murder. The event was largely consistent with socialist and intersectional feminisms. It furthered feminist activism that is global, includes racial and economic justice issues, and prioritizes women's organizations and leadership. Bernie activism benefitted both Sanders' campaign and feminist movements by bringing together a diverse group of feminists in solidarity.

Online and Offline Activism Responds to Gender Conflict

Debates about gender and feminist issues within the movement sparked feminist mobilizations. In February 2016, feminists across the country created rallies, marches, and meetups to build on #NotHereForBoys hashtag organizing (the conflict with Gloria Steinem mentioned in the introduction to this chapter). Activists also responded to the stereotype that all Bernie activists were white and male, or "Bernie Bros" (Hess 2016). For example, at the February 27, 2016 rally in New York City, participants carried signs that read "Babes for Bernie," "Women for Bernie," "Latinas for Bernie" decorated with pictures of Latina grandmothers, and "Vote Nurses Values, Caring compassion community, beRNie," with the R and N bold, signifying an abbreviation for registered nurse. Signs also addressed the Steinem conflict directly, such as "#BernieIsBae But I'm #NotHereForBoys (sorry Gloria) I'm here for the Political Revolution." In addition, the rally prioritized women speakers and leaders. April, a representative from Bushwick Berners, explained she supported Bernie because of his stand on universal healthcare, which she desperately needed when she was raped and doubly harmed by not having health insurance. She paid for the ambulance, rape kit and mental health services herself. By stressing their particular experiences as women, the activists in the #NotHereForBoys marches and rallies made women and feminists' issues visible within Bernie activism. The social media campaigns and street protests linked feminism, economic and racial justice and healthcare.

Experienced feminists created spin-off feminist organizations from within the movement. The largest of these groups was Women for Bernie (or Women4Bernie), which reached more than 100,000 likes on Facebook. They mobilized nationally using social media including Facebook, Tumblr, YouTube and Pinterest. They held a series of grassroots social media coordinated meet-ups on International Women's Day, March 8, 2016. Activists across all 50 states met in their living rooms, shared their grievances, explained why they were participating in Bernie activism, and exchanged organizing strategies. The meet ups became consciousness-raising sessions. The Facebook networks continued to serve as a mobilizing structure for Bernie activism. As Molly Grover, the national Women for Bernie outreach coordinator explained in a June 7, 2016 article in the *New York Times*: "She had been able to meet dozens of like-minded progressive women through her work for the campaign, and felt grateful that it had brought a 'political sisterhood' into her life." Feminism spilled over into Bernie activism when participants used feminist social media, framing and tactics.

Still, feminist and women's issues were subdued within some Bernie activism. For example, two days before the Democratic National Convention, Bernie activists held a "People's Convention," independent of the Democratic Party with an objective to continue Bernie activism regardless of who gained the official presidential nomination. Women participated in and led many meetings and workshops throughout the day. Feminist leaders and Bernie activists Jill Stein and Nina Turner headlined the event. Yet, feminism and gender justice were not explicitly included in any workshop. Also, feminist and gender issues were absent from the Convention's stated goals to: "Ratify a People's Platform of issues that are most pressing to the country's civic health, including: Creating Real Democracy, Climate Justice, Healthcare is a Human Right, Racial Justice, Economic Justice." Debates about how to include feminism within Bernie activism and whether white men dominated the movement were persistent concerns.

Comparing the "Other Spaces"

Contemporary feminism is diverse, uses online organizing, and persists in many different institutional contexts (Reger 2012; Crossley 2017). To understand how current feminist activism influences other social movements, theories about how social movements influence each other need updating. Spillover theory (Meyer and Whittier 1994) accounts for many of the ways that feminists influence other social movements today. I also document how additional spillover mechanisms allow feminists to influence contemporary movements. Still, movements are heterogeneous. Activists in different contexts may use some mechanisms more than others. Next, I compare and contrast the feminist spillover mechanisms used in each movement.

The contemporary *feminist social movement community* fuels spillover by providing legitimacy and resources to new mobilizations from a particularly wide range of institutional contexts. Social movement communities have unique structures that shape opportunities for spillover. In addition, social movement communities are changing; they are becoming increasingly "diffuse" and "decentralized and informal" (Staggenborg 2013: 125–126). Contemporary feminist social movement communities thrive because feminists are distributed throughout a variety of institutions beyond social movement organizations (Taylor and Whittier 1992; Staggenborg and Taylor 2005; McCammon et. al. 2017[2]). Drawing on theory about social movement communities (Meyer and Whittier 1994; Staggenborg 1998; Staggenborg 2013) and theory on how feminism is increasingly distributed in a range of institutional contexts (Staggenborg and Taylor 2005; McCammon et. al. 2017), I reveal how the feminist social movement community in particular facilitated spillover during this wave of protest. Beyond activist or explicitly feminist organizations, the contemporary feminist social movement community thrives in diverse institutional contexts, which provide support and opportunities for other movements. Rosario Dawson, Judith Butler, Patti Smith, Jill Stein, Beyoncé and other individuals who identify as feminist showed up at protests. They gave interviews and contributed analyses, art, music, and social media to endorse the movements. Within their union and throughout medical institutions, National Nurses United (NNU) spread feminist Bernie activism. Contributing resources from academia, feminist professors wrote philosophical essays and popular articles that interwove feminist politics with Occupy's and BLM's goals. Notably, faculty and staff of Columbia University research centers led #SayHerName. Feminists in entertainment industries, academia, public intellectuals, and even elected officials exert their legitimacy from activist and mainstream contexts to support feminist activism within these new movements. Scholars argue that feminism has persisted for decades within social movement organizations and through feminist activism in a range of other institutional contexts (Staggenborg and Taylor 2005). Here I argue that feminists from several institutional contexts, or the wide-ranging *feminist social movement community,* shaped feminist activism within the new mobilizations. Beyond feminist coalitions or social movement organizations, the feminist social movement community was key to bringing feminist framings, leadership, tactics, and goals into these new movements.

Within each movement, *gender conflict* sparked feminist protests and separate spin-off organizations. Scholars and activists recognize that feminists mobilize to respond to gender conflict (Evans 1979; Hurwitz and Taylor forthcoming; Robnett 1997). I argue that gender conflict is also a route that feminists traverse to get involved in and influence other social movements. Each movement omitted or downplayed women's and feminist issues, while prioritizing gender-blind economic justice and racial justice goals. Yet each movement endured different varieties of gender conflict. Many white men dominated speaking positions and sexually harassed women within Occupy encampments. Also, activists failed to recognize women and people of color's distinct grievances and disproportionate economic hardships, which led to a variety spin-off groups and protests. For BLM, activists mobilized around the high profile murders of Black men and marginalized the stories of police violence and harassment against women (Garza 2014; Lindsey 2015). While many feminists chose to participate in Bernie activism that included a wide range of economic and racial issues, feminism was a secondary organizing frame and gender issues tended to be more submerged.

Gender conflict harms activists and organizations, even though it also sparks feminist spillover and positive feminist activism. Gender conflict in the form of violence, harassment and marginalization affected negatively individual feminist activists by undermining their voices. Feminists responded to the devaluation of women's and feminist concerns by organizing feminist spin-off organizations and tactics. Prominent feminists exposed how activists ignored women's issues and leadership. Yet this work taxed pre-existing and new feminist organizations. Gender conflict compelled feminists to expend additional time, monetary resources, and personnel to tackle sexism and gender inequality within the movements rather than address other objectives.

Finally, feminists across each movement used *social media and online activism* extensively. They used social media to recruit other feminists to these not-explicitly-feminist movements. Using online organizing, they publicized feminist tactics that emerged from within each movement. Scholars argue that feminism endures because it persists online with the robust activity of feminists on social media (Crossley 2017; Hurwitz 2017). I argue that feminism not only persists online but feminists also use social media to spread their influence to other social movements. Savvy feminists in each of these movements produced media guides, organized on Facebook and Tumblr, blogged about their successful protest performances, and generated feminist commentary and debate about the "other" movements. Online activism has become a virtual meeting space for feminists and activists from social movement communities. Using social media and online activism, feminists recruited new participants to feminism and other movements. Ultimately, using a variety of spillover mechanisms, feminists diversified and strengthened emerging movements in the cycle of protest.

Conclusion

Women and feminists shaped Occupy, BLM and Bernie activism significantly even though the media and activists have not widely acknowledged women's contributions. Feminists participated in each movement. They used their credibility to publicize the "other" movements. They developed tactics to advocate for women's rights and a variety of feminist goals. They facilitated the inclusion of women participants and leaders in the main movement organizations and in feminist spin-off groups and protests. Yet gender issues, feminism and feminist leaders were often secondary within these "other" movements. Still, feminists are active and committed to "other" movements because feminism is diverse and encompasses a variety of different goals. Each case reveals that feminism persists even within movements that are not explicitly about gender or sexuality issues. The comparative analysis reveals that different feminists participate more or less significantly in "other" movements, but all use a range of spillover mechanisms to influence contemporary movements. I argue that feminists contribute to, critique, diversify, and strengthen emerging movements in this cycle of protest. Also, they use the momentum of the cycle to continue to expand feminist movements. This study fills gaps in theorizing about "movement to movement" influence (Whittier 2004: 548) and theorizing about the persistence of feminism within a variety of institutional contexts (Staggenborg and Taylor 2005).

Future researchers should continue to examine feminism in "other" spaces, especially feminist activism in the most recent U.S. cycle of protest. Additional movements in which to explore feminist contributions include Dreamers and immigration rights activism, the Fight for $15 minimum wage, environmental and climate change movements and transgender rights activism. Like the movements in this study, these additional movements address class, race and some gender inequalities, but most do not explicitly or broadly address the oppression of women. Future researchers might consider under which conditions feminist activism influences "other spaces." Do the feminist spillover mechanisms cited in this study facilitate feminist influence within these additional social movements? What other processes do feminists use to shape "other" contexts? Also, future studies might explore how spillover benefits feminism today. When do "other" not-explicitly-feminist activists join feminist protests? What do they contribute to the fight for women's rights, gender justice, reproductive justice, and activism against sexual harassment and rape? By examining feminist influence even in not-explicitly-feminist or "other" spaces, we can continue to realize the profound versatility of feminism, which persists and changes within a variety of contexts.

Notes

1 In particular, see Part IV: Forums and Targets of Women's Activism.
2 In particular, see Part IV: Forums and Targets of Women's Activism.

References

Buechler, Steven M. 1990. *Women's Movements in the United States*. New Brunswick, New Jersey: Rutgers University Press.

Cohen, Cathy J. and Sarah J. Jackson. 2016. "Ask a Feminist: A Conversation with Cathy J. Cohen on Black Lives Matter, Feminism, and Contemporary Activism." *Signs: Journal of Women in Culture and Society* 41(4):775–792.

Crossley, Alison Dahl. 2017. *Finding Feminism: Millennial Activists and the Unfinished Gender Revolution*. New York, NY: NYU Press.

Evans, Sara Margaret. 1979. *Personal Politics: The Roots of Women's Liberation in the Civil Rights Movement and the New Left*. New York, NY: Vintage.

Garza, Alicia. 2014. "A Herstory of the #BlackLivesMatter movement." October 7, 2014. *The Feminist Wire*. Retrieved September 13, 2017. http://www.thefeminist wire.com/2014/10/blacklivesmatter-2/.

Gould-Wartofsky, Michael A. 2015. *The Occupiers: The Making of the 99 Percent Movement*. New York, NY: Oxford University Press.

Hess, Amanda. 2016. *"Everyone is Wrong about the Bernie Bros: How a Necessary Critique of Leftist Sexism Deteriorated into a Dumb Flame War."* Slate. Accessed September 12, 2017. http://www.slate.com/articles/technology/users/2016/02/bernie_bros_are_ bad_the_conversation_around_them_is_worse.html.

Hurwitz, Heather McKee. 2017. "From Ink to Web and Beyond: U.S. Women's Activism Using Traditional and New Social Media." in *The Oxford Handbook of*

U.S. Women's Social Movement Activism, edited by Holly J. McCammon, Verta Taylor, Jo Reger and R.L. Einwohner. New York/Oxford: Oxford University Press.

Hurwitz, Heather McKee and Verta Taylor. Forthcoming. "Women Occupying Wall Street: Gender Conflict and Feminist Mobilization." In *100 Years of the Nineteenth Amendment: An Appraisal of Women's Political Activism*, edited by Lee Ann Banasak and Holly J. McCammon, New York/Oxford: Oxford University Press.

Katzenstein, Mary Fainsod. 1999. *Faithful and Fearless: Moving Feminist Protest Inside the Church and Military*. Princeton, NJ: Princeton University Press.

Lindsey, Treva B. 2015. "Post-Ferguson: *A "Herstorical" Approach to Black Violability*." *Feminist Studies* 41(1):232–237.

Maharawal, Manissa McCleave. 2016. "Occupy Movements." in *The Wiley Blackwell Encyclopedia of Gender and Sexuality Studies*, edited by N. A. Naples. Oxford: Blackwell.

McCammon, Holly J., Verta Taylor, Jo Reger, and Rachel Einwohner. 2017. *The Oxford Handbook of U. S. Women's Social Movement Activism*. New York/Oxford: Oxford University Press.

Meyer, David S., and Nancy Whittier. 1994. "Social Movement Spillover." *Social Problems* 41(2):277–298.

Reger, Jo. 2012. *Everywhere and Nowhere: Contemporary Feminism in the United States*. New York: Oxford University Press.

Robnett, Belinda. 1997. *How long? How long?: African-American Women in the Struggle for Civil Rights*. New York, NY: Oxford University Press.

Roth, Benita. 2004. *Separate Roads to Feminism: Black, Chicana, and White Feminist Movements in America's Second Wave*. Cambridge: Cambridge University Press.

Shiva, Vandana, and Maria Mies. 2014. *Ecofeminism*. New York, NY: Zed Books Ltd.

Staggenborg, Suzanne. 1998. "Social Movement Communities and Cycles of Protest: The Emergence and Maintenance of a Local Women's Movement." *Social Problems* 45(2):180–204.

Staggenborg, Suzanne. 2013. "Organization and Community in Social Movements." Pp. 125–144 in *The Future of Social Movement Research: Dynamics, Mechanisms, and Processes* edited by Jacquelien Van Stekelenburg, Conny Roggeband and Bert Klandermans. Minneapolis, MN: University of Minnesota Press.

Staggenborg, Suzanne, and Verta Taylor. 2005. "Whatever Happened to the Women's Movement?" *Mobilization: The International Journal of Research in Social Movements, Protest, and Contentious Politics* 10(1):37–52.

Taylor, Verta and Nancy Whittier. 1992. "Collective Identity in Social Movement Communities: Lesbian Feminist Mobilization." Pp. 104–129 in *Frontiers in Social Movement Theory* edited by Aldon D. Morris and Carol M. Mueller. New Haven, CT: Yale University Press.

Whittier, Nancy. 2004. "The Consequences of Social Movements for Each Other." Pp. 531–551 in *The Blackwell Companion to Social Movements*, edited by D. A. Snow, S. A. Soule and H. Kriesi. Oxford: Blackwell.

8 Activism against Sexual Assault on Campus

Origins, Opportunities and Outcomes

Nancy Whittier

Between 2011 and 2018, activism against sexual assault surged with college students—mostly women—speaking out about their experiences of sexual assault and decrying inadequate institutional responses. While sexual assault is an issue off campus and among all age groups, college students have been in the forefront of this movement, not because they are uniquely affected by sexual violence, but because they have a unique mechanism for legal pressure. That mechanism is Title IX of the Civil Rights Act, which bars gender discrimination in education. Using this legal tool, activists have pressured colleges and universities to change their procedures for dealing with sexual assault. Using the strategy of speaking out, activists also have sought to change the culture, promoting better support for survivors and more effective prevention. The upsurge of activism on campus has occurred alongside growing mobilization around other issues, beginning with Occupy Wall Street, Black Lives Matter, and the pipeline protests at Standing Rock (see Chapter 7 this volume) and progressing to protests against President Trump and broad outrage over sexual assault and harassment in the #MeToo movement. A part of this protest cycle, the movement against sexual assault on campus, also has roots in the earlier feminist movement and the policy changes it produced. Campus activism has contributed to the growing resistance to sexual violence across a variety of settings. In this chapter, I trace the movement's origins, give an overview of contemporary campus activism against sexual assault, and show its ongoing effects.

Feminists of the 1960s and 1970s organized extensively against rape, changing cultural beliefs, developing services for those who experienced sexual violence and working to change institutional responses (see Whittier 2018; Bevacqua 2000; Corrigan 2013). Four general outcomes of this movement set the stage for the movement of the 2010s: a tactical repertoire emphasizing visibility; institutionalized women's movement organizations; policy changes; and cultural change. In other words, I argue that political and cultural opportunities—largely created as an outcome of earlier activism—fostered the emergence of campus sexual assault activism after 2011. In turn, the outcomes of that activism include partial successes and new opportunities that spurred subsequent organizing against sexual assault.

After a brief overview of the issue, I briefly outline the history of the movement from 1970–2010. I then describe how a newly invigorated movement grew from 2011 onwards and show how political opportunities under the Obama administration facilitated this movement. I then show how the election of President Trump both foreclosed political opportunities and opened cultural ones. I conclude by discussing the outcomes of this movement for policy, culture and subsequent mobilization.

An Overview of Sexual Assault on Campus

Sexual violence is a serious problem on and off college and university campuses. It is difficult to know precisely how many people are raped, sexually assaulted or harassed, or experience attempted sexual assault, because most such incidents are not reported to authorities or even on anonymous surveys. Estimates of college sexual assault rates vary from 25 to 17 percent of women, slightly higher percentages of transgender and gender nonconforming people, and around 5 percent of men (Richards et al. 2017; Cantor et al. 2017). The large and well-designed American Association of Universities (AAU) study of 27 different institutions found that schools varied widely in their rate of sexual assault, with, for example, the rate of sexual assault due to physical force or incapacitation for women varying between 15 and 30 percent (Cantor et al. 2017: x). By the time students are seniors, Cantor, et al. (2017: 14) found 26.1 percent of women, 29.5 percent of transgender and nonconforming people, and 6.3 percent of men had experienced "penetration or sexual touching as a result of physical force or incapacitation," with 11.3 percent of women and 12.6 percent of transgender and gender nonconforming people having experienced penetration, meeting the legal definition of rape. Including unwanted penetration or sexual assault due to coercion or absence of affirmative consent, rates among college seniors were 39 percent for transgender or gender nonconforming people and 33 percent for women (Cantor et al. 2017: 14).[1] As Grigoriadis (2017) points out, about half of the women who fit the criteria for attempted or actual sexual assault do not label their experiences as assault. The majority of sexual assault is committed against women and transgender or gender nonconforming people, by men, but men and people of other genders are also assaulted and people of all genders commit assault (Cantalupo 2012; Grigoriadis 2017).

Sexual violence rates are high on college campuses because of both the age of students and the institutional context. High school and college-aged women, between the ages of 16–24, have among the highest rates of rape overall, and younger women have higher rates of rape than older women; an estimated 51 percent of all female forcible rape victims are under the age of 18 (Langan and Harlow 1994).[2] In addition to age, college brings its own risks. Most research finds that women enrolled in college are more likely to be sexually assaulted than similar-aged women who are not in college, and sexual assault is most likely in the first weeks to months of college (Cantalupo 2011:210; Grigoriadis 2017:37).[3] College—especially residential college—is risky because of a male-dominated party culture, in which sexual aggressiveness is rewarded for men, sexual shame is common for women, and insular organizations like fraternities control access to alcohol and social life (Grigoriadis 2017; Jozkowski and Wiersma-Mosley 2017; Armstrong, Hamilton and Sweeney 2006).[4]

Colleges and universities have unique legal obligations under the Clery Act and Title IX of the Civil Rights Act. They are required to report sexual assaults on their campus in an annual public report, to ameliorate the difficulty victims face when they may encounter their assailants (in classes or residences, for example), and to punish assailants. These are not new responsibilities, but it is only since 2011 that the federal government has enforced institutional responses to sexual assault through Title IX, which bars gender discrimination in education. (Title IX is the same law that requires equity in women's and men's sports.) Under the Obama administration's interpretation of Title IX, schools were responsible for promptly adjudicating reports of sexual assault, using specific procedures, and could be held liable not only for violations in particular cases but for overall failure to address sexual assault in a way that interfered with women's access to equal education.

Many wonder why colleges and universities are involved in addressing sexual assault at all. Indeed, sexual assault is a criminal offense, and can be reported to law enforcement. But although many police departments have specialized responses for sexual assault, the process of reporting and pressing charges is stressful, time-consuming and only rarely results in prosecution or conviction. In addition, people of color from over-policed communities and undocumented people are reluctant to involve the same law enforcement agencies that often cause them harm (Richie 2012). As a result, few sexual assaults are reported to police. Even when they are, campus resources can be deployed more quickly and can include responses short of incarceration. As a result, feminist activists have long sought a range of responses to sexual violence.

Feminist Activism Against Sexual Violence, 1970–2010

Sexual violence has been a central issue in every incarnation of the women's movement. Rape was one of the first issues that feminist activists raised in the late 1960s and early 1970s. This organizing, and ongoing feminist anti-violence in the decades that followed, established a framework for understanding sexual violence, built local organizations that provided services to victims, established institutionalized social movement organizations that lobbied for federal law on violence against women. In turn, that law funded grassroots organizations and built support among politicians for subsequent enhancements in Title IX enforcement. Combined with a small but persistent grassroots movement in the 1990s and 2000s, these factors enabled the resurgence of activism around the issue in the 2010s.

Much of the early activism emerged from consciousness-raising groups in which participants discussed their experiences, realized that sexual violence was widespread and constructed a new analysis of the experience and its causes. Much of what we now take for granted about it grew from these efforts, such as its commonality and the idea that it is an act of violence and domination that is neither the woman's fault nor the result of men's over-powering lust (Martin 2005; Matthews 1994). Feminists developed peer-run rape crisis hotlines, accompanied women to court hearings, taught self-defense classes, campaigned against the idea that women incited rape through provocative behavior and pushed for police, hospitals and other institutions to treat women reporting rape more humanely. Their activism was based on the view that violence against women and children was a manifestation of male domination and a systematic way that women and children were oppressed (Whittier 2009). Over time, activists began to address violence against men, transgender and gender nonconforming people and children (Whittier 2009). Activists grappled with the impact of race and class, in terms of both the greater vulnerability of women of color and low-income women to sexual assault and in terms of the elevation of a raced and classed ideal of sexual purity, and they grappled with race and class dynamics within the movement itself (Richie 2012; Crenshaw 1991). Although the analysis of rape as an expression of both gendered and racial power was new to many feminists in the early 1970s, it was not new to long-time African American activists, who had long understood rape by white men in similar terms (Freedman 2013; McGuire 2010).

By 1980, feminists had founded numerous organizations around the country to combat rape and child sexual abuse. The first rape crisis center was founded in Florida in 1972; many others followed (Martin 2005; Matthews 1994). Bearing variations on the name "Women Against Rape," anti-rape organizations sprang up in most cities and towns around the country, from New York (Brownmiller 1999) to Columbus, Ohio (Whittier 1995), Lawr-ence, Kansas (Bailey 1999), Washington DC (Bevacqua 2000) and countless other locales. Most served both as support groups and as activist organizations seeking to change societal responses to sexual violence. Activists organized marches, speakouts and self-defense training; some used dramatic tactics like mailing blood or severed animal testicles to recalcitrant judges (Gavey 2009; McCaughey 1997; Whittier 1995). While many rape crisis centers were pre-dominantly white, others were multi-racial. For example, the Washington DC rape crisis center was at the center of Black feminist organizing in the city and sponsored an influential 1980 conference on Third World Women and Violence (Bevacqua 2000) and the East Los Angeles Center was organized by and for Latinas (Matthews 1994).[5]

Activists targeted institutions for change. They accompanied women who had been raped to the hospital and to interviews with police to ensure that they were treated with respect. When they discovered that evidence was rarely collected, they pushed hospitals to do so. They shadowed rape trials and collected evidence of bias. They pushed for change in the law to outlaw marital rape and exclude women's prior sexual history from being used in trials. Over time, these initiatives led to the institutionalization of such efforts. In other words, many institutions that activists targeted adopted new procedures, and many feminist groups received funding to hire professional staff and began to function more like the organizations they targeted. Efforts to change how police and hospitals responded to victims led to contracts for training programs in which activists taught detectives, district attorneys, medical professionals, and teachers how to respond to victims (Bevacqua 2000; Corrigan 2013; Rentschler 2011). Efforts to change psychotherapy inspired feminists to become credentialed therapists and social workers. But grassroots feminist organizations struggled to balance their social change agendas with the deluge of cases and bureaucratic requirements that came with government funding. By the late 1980s, many service organizations had been absorbed by schools or hospitals and countless others were run by professionals with a relatively political neutral orientation (Bevacqua 2000; Corrigan 2013; Gottschalk 2006; Martin 2005; Matthews 1994).

By 1990, national feminist organizations like NOW (National Organization for Women), the pro-choice group NARAL (National Abortion Rights Action League) and Planned Parenthood had grown and acquired professional staff and lobbyists. NOW worked with Congress, primarily with then-Senator Joe Biden and his senior staff member Victoria Nourse, to write federal legislation on rape and domestic violence. The result, the Violence Against Women Act (VAWA), passed in 1994. VAWA funded numerous service, policing and prosecution initiatives. It also contained a controversial provision allowing people to sue their assailants in federal court if an assault could be shown to be motivated by "gender animus," essentially conceptualizing violence against women as a violation of their civil rights. This provision was overturned by the Supreme Court in 2000, but the rest of VAWA was reauthorized and modestly expanded in 2000 and 2006 with strong bipartisan support, and ultimately reauthorized again in 2013 after more contentious debate (Whittier 2018, 2016).

Grassroots activists, including younger feminists, were not engaged with the effort to pass VAWA and there was very little coverage of VAWA in the feminist press, except when the civil rights provision was overturned (Whittier 2018). Nevertheless, VAWA funding bolstered many organizations that sustain anti-rape activism at the grassroots, including crisis centers and educational offices. It enabled groups not only to offer more services, but to engage in more outreach to police, schools, hospitals, communities of color, and younger women who might serve as interns or paid staff. In addition, the VAWA hearings cultivated support for a dominant frame within Congress of violence against women as a gendered crime (Whittier

2016). This helped build support for later legislation and policy initiatives, such as expansions in the enforcement of Title IX and 2013 expansions to the Clery Act that required "educational institutions to educate staff and students about campus sexual assault, including…definitions of sexual assault and consent, [and] bystander tools" for intervention to prevent assault (Silbaugh 2015: 1073–4).

Despite progress on the legislative front, grassroots feminist activism on sexual assault was minimal in the 1990s and early 2000s. Between the 1990s and 2010, activism against sexual assault on campus existed at a steady, but relatively low, level. Activists at many institutions organized annual events like Take Back the Night marches and exhibits of the Clothesline Project, which displays T-shirts with messages written by survivors of sexual assault and child sexual abuse (Whittier 2009). Survivors' support and activism groups existed at numerous campuses, but activism was not formally coordinated across campuses and, before social media, geographically dispersed activists could not easily share information or support. Short-lived more visible campaigns emerged sporadically, such as in the early 1990s around date rape. At Brown University, Wesleyan and other schools, activists wrote the names of men they said had assaulted them in bathroom stalls (Grigoriadis 2017). A related push for what we now call affirmative consent also grew, led by a policy at Antioch College that required explicit verbal approval for each sexual act. Although these protests were not large or sustained, they helped keep the feminist critique of sexual violence on the radar, which enabled the rapid spread of protest around 2011.

A Resurging Movement, 2011–2018

In 2011, widespread protest against sexual violence emerged among younger women. Through marches, speakouts, art and protests over the treatment of survivors, they garnered widespread attention. Student activists targeted their colleges' procedures for addressing sexual violence directly with all these tactics, as well as the legal tool of Title IX. Their protests built on the frames and tactical repertoires of previous activism against sexual violence, but also changed in important ways.

The first uprisings came in response to a Toronto police officer's comment that women could prevent rape by not dressing as sluts; a group of activists organized a protest march that they called a SlutWalk. They protested "slut shaming," and proclaimed that "[b]eing in charge of our sexual lives should not mean that we are opening ourselves to an expectation of violence" (quoted in Reger 2014: 50). The initial slutwalks garnered extensive media attention and women across the United States and worldwide organized similar marches in 2011 and 2012. Reger (2014) counted 53 slutwalks in the United States and Canada, in both conservative and liberal areas, and another 33 worldwide. The slutwalks were the first feminist antiviolence protest form to go viral, spreading through social media and feminist news and opinion websites, they drew on the legacy of Take Back the Night marches, combined with the long-standing strand of feminist sex-positivity (Reger 2014). Participants in the initial march dressed in exaggerated versions of attire labeled "slutty," such as underwear or revealing clothing; some of the other marches followed suit while others did not. They shared the political perspective that women were entitled to pursue and enjoy whatever form and amount of sex they desire without vulnerability to sexual assault.

The slutwalks sparked criticism from older generations of feminists and from women of color. As Reger (2014) explains, many older feminists saw the reclaiming of "slut" as a misguided collusion with women's sexual objectification, not a challenge to it. Feminists of color argued that reclaiming a stigmatized identity like "slut" might carry a transgressive meaning for white women, who are culturally defined as sexually pure, but the meaning for women of color, who have been defined as sexually immoral or hypersexual, is quite different. Black Women's Blueprint (2016 [2011]) circulated an influential letter about the slutwalks that helped spark a discussion about how to protest sexual violence while being conscious of the different ways that it plays out according to race and class. These conversations and critiques have continued and are one of the key characteristics of the contemporary movement, as we will see.

Shortly after the slutwalks, activism against sexual assault on campus mushroomed. These were separate campaigns, but the slutwalks and the conversations around them clearly influenced the activism that followed. While slutwalks often originated among college students, they targeted rape culture and law enforcement broadly, not school administrators. They led, however, to increased visibility of the issue. As college students began speaking out about assault on campus, they gained a broad platform through social media, especially the micro-blogging site Tumblr. A vivid letter written in the fall of 2012 by Amherst College student Angie Epifano about the administration's hostile and inept response after she reported being raped by another student went viral (2012). Epifano's account highlighted the many ways her college failed to follow federal law, including failure to report incidents of sexual assault and failure to follow any reasonable procedure for determining what had happened, mistreating Epifano and failing to sanction the alleged assailant. As her story gained attention, other students and alumni at Amherst and numerous other institutions shared similar stories. As these stories spread over social media, the emerging network built cross-campus ties and strategies. For example, Andrea Pino (who later became one of the central subjects of the documentary about sexual assault on campus, *The Hunting Ground*) explained that, "I came out as a survivor in October of 2012, reading the powerful stories of Angie Epifano, Dana Bolger, and the other strong survivors who fought back at Amherst College." Pino and other students filed a Title IX complaint against the University of North Carolina, Chapel Hill and founded the group End Rape on Campus (Pino 2013).

Protests across campuses focused on how institutions failed to follow procedures and mistreated survivors. For example, protests over a series of acquaintance rapes at the University of Montana in 2011 that were treated dismissively by Missoula police produced an investigation and a best-selling exposé (Krakauer 2015; New 2015). In the spring of 2011, 300 Dickinson College students occupied the administration building to protest the handling of sexual violence cases (Gilmore 2011). Also in 2011, after fraternity members at Yale chanted, "No means yes, yes means anal," students protested and filed a Title IX complaint. The administration quickly banned that fraternity. In 2014, students and faculty at Texas Tech protested a fraternity party that included the same infamous chant (Sharp et al. 2017), and University of Delaware students demonstrated against both sexual assault and the university's responses to it (Leon 2016).

Most prominently, in the 2014–15 academic year, Columbia University student Emma Sulkowicz carried her dorm room mattress everywhere she went, as a protest against Columbia's inaction after she reported having been raped the previous year and as her senior thesis in art. Columbia had already been under pressure, with 23 students bringing Title IX complaints against the school in 2014 (Mitra 2015). Sulkowicz's dramatic tactic brought national attention to the problem. "Carry That Weight," the title of Sulkowicz's project, became the name of an emerging activist group. Another group, "No Red Tape," founded at Columbia in the 1990s, gained new life in 2014 as it targeted the university's reluctance to release information about sexual assaults and its foot-dragging in addressing assault (Mitra 2015). No Red Tape's name led to a cross-campus action where activists attached pieces of red tape to clothes or campus statues (Mitra 2015). The Day of Action organized by these groups in October 2014 included 130 schools in five countries. Students followed Sulkowicz's lead, bringing their mattresses or pillows to demonstrations, speaking out about their sexual assaults, and calling for change in institutional procedures (Grigoriadis 2017; Mitra 2015).

These tactics are oriented toward visibility and cultural change. Speaking out occurred at rallies, in print, and online. Speakouts served multiple functions. They called attention to the problem and its widespread nature and worked to change survivors themselves, symbolically throwing off the shame and secrecy that characterize sexual violence (Whittier 2009, 2012; Haaken 2017). They aimed to change the culture, suggesting that experiences that both had been understood as normal or unproblematic were in fact rape or sexual assault. Speakouts were a well-established tactic of the movement against sexual violence. Similarly, the use of art—as in Sulkowicz's mattress project—reflected a longstanding use of art in related movements (see Whittier 2009).

Students also took advantage of Title IX as a tool to compel change in a new way. Students at numerous institutions filed Title IX complaints and created cross-campus organizations to share knowledge and encourage action, including Know Your IX, which helped students bring Title IX complaints and learn "direct action skills" (Grigoriadis 2017: 82). The strategy of Know Your IX is stated in the group's name: using federal law to compel institutional change. The number of Title IX complaints sky-rocketed from 32 complaints in 2013 to 102 in 2014 and 320 in 2017 (Grigoriadis 2017: 88). Student activists also successfully worked with lawyers and faculty to pressure schools through negative media coverage (Grigoriadis 2017: 90). *Time* magazine had a cover story in 2014 on sexual assault on campus (Gray 2014), Krakauer's *Missoula* was published in 2015, and the documentary *The Hunting Ground* was released in 2015.

Like the women's movement overall, the campus activists struggled with issues of race. Although there is no solid data, both researchers and activists remarked on how campus activists were disproportionately white. At the same time, many organizers worked to incorporate women of color into the movement and to build connections with movements for racial equality. For example, Mitra (2015: 394) says that the Columbia student movement "thought long and hard about" how to make the rally "broad [and] inclusive," and recounts a student speaker who focused on victimi-zation of people of color and trans people. Speaking at the Day of Action at Columbia in 2014, the African-American New York City public advocate, Letitia James connected the sexual assault movement to the civil rights struggle, noting that the Columbia steps where they gathered were "the steps from which the civil rights movement in Harlem was launched" (Mitra 2015: 394). Nevertheless, both white and black participants in the Columbia protests noted that "a lot of this discussion is centered around white women" and that relatively few people of color participated in the protests (Avila-Chevalier 2014). Nevertheless, one study found that both male and female students of color were "more supportive" of sexual assault education and prevention programming than white students (Worthen and Wallace 2017: 186).

One result of these efforts was a clear articulation of how race, class, gender and sexuality intersect to shape sexual assault and institutional responses to it. This combined with increasing attention to the dis-proportionate rates of assault against transgender women of color. The movement's frames explicitly connected sexual violence to inequalities around multiple forms of inequality. For example, the Know Your IX website states that, "sexual and dating violence are manifestations of sys-temic gender oppression, which cannot be separated from all other forms of oppression, including but not limited to imperialism, racism, classism, homophobia, transphobia, and ableism" (https://www.knowyourix.org/our-values/). Targeting campus responses to sexual violence, then, could be a tactic in what activists saw as a larger effort to end oppression. At the same time, the immediacy of personal experiences and the close commu-nity of college campuses meant that the specific issue—and specific cases—remained priorities as well.

Origins and Opportunities

Two major forces shaped the growth of the movement in the 2010s: prior activism against sexual violence and new political and cultural opportunities. Prior grassroots anti-violence activism, discussed above, was an important influence. Beyond the grassroots, the institutionalized women's movement (which many younger sexual assault activists did not see themselves part of) had long pushed for policy change around issues of sexual violence. These efforts produced the new political opportunities that spurred campus activism. Specifically, increased and broadened enforcement of Title IX under the Democratic Obama administration presented activists with an opportunity that applied specifically to activists targeting sexual assault at educational institutions.

The idea that sexual harassment or assault on campus could be a violation of Title IX was pioneered in 1977, in a case at Yale argued in part by ground-breaking feminist lawyer Catharine MacKinnon (Grigoriadis 2017: 74).[6] The activists at Yale who filed an influential Title IX complaint in 2011 included the daughters of one of the leaders of the 1977 Yale student movement (Grigoriadis 2017: 81). This direct personal connection between that history and the recent movement enabled the passing on of crucial knowledge. It wasn't until the Obama administration redefined enforcement, however, that the movement took off. Under the Obama administration, the Office of Civil Rights in the Department of Education stepped up enforcement of Title IX, and in 2011 released guidance for institutions in a letter known as the "Dear Colleague" letter. This guidance required schools to have a clear process for addressing and resolving reports of sexual violence, to resolve cases promptly, and to offer accommodations to victims in terms of housing, class schedule, and academic extensions. In hearings, schools were advised to use the lesser standard of proof used in civil law, the preponderance of evidence (often explained as "more likely than not"), rather than a stricter standard of proof (Grigoriadis 2017: 78–9; Silbaugh 2015). In addition, the "Dear Colleague" letter encouraged schools to expand their own institutional bureaucracy for dealing with sexual assault, hiring a dedicated Title IX coordinator and, often, additional staff.

The administration investigated numerous colleges and universities, finding prominent institutions out of compliance with Title IX, and threatening to eliminate federal funding to institutions that did not come into compliance. This gave activists a powerful tool: leverage over their institutions. They trained each other in what Title IX required and how to report violations. While the new requirements do not necessarily reduce sexual assault or improve institutional responses, they do signal a cultural and institutional opening. They tell activists where to target their efforts for change (e.g., the Title IX coordinator, other school administrators, and the federal Department of Education), establish expectations about how reports will be treated, and convey a cultural value of condemning and responding to sexual violence.

The Obama administration did not decide to increase enforcement out of the blue. Congressional hearings on VAWA took four years and involved many feminist activists, experts and service providers around sexual and intimate partner violence. Through the process of passing the bill, legislators across the political spectrum learned a great deal about the phenomenon of sexual violence and institutional shortcomings in dealing with it (Whittier 2018). VAWA funding also bolstered organizations dealing with sexual and intimate partner violence, which then were in place to support the burgeoning activism. When Biden became the Vice President, he adopted violence against women as one of his priorities and spearheaded the White House Task Force to Protect Students from Sexual Assault, which was housed in the Office on Violence Against Women, the federal office established by VAWA. The task force issued reports on the scope of the issue, brought together researchers and advocates, and played a role in rethinking how to use Title IX to reduce sexual violence on campus. In addition, grant funding available to campuses through the Office on Violence Against Women supported the creation of dedicated offices for dealing with sexual assault that, in turn, increased reporting rates on campus as victims learned how to report and what the consequences of reporting would be (Palmer and Alda 2016).

The White House Task Force also developed the public education campaigns, "It's On Us" and "Not Alone." Not Alone provided resources to students and schools about how to respond to sexual assault, while It's On Us sought to encourage bystanders to speak up to prevent sexual assault. It's On Us was the higher-profile, public health campaign, with posters, t-shirts, an online pledge, all materials raising awareness and reminding especially men that they should intervene (http://www.itsonus.org/.) Biden was a visible spokesperson for the campaign and continued to speak with campus organizations, at sports events, and to fraternities and sororities as of 2018 (Tatum 2017). The task force reports, lobbying by advocates from organizations, including Know Your IX and SurvJustice (Richards et al 2017), and Biden's own efforts led to the issuance of the "Dear Colleague" letter and, in turn, to the burgeoning campus movement. In sum, prior grassroots and campus activism shaped newer activists' tactics and frames, while institutionalized feminism helped produce VAWA and ultimately the expansion of Title IX expansion. This in turn provided an opening for the new round of activism. Much of this shifted as the Obama administration ended.

Opening and Closing Opportunities under the Trump Administration

The Trump administration obviously was less receptive to the movement, but it also facilitated increased opportunities for activists in other ways. On the political side, because the new interpretation of Title IX under the Obama administration was a matter of rules issued by the Department of

Education, not legislation, it could be easily over-turned under a new administration. Unsurprisingly, in September 2017, Trump's Secretary of Education, Betsy DeVos, withdrew the 2011 "Dear Colleague" letter and issued new guidance. Under the new guidance, colleges could choose a higher (clear and convincing evidence) or lower (preponderance of the evidence) standard of proof for accusations of sexual misconduct but could not use a lower standard of evidence for sexual misconduct than for other types of misconduct; could resolve cases through mediation; did not have to resolve cases within a specified timeframe; and had to provide interim accommodations to both parties, as needed, without assuming guilt or innocence (United States Department of Education 2017). Meanwhile, a number of men accused of sexual assault have sued their colleges or universities for violations of due process, and some have won. Without the Department of Education enforcing strict standards for sexual assault adjudication, schools have less incentive, and more risk, if they continue to pursue cases aggressively. It seems likely, therefore, that schools who had not yet adopted the Obama-era procedures will not do so and that many of those who had will roll them back. The federal government no longer gives activists leverage over their schools. Instead, the federal government has become a potential target for change. Similar to other movements, activists against sexual assault have resorted to legal challenges to the Trump administration; a coalition of advocates is suing Secretary of Education Betsy DeVos over the rule changes (Green 2018).

Despite these roll-backs, the federal Office on Violence Against Women remained, as of 2018, headed by a deputy director appointed by Trump, yet remains without a director (United States Department of Justice 2018). The Office on Violence Against Women website continued to host the reports of the Obama-Biden White House Task Force, posting the final reports in early 2017 (https://www.justice.gov/ovw/protecting-students-sexual-assault). The reports and other materials from the Task Force are also housed on the website of the Center for Changing Our Campus Culture (http://changingourcampus.org/), which as of early 2018 was funded by VAWA through the Office on Violence Against Women. The It's On Us materials are housed on a dedicated, non-governmental website. Because the Trump administration has removed material from government websites and is working to defund many federal agencies, it is uncertain what will remain online.

At the same time that the Trump administration closed opportunities for federal policy, it created new cultural openings. The high-profile sexual assault and harassment accusations against Trump, which fueled countless other accusations, has kept the issue in the spotlight and expanded the movement beyond college campuses to the media, entertainment, and workplace. During the 2016 campaign, when numerous women alleged that Trump had grabbed, fondled and forcibly kissed them, his opponents framed him as an unrepentant sexual assaulter. The release during the campaign of the Access Hollywood tapes, in which Trump bragged of such actions, led to a spate of disclosures of sexual harassment and conversations as women around the country began speaking with their family and friends about their own experiences of sexual harassment and assault (PBS News Hour 2016). The 2017 Alabama Senate candidacy of Roy Moore, who was accused of sexual assault by multiple under-aged girls, in Alabama led to another nationwide conversation, in media and daily life, about statutory rape, predatory older men, the sexualization of teenaged girls and—again— Trump's condoning of these things. The 2018 firing of White House aides Rob Porter and David Sorensen for domestic violence again focused national attention on that issue. In other words, the election of Trump helped connect the campus sexual assault campaign to a broader movement. It is no coincidence that activists framed mass protests after Trump's election as a *women's* march. Sexual assault was a key issue for protesters and sparked the iconic "pussy hats" and slogans like "pussy grabs back" (Puglise 2016). At the same time, the marches included people of all genders and diverse issues including sexism, racism, immigration, homophobia, reproductive rights, sexual assault, environmental protection and climate change, labor, democracy, and more (Fisher et al. 2017). (See Chapter 1 on the women's marches.)

Conclusions: The Outcomes of the Movement

Social movements can change policy, the broader culture, and mobilization (Staggenborg 1995). In the end, the campus sexual assault movement produced change in all three areas. In terms of *policy*, the expansion and enforcement Title IX under Obama, although temporary, did affect schools' responses to sexual violence for a time, and may ultimately influence them in the longer term. At the same time, that redefinition likely also contributed to a backlash and to the stricter rules imposed under Trump. Further, even where Title IX produced changes in procedures, these may have been more a matter of symbolism and increased bureaucratic procedures and less a matter of meaningful change (Leon 2016). The Obama administration attempted to use Title IX in a very broad way, to change campus culture and prevent sexual assault. Because this is not spelled out in the legislation itself, such efforts will continue to be vulnerable to reversal as federal power shifts.

Activists interested in the prevention of sexual assault might instead work to get colleges to approach prevention through a public health approach, rather than the enforcement approach reflected in Title IX (Potter 2016). The Centers for Disease Control and the It's On Us and Not Alone campaigns have encouraged this kind of approach, which develops programming, trains bystanders to intervene, examines alcohol policy, and works to regulate and intervene in fraternities and sports teams, which traditionally have high rates of sexual assault (Silbaugh 2015). Activists might also explore reviving feminist self-defense (McCaughey and Cermele 2017). Activists who want more lasting change may pursue legislation, either at federal or state levels. In fact, several states recently passed legislation requiring colleges and universities to adopt an affirmative consent standard in determining whether sexual activity is consensual or not (Cooney 2018). This standard presumes sexual activity is not consensual unless both parties affirmatively indicate consent, rather than assuming it is consensual as long as neither party says "no."

As the example of affirmative consent indicates, *cultural change* has been significant. Affirmative consent and public health-style campaigns that might reframe the culture and sexual script have been largely limited to campuses. The "yes-means yes" state laws suggest a potential for broader impact. Further, there is evidence that the idea of affirmative consent may be reshaping how current high school and college-aged people view sexuality and consent, at the same time that substantial barriers remain to clear sexual communication (Curtis and Burnett 2017; Williams 2018).

Finally, the campus sexual assault movement has contributed to the upsurge in feminist and anti-violence *mobilization* following Trump's election. The mass mobilization of the women's marches, Trump's sexism and the campus organizing together fueled the #MeToo and Times Up movements that focused on speaking out about sexual violence and harassment and demanding individual and institutional responses. #MeToo as an organizing frame, coined in 2006 by activist Tarana Burke, spread exponentially in 2017 (Garcia 2017). The cultural visibility of sexual assault and harassment that began after Trump's recorded comments combined with the viral hashtag to produce something unprecedented. #MeToo is a cultural change in itself, as well as an activist campaign. As a cultural change, it reflects the acknowledgment of widespread sexual assault, encourages visibility as women and people of other genders "come out" about their experience, and frames sexual harassment and violence as a result of power. The many men (and the few women) in government and entertainment who have lost their positions suggests a concrete, albeit individual, outcome and the potential for institutional change in toleration of sexual harassment. Expanding beyond high-status occupations, the #MeToo movement is beginning to highlight an intersectional lens. For example, prominent actresses brought activists from groups like the National Domestic Workers' Alliance to the Golden Globe awards to bring attention to sexual harassment in less-visible, less-powerful industries (Buckley 2018). Because sexual harassment and assault are already illegal, activists' goals center on cultural change, including enforcement of existing law and changes in norms of interaction, views of gender and practices of sexual consent.

Sexual violence has been an enduring issue in organizing by women across race and class. The campus sexual assault movement mobilized a cohort of activists who are likely to remain politically committed over the long haul (Whittier 1997). It responded to openings under Obama, and helped create cultural openings for further activism in the Trump era. Thus far, its outcomes for policy, culture, and mobilization suggest that the movement had both short-term outcomes, and longer term ones that are not yet clear. Scholars and activists should watch to see whether the various strands of contemporary organizing against sexual harassment and assault gel into a durable movement and what the place of activism against sexual violence is in the larger anti-Trump coalition over time.

Notes

1 These estimates define sexual assault as involving "nonconsensual sexual contact by physical force, threats of physical force, or incapacitation," including both penetration and sexual touching (Cantor et al. 2017: viii). The figures reported are for undergraduates. Rates for graduate students are much lower. Non-heterosexual students and those with a disability reported higher rates of victimization (Cantor et al. 2017: xx). Oddly, this study does not report characteristics of the assailant.

2 These figures exclude statutory rape and are based on reports to law enforcement in 12 states that collected data on the age of the victims.

3 Cantor et al. (2017: ix) find that 16.9 percent of freshman women "reported sexual contact by physical force or incapacitation" that academic year compared to 11.1 percent of seniors.

4 Some research suggests that rates of sexual violence are comparable or higher among young women who are not enrolled in college (Rennison and Addington 2014, cited in Grigoriadis 2017: note 115).

5 The trial of Joann Little, an African American woman who killed a prison guard who attempted to rape her, generated a major cross-racial coalition that included NOW, the NAACP, and many grassroots activists (McGuire 2010).

6 A 1999 case about an elementary school confirmed that harassment by other students (not just by faculty) was a Title IX violation (Grigoriadis 2017: 76).

References

Armstrong, Elizabeth A., Laura Hamilton and Brian Sweeney. 2006. "Sexual Assault on Campus: A Multilevel, Integrative Approach to Party Rape." *Social Problems* 53(4):483–499.

Avila-Chevalier, Darializa. 2014. "Sister Outsider: Examining the Intersection between Race and Sexual Assault at Columbia." *Columbia Spectator*. Oct. 16. Retrieved March 1, 2018. http://features.columbiaspectator.com/blog/2014/10/16/sister-outsider/.

Bailey, Beth. 1999. *Sex in the Heartland*. Boston: Harvard.

Bevacqua, Marie. 2000. *Rape on the Public Agenda*. Boston: Northeaster.

Biden, Joe. 2017. "I Was Heartbroken." *Marie Claire*. Sept. 25. Retrieved March 2, 2018. https://www.marieclaire.com/culture/news/a29656/joe-biden-its-on-us-essay/.

Black Women's Blueprint. 2016 [2011]. "An Open Letter from Black Women to the Slutwalk." Reprinted in *Gender & Society* 30(1):9–16.

Brownmiller, Susan. 1999. *In Our Time: Memoir of a Revolution*. New York: Delta/Dell Publishing.

Buckley, Cara. 2018. "Stars Will Take Activists to the Golden Globes Red Carpet." *New York Times*. Jan. 7. Retrieved March 1, 2018. https://www.nytimes.com/2018/01/07/movies/golden-globes-2018-activists-metoo-red-carpet.html.

Cantalupo, Nancy C. 2011. "Burying our Heads in the Sand: Lack of Knowledge, Knowledge Avoidance, and the Persistent Problem of Campus Peer Sexual Violence." *Loyola University Law Journal* 43:205–266.

Cantalupo, Nancy Chi. 2012. "'Decriminalizing' Campus Institutional Responses to Peer Sexual Violence." *Journal of College and University Law* 38:481–524.

Cantor, David, Bonnie Fisher, Susan Chibnall, Reanne Townsend, Hyunshik Lee, Carol Bruce and Gail Thomas. 2017. Report on the AAU Campus Climate Survey on Sexual Assault and Sexual Misconduct. Retrieved March 8, 2018. https://www.aau.edu/sites/default/files/AAU-Files/Key-Issues/Campus-Safety/AAU-Campus-Climate-Survey-FINAL-10-20-17.pdf.

Cooney, Samantha. 2018. "The Aziz Ansari Allegation Has People Talking About 'Affirmative Consent.' What's That?" *Time*. Jan. 17. Retrieved March 2, 2018. http://time.com/5104010/aziz-ansari-affirmative-consent/.

Corrigan, Rose. 2013. *Up Against a Wall: Rape Reform and the Failure of Success*. New York: NYU.

Crenshaw, Kimberle. 1991. "Mapping the Margins: Intersectionality, Identity Politics, and Violence Against Women." *Stanford Law Review* 43(6):1241–1290.

Curtis, Jena, and Susan Burnett. 2017. "Affirmative Consent: What Do College Student Leaders Think About 'Yes Means Yes' as the Standard for Sexual Behavior?" *American Journal of Sexuality Education* 12(3):201–214.

Epifano, Angie. 2012. "An Account of Sexual Assault at Amherst College." The Amherst Student. Oct. 17. http://amherststudent.amherst.edu/?q=article/2012/10/17/account-sexual-assault-amherst-college.

Fisher, Dana R., Dawn M. Dow and Rashawn Ray. 2017. "Intersectionality Takes It to the Streets: Mobilizing Across Diverse Interests for the Women's March." *Science Advances* 3(9). http://advances.sciencemag.org/content/3/9/eaao1390.full.

Freedman, Estelle. 2013. *Redefining Rape*. Cambridge, MA: Harvard University Press.

Garcia, Sandra. 2017. "The Woman Who Created #MeToo Long Before Hashtags." *New York Times*. Oct. 20. Retrieved March 1, 2018. https://www.nytimes.com/2017/10/20/us/me-too-movement-tarana-burke.html?_r=0.

Gavey, Nicola. 2009. "Fighting Rape." Pp. 96–124 in *Theorizing Sexual Violence*, edited by Renee Heberle and Victoria Grace. NewYork: Routledge.

Gilmore, Stephanie. 2011. "'Everything We're Doing Here, We Learned in Class': Views On The Protest Against Sexual Violence at Dickinson College." *Feminist Studies* 37(1) (Spring 2011):214–217.

Gottschalk, Marie. 2006. *The Prison and the Gallows: The Politics of Mass Incarceration in America*. Cambridge, UK: Cambridge University Press.

Gray, Eliza. 2014. "The Sexual Assault Crisis on American Campuses." *Time Magazine*. May 15. Retrieved March 1, 2018. http://time.com/100542/the-sexual-assault-crisis-on-american-campuses/.

Green, Erica. 2018. "Education Secretary Betsy DeVos is Sued over Sexual Assault Guidance." *New York Times*. Jan. 25. Retrieved March 2, 2018. https://www.nytimes.com/2018/01/25/us/politics/betsy-devos-sexual-assault-guidelines-lawsuit.html.

Grigoriadis, Vanessa. 2017. *Blurred Lines: Rethinking Sex, Power, and Consent on Campus*. New York: Eamon Dolan/Houghton Mifflin Harcourt.

Haaken, Janice. 2017. "Many Mornings After: Campus Sexual Assault and Feminist Politics." *Family Relations* 66:17–28.

Jozkowski, Kristen N. and Jacquelyn D. Wiersma-Mosley. 2017. "The Greek System: How Gender Inequality and Class Privilege Perpetuate Rape Culture." *Family Relations* 66(1): 89–103.

Krakauer, Jon. 2015. *Missoula: Rape and the Justice System in a College Town.* NY: Doubleday.

Langan, Patrick and Caroline Harlow. 1994. Child Rape Victims, 1992: Crime Data Brief. Washington, DC: U.S. Department of Justice. http://www.bjs.gov/ con tent/pub/pdf/crv92.pdf.

Leon, Chrysanthi S. 2016. "Law, Mansplainin', and Myth Accommodation in Campus Sexual Assault Reform." *Kansas Law Review* 64(4):987–1025.

Martin, Patricia Y. 2005. *Rape Work.* New York: Routledge.

Matthews, Nancy. 1994. *Confronting Rape.* New York: Routledge.

McCaughey, Martha. 1997. *Real Knockouts.* New York: NYU.

McCaughey, Martha and Jill Cermele. 2017. "Changing the Hidden Curriculum of Campus Rape Prevention and Education: Women's Self-Defense as a Key Protective Factor for a Public Health Model of Prevention." *Trauma, Violence & Abuse* 18:287–302.

McGuire, Danielle. 2010. *At the Dark End of the Street.* New York: Knopf.

Mitra, Shayoni. 2015. "'It Takes Six People To Make A Mattress Feel Light…': Materializing Pain in Carry That Weight and Sexual Assault Activism." *Contemporary Theatre Review* 25(3):386–400.

New, Jake. 2015 "Missoula's Mistakes." *Inside Higher Ed.* April 24. Retrieved January 8, 2018. https://www.insidehighered.com/news/2015/04/24/new-book-details-u-montanas-citys-mishandling-sexual-assault.

Palmer, Jane E. and Erik Alda. 2016. "Examining the Impact of Federal Grants to Reduce Violent Crimes Against Women on Campus." *Review of Higher Education* 40:63–89.

PBS News Hour. 2016. "Why the Trump Tape Started a National Conversation about Sexual Assault." Oct. 12. Retrieved March 1, 2018. https://www.pbs.org/newshour/show/trump-tape-started-national-conversation-sexual-assault.

Pino, Andrea. 2013. "Why Filing an Office for Civil Rights Complaint against UNC is Bigger Than Me." *Huffpost.* Jan. 19. https://www.huffingtonpost.com/a ndrea-pino/unc-sexual-assault-_b_2497326.html.

Potter, Sharyn J. 2016. "Reducing Sexual Assault on Campus: Lessons from the Movement to Prevent Drunk Driving." *American Journal of Public Health* 106:822–829.

Puglise, Nicole. 2016. "'Pussy Grabs Back' becomes Rallying Cry for Female Rage Against Trump." *The Guardian.* Oct. 10. Retrieved March 1, 2018. https://www.theguardian.com/us-news/2016/oct/10/donald-trump-pussy-grabs-back-mem e-women-twitter.

Reger, Jo. 2014. "Micro-Cohorts, Feminist Discourse, and the Emergence of the Toronto SlutWalk." *Feminist Formations* 26:49–69.

Rentschler, Carrie A. 2011. *Second Wounds: Victims' Rights and the Media in the U.S.* Durham, NC: Duke University Press.

Richards, Tara N., Kathryn A. Branch, Ruth Fleury-Steiner and Katherine Kafonek. 2017. "A Feminist Analysis of Campus Sexual Assault Policies: Results from a National Sample." *Family Relations* 66(1):104–115.

Richie, Beth. 2012. *Arrested Justice: Black Women, Violence, and America's Prison Nation*. New York: NYU.

Russlynn, Ali. N.D. "'Dear Colleague Letter' Sexual Violence." US DOE Office for Civil Rights. Retrieved March 1, 2018. https://www2.ed.gov/about/offices/list/ocr/letters/colleague-201104.html

Sharp, Elizabeth A., Dana A. Weiser, Don E. Lavigne and R. Corby Kelly. 2017. "From Furious to Fearless: Faculty Action and Feminist Praxis in Response to Rape Culture On College Campuses." *Family Relations* 66(1):75–88.

Silbaugh, Katharine. 2015. "Reactive to Proactive: Title IX's Unrealized Capacity to Prevent Campus Sexual Assault." *Boston University Law Review* 95(3):1049–1076.

Staggenborg, Suzanne. 1995. "Can Feminist Organizations be Effective?" In *Feminist Organizations*, edited by Myra M. Ferree and Patricia Y. Martin. Philadelphia: Temple.

Tatum, Sophie. 2017. "Biden: 'New Challenges' On Campus Sexual Assault." CNN. Sept. 19. Retrieved March 2, 2018. https://www.cnn.com/2017/09/19/politics/joe-biden-its-on-us-three-year-anniversary/index.html.

United States Department of Education, Office of Civil Rights. 2017. "Q&A on Campus Sexual Misconduct." Retrieved March 2, 2018. https://www2.ed.gov/about/offices/list/ocr/docs/qa-title-ix-201709.pdf.

United States Department of Justice. 2018. "Meet OVW Leadership." Retrieved March 2, 2018. https://www.justice.gov/ovw/staff-profile/meet-ovw-leadership.

Whittier, Nancy. 2018. *Frenemies: Feminists, Conservatives, and Sexual Violence*. New York: Oxford University Press.

Whittier, Nancy. 2016. "Carceral and Intersectional Feminism in Congress: The Violence Against Women Act, Discourse, and Policy." *Gender & Society* 30 (5):791–818.

Whittier, Nancy. 2012. "The Politics of Visibility: Coming Out and Individual and Collective Identity." Pp. 145–169. In *Strategies for Social Change*, edited by Jeff Goodwin, Rachel Kutz-Flamenbaum, Greg Maney and Deana Rohlinger. Minneapolis: University of Minnesota Press.

Whittier, Nancy. 2009. *The Politics of Child Sexual Abuse*. New York: Oxford.

Whittier, Nancy. 1997. "Political Generations, Micro-Cohorts, and the Transformation of Social Movements." *American Sociological Review* 62 (October):760–778.

Whittier, Nancy. 1995. *Feminist Generations*. Philadelphia: Temple University Press.

Williams, Alex. 2018. "#MeToo Men." *New York Times*. Feb. 27. Retrieved March 2, 2018. https://www.nytimes.com/interactive/2018/02/27/style/me-too-men-consent-pledge.html.

Worthen, Meredith G. F. and Samantha A. Wallace. 2017. "Intersectionality and Perceptions about Sexual Assault Education and Reporting on College Campuses." *Family Relations* 66:180–196.

9 The Messy Politics of Menstrual Activism

Chris Bobel and Breanne Fahs

What We Talk About When We Talk About Menstruation

When we pay attention to menstrual health and its potential to inspire political resistance, we tap into a complex and enduring project of loosening the social control of women's bodies. Menstrual activism works to move embodiment from object to subject status–to see the body not as trivial or unimportant, but as something foundational, urgent and politically relevant. When we take seriously the (menstruating) body, we link up with others who engage in critical embodiment work, from human trafficking to eating disorders to sexual assault. This is why #menstruationmatters (https://twitter.com/hashtag/menstruationmatters) really should be a rallying call for *everyone* who cares about social justice and gender equality. Menstruation unites the personal and the political, the intimate and the public, the minutiae and the bigger stories about the body. *It IS about so much more than blood.*

It may not be obvious at first but those working to improve menstrual health—whether using humor, poetry, empirical research, school curricula, or promoting a better menstrual absorbent—must counter the internalization of destructive messages about womanhood including notions of bodies as messy, unruly things that need to be tidied up, medicated, plucked, smoothed and trimmed. "Managing" menstrual cycles evokes the range of activities and practices that women do to "manage" other parts of their bodies, including grooming body hair, making fashion choices, hiding breastfeeding, losing weight and more. In this chapter, we argue that feminists must challenge generations of silence and shame that obstruct evidence-based, student-centered, body-positive quality menstrual health education. We must also promote a culture of curiosity and informed decision-making about caring for our bodies. Finally, we must counter the assumption that menstruation matters *only* to menstruators.

When we pull back and see menstrual health in context, we can see what is really at stake in menstrual activism. Because a challenge to the menstrual status quo is itself a critique of gender norms about embodiment, it productively leads us to ask some tough questions about what we take for granted. What can we learn about our cultural value systems when we consider enduring menstrual restrictions? What can we learn about gender, bodies and power when we look at our actions as consumers (e.g., buying skin lightening creams or diet pills)? Who benefits from these values-in-practice? Who suffers?

Certainly, menstruation is personal, but feminists have long understood that the personal *is* political, that is, while we may experience something—a monthly period, an act of intimate partner violence, an unplanned pregnancy—the way we respond to these events and the support, or lack of support, we can access is the consequence of something far bigger than ourselves. As Carol Hanisch, an American radical feminist, wrote in 1969: "...personal problems are political problems. There are no personal solutions at this time. There is only collective action for a collective solution." Hanisch, here, calls for remedies to the injustices of women's lives that compel us all. That's what menstrual activism is—a mobilizing effort that challenges menstrual taboos and insists that menstruators have the support they need to live healthy happy lives, throughout their cycles and throughout their lives. When we pay attention to menstruation, we work toward a world that is safer and more just, a world where everyone is supported in whatever body they inhabit.

Taking seriously the call for collective action, this chapter first describes a brief history of menstrual activism alongside its more recent iterations in both policy and radical social activism. This is followed by an analysis of menstrual humor, menstrual art and menstrual activism today. We then turn toward the hazards and possibilities of doing menstrual activist work, including politics of menstrual language and the trivializations and hostilities that can plague this work, followed by a politically charged outline for the future of menstrual activism.

A Movement Dawns, and Finally Gets Brighter

In April 2016, *Newsweek* ran a feature on menstrual activism. The cover featured an unwrapped tampon against a deep red background. The words, large, bold and in contrasting white, read: "There Will Be Blood. Get Over It. Period Stigma is hurting the economy, schools and the environment. But the crimson tide is turning." When a mainstream, high-circulation news organization ran a feature like this, it signaled that something had shifted, a new urgency around menstrual culture was surfacing. Despite what many assume, menstrual activism is *not* new. It has been picking away at the edges of body-based shame and stigma for decades. According to Bobel (2007, 2010), "feminist spiritualist menstrual activists" broke ground in the late 1960s with their reframing of menstruation as a source of power and sisterhood. They refused the taken-for-granted assumption that menstruation was merely a nuisance, a "curse," and offered a conceptual reframing through art, including filmmaking, music, poetry and ritual. They built upon a second wave cultural feminist (that is, the embrace of women's differences and the assertion that women need to value their "womanness") sensibility that embraced rather than obscured sexual differences.

Concurrently, the women's health movement emerged, cultivating a robust resistance to the androcentric and often patronizing medical establishment. These activists spurred a healthy scrutiny of many tacit practices, especially those around reproductive health care which led to attention to menstrual and menopausal health care. Animated by a need for bodily sovereignty and the tools and resources to make informed choices regarding providers, diagnoses and treatments, these activists joined consumer rights advocates when thousands of women developed Toxic Shock Syndrome (TSS), and 38 died, as a result of a new super absorbent, fully synthetic tampon call Rely ("It Even Absorbs the Worry" was its tagline). Rely's makers, Procter & Gamble, pulled the tampon from the shelves because it was an aggressive incubator for the potentially lethal bacterial strain staphylococcus aureus. This tragedy led activists to work with the U.S. government to better regulate the industry, leading to mandated TSS warnings in tampon packages and standardized absorbency ratings to help consumers choose the appropriate tampon to meet their needs.

Some environmentalists also became menstrual activists, adding to the critique of conventional care by bringing to light the polluting effects of single use menstrual care products and promoting greener alternatives such as organic tampons and pads, reusable cloth pads, cups and sponges. Further, as third-wave feminism (that is, feminism from the 1990s onward that focused on diversity, intersectionality, and activism) took shape, it found alignment with Punk and anarchism's anti-capitalism and Do It Yourself ethos (LeBlanc 1999; Marcus and McKay 2010). This intersection became a site for the emergence of what Bobel terms the "radical menstruation" wing of the movement (2010). Alternative products were championed, as well as free bleeding, as were zine making, early blogging and menstrual health education. Creative actions such as tampon art and tampon "send backs," in which activists return menstrual products to their manufacturers, defined menstrual activism through the turn of the century.

Another hallmark of the radical menstruation activist approach was its disinterest in structural reform. While earlier activists worked tirelessly with both government and industry to protect consumers, radical menstruation activists took a more cultural approach, instigating attitudinal change through visual art, performance, and humor. While feminist spiritualists promoted personal transformation through a celebration of menstruation, radical menstruation focused on building a more inclusive movement and "undoing gender," in the words of theorist Judith Butler (1990). Some began to use the word "menstruator," a term that embraced anybody that menstruated, heretofore assumed to be women. This linguistic move splits the biological (menstruation) from the socio cultural (the social construction of gender).

Today's menstrual activism is difficult to categorize, revealing its dynamism and its responsiveness to an ever-globalizing world where boundaries around identities are shifting. Accordingly, scholarship on menstrual activism is emerging and complicating definitions and categorizations (see Barkardóttir 2016; Fahs 2016; Kafai in press; Tarzibachi 2017). Persdotter, for example, situating her inquiry in western Europe, refers not to menstrual activism, but instead to the "menstrual Countermovement": "the mass of actions, and agents that purposefully work towards challenging the repressive mainstream menstrual discourse of shame and silence" (2013: 13). She argues for a more nuanced and diverse categorization that makes room for consumer-oriented change makers, such as those who produce and sell alternative menstrual products, ritualists, and others whose work is at once activist and income generating. With this historical overview in mind, we turn now to selected activist actions, moving between past and present. Our aim is to illustrate both important continuities with and key departures from menstrual activism's little known history.

Everything Old is New Again

Laughing While Bleeding: Using Humor to Break the Silence

In 1978, Gloria Steinem penned her now iconic satire "If Men Could Menstruate." The essay, what she dubbed "a political fantasy," first appeared in *Ms.* and has been widely and regularly republished and excerpted since. Cleverly using satiric humor, Steinem guides the reader through a thought experiment led by the question: "So what would happen if suddenly, magically, men could menstruate and women could not?" She goes on: "Clearly, menstruation would become an enviable, worthy, masculine event. Men would brag about how long and how much. Young boys would talk about it as the envied beginning of manhood. Gifts, religious ceremonies, family dinners, and stag parties would mark the day" (Steinem 1978: 110). A few years later, "If Men Could Menstruate" was republished in a collection of feminist humor titled "Pulling Our Own Strings" (Kaufman and Blakely 1980), which included several menstrual-themed pieces in the book's lead section titled "Periodic Hysteria." The book opens with an introduction explaining what makes humor feminist: at once an acknowledgement of sexist oppression and a vision of change. The book includes an argument for feminist menstrual humor in which "the attitude is that menses is not to be hidden (as shameful) but to be joked about (as normal) or even celebrated (as naturally female)…the expression of such humor attacks the unhealthy and oppressing idea cultivated for thousands of years that women's bodies are foul" (Kaufman 1980: 14).

This claim similarly animates contemporary menstrual activist humor. The Crimson Wave is a stand-up comedy duo of Natalie Norman and Jess Beaulieu from Toronto, Canada that describes their feminist podcast as being "about periods/vaginas/Beyonce's vagina where guests tell hilarious stories, anecdotes, and theories about their lovely menses." In this same vein, U.K.-based solo comedian, educator and activist Chella Quint performs her gender-inclusive show aimed at menstrual stigma through playful deconstruction of vintage menstrual product ads. In her shows, she introduces her tongue-in-cheek "product": Stains™. The use of the bright red stain—as earrings, as cufflinks, as felt stains ready to be pinned to any part of the body—deploys the visual to challenge menstrual invisibility. The use of the visual has been a mainstay of menstrual activists since the dawn of the movement.

The Visual is Political: Menstrual Art as Change Agent

In 1971, Judy Chicago, feminist art pathbreaker, created a shocking photolithograph: a self-portrait of Chicago, legs spread, withdrawing a tampon from her vagina. Titled "Red Flag," the piece, reports Chicago, represented something so profoundly absent from our visual landscape that many people assumed the object was a penis.

The following year, Chicago further explored menstrual realities when she created "Menstruation Bathroom" in her multiroom installation collaboration with Judith Schapiro, "Womanhouse." In Menstruation Bathroom, numerous tampons and pads (both single use and reusable cloth), used and unused, are strewn throughout the room. They sit on shelves, piled in the trash bin, on the floor and hanging on the clothesline. Here, one encounters the scope and scale of menstrual care across many cycles, even years. Interestingly, the blood in this piece is relatively contained—only a few splatters appear on the floor. The lid to the toilet is closed.

Some 40 years later, self-described "menstrual designer" Jen Lewis and collaborator and photographer Rob Lewis lifted the lid in their work and began showing portraits of menstrual blood moving through water. As a menstrual cup user, Lewis grew fascinated by the designs she observed as she emptied her menstrual cup in the toilet. Her work has been featured in mainstream and fringe media and widely circulated across social media. In 2015, she curated

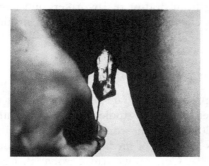

Image 9.1 Judy Chicago, *Red Flag*, photolithograph, 20 x 24 in., 1971.
© 2017 Judy Chicago / Artists Rights Society (ARS), New York.

the largest art show featuring menstrual art, "Widening the Cycle: A Menstrual Cycle and Reproductive Art Show." Framing menstrual art as part of the reproductive justice movement, the show displayed the work of 38 artists from 10 countries "to disrupt the current cultural narrative and replace it with one that reflects the real thoughts, emotions and experiences of menstruators" (http://www.wideningthecycle.com/). Soon after, "Our Bodies Our Blood," "an art project about creating a safe space to express thoughts on menstruation, cultural shame and our stories," (https://www.facebook.com/pg/ourblood. artproject/about/?ref=page_internal) went on view in Nova Scotia. In 2017, there were two menstrually-focused group art shows, "Period" in Miami, Florida (http://rojasrubensteenprojects.com/new-page/) and "The Crimson Wave: Art About and With Menstrual Blood" in Bangalore, India (http:// www.boondh.co/the-crimson-wave.html). These shows are evidence that menstrual artists form a crucial part of the battle to make menstruation visible and culturally-relevant.

Along these lines, 2015 was the same year *Cosmopolitan* dubbed "the year the period went public" evinced by an illustrated timeline cataloguing "The 8 Greatest Menstrual Moments of 2015." The 12-month history included Instagram's much maligned decision to twice remove a photo of artist and *New York Times* bestselling poet Rupi Kaur lying in bed wearing period-stained pants. The photo quickly went viral. Cosmo's timeline also included reference to Kiran Gandhi's decision to free bleed while running the London Marathon. Initially, Gandhi chose to go without menstrual absorbent for ease and comfort, but as she ran, she began to consider the political implications of her act, transforming her personal decision into a moving protest, a type of circumstantial performance piece (Gandhi 2015). Gandhi has continued her menstrual activism, with a focus on menstrual product access (https://madamegandhi.blog/hi/) and legislative action. Her turn to legislative action represents a return to the roots of menstrual activism, when collaborations between feminist health and consumer rights advocates pressured the government to provide more careful oversight of the industry. While menstrual activists of the late 20th and early 21st centuries showed disinterest, springing from distrust of lawmakers and corporate players, the newer crop of social change has doubled down on making change through legal reform.

Menstrual Activists (Go Back) to Washington

In some menstrual products there are trace amounts of dioxins, which are potentially carcinogenic. Recent studies have found phthalates and furanes as well (Gloaguen 2017), but the contents of menstrual products, classified in the United States as a class of medical devices, are not made available to the public. Since 1997, Congresswoman Carolyn B. Maloney has brought the bill the Tampon Safety and Research Act before Congress nine times, and each time it languished in committee. Her most recent version is the

Robin Danielson Feminine Hygiene Product Safety Act of 2015, named after a woman who died in 1988 of Toxic Shock Syndrome. Maloney proposes the National Institute of Health fund research on the synthetics and chemicals used in menstrual products and test for reproductive problems as well as common health conditions "to close this research gap" (O'Hara 2015). In addition, the Federal Drug Administraton (FDA) would check manufacturers' data and make this information available to the public (O'Hara 2015). Maloney's bill is now joined by U.S. Rep. Grace Meng's introduction of the Accurate Labeling of Menstrual Products Act of 2016, which calls for menstrual product companies to disclose the ingredients of their products.

As menstrual activism gains force, some legislators are linking issues of safety to broader issues of access and affordability. In New York City, Mayor Bill de Blasio signed legislation to provide public school grades 6–12, homeless shelters and correctional facilities with free pads and tampons. Meng proposed a second menstrual-related bill: the five-part Menstrual Equity Act of 2017, the product of a recent spate of interest and energy around the cost of menstrual products. The fact that many cities, states, and countries tax menstrual products, commonly referred to as the "tampon tax," has become a lightning rod for those frustrated by gender inequality. Considering that items such as men's shaving cream, Viagra, candy and soda do not carry this added tax, it is easy to regard the extra cost as a form of discrimination against females *qua* females. For menstruators, menstrual supplies are as essential as toilet paper.

No doubt, the reach of social media and an evolving public attitude toward menstruation facilitated high profile efforts such as Jennifer Weiss-Wolf's joint campaign with *Cosmopolitan* magazine; "Stop Taxing our Periods! Period." To date, it has garnered over 68,000 signatures. Weiss-Wolf coined the phrase "menstrual equity," a frame that asserts that "in order to have a fully equitable and participatory society, we must have laws and policies that ensure menstrual products and affordable and available for those who need them" (2017: xvi). Menstruation, she claims "transcends all the other things about women's bodies that make us targets for the right, and this one doesn't" (Arriaga 2017). This may explain bipartisan support for removing the "tampon tax" in a climate where other reproductive issues garner little Republican support.

Access and Affordability: Today's Menstrual Activism's Rallying Cry

In a marked departure from their predecessors who, for the most part, had not yet taken stock of the particular realities of various populations, with the exception of trans and genderqueer menstruators among those in the radical menstruation wing, today's activists are keen to address the menstrual needs of the marginalized. For low-income, homeless and incarcerated menstruators, removing a tax or testing for potential health risks is less a priority than gaining access to menstrual products. A 2011 Feeding America Survey places menstrual products among the top eight basic essentials; however, they are not covered by food stamps. Many low-income menstruators cannot afford the products they need—even without taxes in certain places. The cost is estimated at approximately $2,500 over the course of a lifetime (Meng 2017).

Homeless menstruators face not only a lack of access to menstrual products but also to clean spaces in which to care for their menstruating bodies. A handful of campaigns and organizations are distributing menstrual care products to low income and homeless menstruators. #HappyPeriod, Support the Girls, and Period: the Menstrual Movement are three such organizations, based in the United States with ever growing rosters of chapters. U.K.-based #theHomelessPeriod is another. All are relative newcomers to the movement. Some have successfully partnered with big business players, such as Procter & Gamble, by negotiating product donations. Theirs is a bounty that earlier menstrual activists would surely eschew given their critiques of the menstrual product industry as purveyors of toxic, polluting products that use body shame to sell.

Schools of various kinds are also sites in need of reform, say today's menstrual activists. While schoolgirls in the global South have captured the attention of development agencies, NGOs and social entrepreneurs for more than a decade (Sommer et al. 2015), U.S. middle and high schools and universities and colleges have increasingly been challenged to provide free menstrual products to their students. Many of the new activists are under 30. Their age may explain a growing sensitivity to the needs of menstruators in schools, including not only the cost of products but also access to supplies in school bathrooms. The argument put forth here centers on the importance of providing the means to care for menstrual flow so that students can focus on their education despite their income or level of preparedness—or gender identity. For example, a student-led initiative at Brown University put free pads and tampons in women's, men's and gender inclusive bathrooms around campus. Other schools—such as Emory, University of Arizona, Reed College, University of Minnesota-Twin Cities, and the University of Wisconsin at Madison—have followed suit with similar programs. Efforts to ensure access to menstrual products is an interesting and some would argue, controversial, shift in campus-centered menstrual activism. As Bobel (2010) found, much of the college student-led work on campuses from the late 1990s forward had centered on workshops and tabling about the health and environmental hazards associated with single use pads and tampons and the promotion of *alternative* options, such as cloth pads, Do It Yourself (DIY) cloth pads, menstrual cups and sponges. For example, "Ax Tampax" was a slogan (and zine title) used by trailblazing Montreal-based menstrual activists, the Bloodisters (Bobel 2010).

Another profoundly marginalized population, incarcerated menstruators, has become a focus of some activists. In prisons and jails, menstrual products are often rationed, restricted, traded, or used by guards in power games. The lack of menstrual supplies among inmates affects not only their hygiene but also their self-esteem. Chandra Bozelko, a former inmate, said, "To ask a macho guard for a tampon is humiliating. But it's more than that: it's an acknowledgement of the fact that, ultimately, the prison controls your cleanliness, your health and your feelings of self-esteem" (Ronan 2015). Not only is there a dearth of materials, but also the ones provided are small, poor quality and lack adhesive. Some incarcerated menstruators are forced to wear these for multiple days, which can cause bacterial or fungal infections, or lead to bleeding through clothes.

In April 2017, Colorado passed an amendment agreeing to spend $40,000 to provide tampons for female inmates. Senators Elizabeth Warren and Cory Booker introduced the Dignity for Incarcerated Women Act on July 11, 2017; the legislation proposes distributing free quality pads and tampons to inmates. Soon thereafter, and ostensibly to avoid a legislative mandate, the U.S. Department of Justice issued an Operations Memorandum in August 2017 that "ensures that female inmates have access to a range of feminine hygiene products related to menstruation" (https://www.bop.gov/policy/om/001_2017.pdf). Because the mandate does not apply to state and municipal facilities, the fight continues. As Bozelko (2017) forcefully writes:

> Talking openly about menstruation can't be restricted to hygiene, as important as it is. The appeal to public health sidles up to the issue by making it seem like it's everyone's problem. That just gets us halfway there. The truth is that it shouldn't be anyone's problem because your period really isn't a predicament. It's proof of life.

Bozelko's observation resonates. While early menstrual activism of the past did attend to products, the focus was safety and promoting alternative, more environmentally friendly cups and cloth pads in a context of creative resistance to menstrual invisibility. Today, the product focus dominates the activist landscape, one centered on product access and affordability. While these are worthy projects indeed, they are narrowly focused on what Sharra Vostral (2011) calls "technologies of passing," that enable menstruators to "pass" as non-menstruators in order to comply with the cultural norms—keep it hidden, keep it quiet. As such, products serve merely to accommodate rather than resist the menstrual mandate of shame, silence and secrecy. In this way, contemporary menstrual activism has dulled its radical edge through a neoliberal engagement with menstrual *management*. When menstrual activism's main focus devolves to a preoccupation with "something to bleed on," it betrays its feminist roots of challenging the misogynist framing of the polluted and disgusting menstrual body.

Hazards and Possibilities of the Work

Identity Politics

Menstrual activism is uniquely positioned to push feminists and other critically minded scholars and activists toward thinking about the complexities of gender and the body. That said, the hazards of doing justice to the menstrual experience—particularly with regard to gender identity—have been particularly messy in recent years. Menstruation is, at once, deeply gendered and coded as women's experience and also expansive and transgressive in its gender politics. Many women menstruate but not *all* women menstruate. Some women, such as women who have gone through menopause, those who have had hysterectomies, pregnant women, young women, women with severe eating disorders, women suppressing their periods, women on certain kinds of birth control and some competitive athletes do not menstruate; this then complicates simplistic notions that *all women menstruate.*

Similarly, *some* men do menstruate. Trans men often still menstruate, particularly if they are not on testosterone hormone therapies. Further, trans men who menstruate often report distress and body dysmorphia during their menstrual periods, while other trans men associate menstruation more positively (Fahs 2016; Reading 2014). Holly Devor (1999) found that trans men reported intensely negative emotions about menstruation, with 51 percent saying they felt emotional discomfort. Trans men and transmasculine people's menstrual experiences are under-researched, in part because menstrual bleeding is not typically associated with cultural ideals about masculinity. This can lead not only to trans men feeling distress about their periods but also, as one recent study found, avoiding restrooms and working toward menstrual suppression (Chrisler et al. 2016).

Endometriosis—where tissue that normally lines the uterus grows outside of the uterus and causes pain—also complicates the "who menstruates?" question. Cara Jones (2016) has argued that not all bodies with endometriosis are female and that endometriosis has been found in infants, postmenopausal bodies, post-hysterectomy bodies, trans men and cisgender men. At the same time, trans women and transfeminine people's experiences who undergo hormone replacement therapy often report "menstrual" symptoms and pain such as soreness, swelling, nausea, cramping, dizziness, migraines, muscle fatigue, joint pain, bloating, depression, and mood changes on a cyclical basis; researchers have largely ignored this (Riedel 2016).

The move to recognize the breadth of the menstrual experience has appeared more vividly in recent years. While little research has examined non-binary gender identity and menstruation, some activist and "artivist" work has started to make room for these experiences; for example, Cass Clemmer (https://www.tonithetampon.com/) developed the character "Toni the Tampon" for a coloring book about menstruation in order to broaden cultural ideas about who menstruates. In July 2017, Clemmer posted a photo on Facebook that showed Clemmer with obvious menstrual blood on their pants; the photo went viral and inspired a series of news articles and commentaries (Dupere 2017).

The move from gendered language to non-gendered language creates a conversation that, on the one hand, expands notions of "who menstruates" and, on the other hand, erases some of the ways menstruation is coded as a cisgender female experience. Some menstrual activists argue that non-gendered language of "menstruators" should be used in tandem with "women" and "girls" as a way to both broaden the language of menstruation while still marking menstruation as feminized and menstrual negativity as grounded in misogyny (Przybylo and Fahs in press). How to best challenge the frank sexism of much menstrual discourse remains an open question that menstrual activists are continuing to take up. Expanding the existing circle of menstruators better represents the wide swath of people affected by menstrual cycle changes. Thus, "Menstrual bleeding in this sense is complex: it is both highly gendered and not attached as a material reality to only one gender" (Przybylo and Fahs in press).

Image 9.2 Cass Clemmer. Instagram Post. July 12, 2017.
Photo Credit: Jocelyn Daily.

Additionally, menstrual activism has also grown savvier in recent years in its approach to race and class diversity, particularly as menstrual activists recognize that different groups of menstruators have different needs. There has been a major push toward thinking about menstrual health as more of a *global* issue rather than a solely Western issue; this means that menstrual activists may simultaneously work within the contexts of the United States and the Western world and in the global South. In the last several years, a development subsector referred to as "Menstrual Hygiene Management," has rapidly proliferated. Using human rights (Boosey and Wilson 2014; WASH United and Human Rights Watch 2017; Winkler and Roaf 2014) and public health frames (Sommer et al. 2015), Menstrual Hygiene Management advocates seek to challenge menstrual shame, silence and stigma through initiatives that provide girls and women access to menstrual care products, improved infrastructure (access to toilets, water and soap) and puberty education.

Policy efforts are sometimes engaged as well, such as persuading governments to provide menstrual care resources–including menstrual products and menstrual health education–in government schools (Bobel 2015). For example, Menstrual Hygiene Day now has a global platform with 350 events in 54 countries as of 2017, including educational events in schools, community rallies, concerts to raise awareness about menstrual health needs, advocacy workshops with governments, and product donations. India was the most active of all nations with 67 separate events. Online media coverage has been abundant, with pieces in *Huffington Post*, *The Guardian*, *El Pais*, *Metro*, and *Glamour*, just as digital campaigning has been abundant and successful. All key development partners working in the field of menstrual health management participated in menstrual hygiene day (e.g., UNICEF, WaterAid, WSSCC, Global Citizen, USAID, PLAN International, and PATH). These efforts are part of a larger global trend of centering development efforts on girls, a move that has garnered some feminist critique as overly instrumentalist and only superficially focused on girls' most acute needs (Hayhurst 2011; Koffman and Gill 2013).

As discussed earlier, social class issues have also been foregrounded in the recent policy work of menstrual activists, particularly as menstrual activists recognize the importance of addressing underserved populations like homeless and incarcerated menstruators. As noted, initiatives to give homeless menstruators access to menstrual products have begun, as have policies to make high quality tampons and pads available to those in prison. Beyond this, the push toward reusable products as a *class-based* issue has also occurred; rather than framing reusable products only as an environmentally-friendly choice, menstrual activists have encouraged women and other menstruators to see these products as ways to cut ties with corporate control over periods *and* save money while doing so (Edwards 2015; Mok 2004).

Corporate and Media Appropriation

As with any resistance movement, one of the dangers of pushing for progressive social change is that the work is often swiftly appropriated, distorted, and/or used for unintended purposes. For example, for years, menstrual activists critiqued the use of "blue liquid" to signify menstrual blood, noting that it distorted the ordinariness of the menstrual experience by erasing blood. This has recently been taken up in an advertisement for Kotex that makes fun of the blue liquid commercials in order to *sell* disposable tampons and pads (https://www.youtube.com/watch?v=lpypeLL1dAs).

Similarly, activists' efforts to promote the empowerment of women have been distorted by corporate and media entities as "girl power" packaged to sell products, particularly in menstrual advertisements. Products that purport to "empower" women, like tampon subscription services, often end up merely recreating menstrual shaming and taboo; for example, Club Monthly advertises, "Feminine products at your door, without the shame of the store" (Davis 2014). Many menstrual products have "better and better" technologies that serve to better hide or mask menstruation. Tampon companies inject scented perfumes into tampons to "deodorize" the vagina, just as disposable pad companies design products to be better absorbent and "leak proof." The language of appropriation used to sell tampons and disposable pads exemplifies one of the hazards of menstrual activist work and serves as a reminder of why menstrual activists must always remain one step ahead of such corporate and media appropriation.

Hostilities and Trivialization

Menstrual activists have also faced hostilities from right wing internet trolls, bloggers, and journalists for the work they do, resulting in painful clashes about the value of making menstruation more public. Given that menstrual activist work is often in the public eye, such hostilities have intensified in recent years. The hostile climate of the Trump presidency and his policies and practices of xenophobia, racism, sexism, and classism have only worsened these attacks. Clemmer grappled with a host of negative reactions to their work on gender-inclusive menstrual education and their "Toni the Tampon" character (2017). Their work has been met with harsh criticisms and hateful, vitriolic rhetoric from some conservatives (we avoid replicating that here in order to not further and reproduce hate speech) and even some doctors. We, too, have dealt with such hostilities. Breanne Fahs's recent book cover for *Out for Blood*—which features a realistic depiction of menstrual blood running down a woman's leg—started a tweetstorm online in early 2017 after some right-wing bloggers found it "disgusting"; later in 2017, Fahs also watched conservative internet trolls move freely from mocking and trivializing her work on fatness narratives to mocking and trivializing her work on menstruation.

Menstrual activists also face numerous other obstacles related to the trivialization of their work, particularly as many activists work to get policies changed, funding secured, or research published. Those working within the academy face critiques that their work is not on a "serious" subject, or that it is of little academic value (Fahs, Plante and McClelland in press). The taboo of menstruation, or beliefs that people should not discuss menstruation publicly, have negatively impacted public conversations about governmental policy initiatives and media coverage for menstrual activist work (Bobel 2007, 2010). Recent debates concerning menstrual leave in the workplace reveal the enduring perception of menstruation as a minor matter that should be quietly managed. This view often stems from a liberal feminist ideology that fails to engage the complexity of menstrual experience as at once biological *and* sociocultural. As long as menstruation is portrayed as trivial, silly, gross, or unimportant, much of the important work on menstruation continues to get sidelined.

The Future of Menstrual Activism

After reviewing some of the major accomplishments of menstrual activism, and some of the recent hazards and challenges of doing menstrual activist work, we turn an eye toward the future of menstrual activism. Ultimately, we argue that menstrual activism has radical potential to deeply unsettle many assumptions about gender, bodies, political activism, embodied resistance, and feminist coalition-building. Indeed, menstrual activism has at its core a vision of radical politics that we find exciting, timely, and relevant—one that digs deep into the root structures of inequalities to expose some of the fundamentally problematic aspects of misogyny, sexism, racism, homophobia, and classism. That said, menstrual activism also has the potential to shun its political roots and move toward assimilationist or liberal politics; such a move could have many problematic consequences—for example, without radical energies menstrual activism is more vulnerable to appropriation in ways that serve corporate and/or pharmaceutical interests, just as it could become reduced to "liking your body" or "girl power."

We assert that menstrual activism has the potential to fight back against the forces that silence and shame women's bodies. In these regressive and conservative times, menstrual activism has even more relevance and importance, but if it succumbs to its more assimilationist/liberal impulses, it will diminish some of its major successes and fracture some of its major inroads as a global powerhouse. As such, we end this chapter with a call to action for the vision of (radical) menstrual activism we find most exciting and impactful:

- Menstrual activism must continue to prioritize underserved populations and engage in activism that prioritizes these groups' needs. A major thread of its work is to keep a close eye on menstruators who are overlooked and ignored. This may include menstruators who are: incarcerated, disabled, trans/non-binary, homeless, low-income, HIV-positive, refugees, pre-menarche, indigenous, in the military, outside of Western contexts, rural and who have undergone forced sterilization.

- Menstrual activists must continue to work with other progressive social movements and groups, forging alliances that will be productive and co-constructed. This may include groups that prioritize issues such as anti-xenophobia, anti-racism, sustainability, homelessness, LGBT justice, transnational feminism, disability rights, immigrant rights, anti-femicide, sexual violence prevention, education, reproductive justice, abortion rights and the social class struggle.

- The notion of what menstrual activism is, and the work these activists do, must move from a primary focus on menstrual products and instead emphasize a much wider array of menstrual activist priorities including mental health, global feminisms, cultural critiques, humor and mockery and educational changes as means to promote menstrual literacy and to fight stigma.

- Menstrual activism must prioritize work that speaks to the immediate, urgent issues of the day, just as they must work on long-range projects with long-term impacts. This means that menstrual activists have a special responsibility to see their work as connected to the political climate of their time. Some ways that menstrual activists could directly combat the existing political climate of repression, xenophobia, misogyny, and classism include: flash mob workshops, tweeting (#period-sarenotaninsult), free bleeding in public as a form of protest, making snarky or satirical menstrual ads, menstrual performance art (see Raegan Truax's 2017 piece called *Sloughing* for an example), engaging in open dialogue about menstruation, turning toward old-fashioned consciousness-raising, educational disruptions, art and storytelling, menstrual humor and clowning and remembering that we can use our everyday bodies as a form of political protest.

- Menstrual activism must resist letting go of its radical impulses; it must always push to become *more* radical. This means thinking deeply about the root structures of menstrual negativity and taboo, and working to link the inequalities that surround menstruation to deeper stories about power and identity. For example, menstrual activists could work to link menstrual activist work to conscious capitalism, pushing back against co-optation of menstrual activist work, confronting and changing menstrual narratives, working on connecting other kinds of policies (e.g., breastfeeding, menstrual leave) to existing activist work, continuing to engage in internal critiques of the work ("productive unsettling"—see Bloomfield 2015), engaging in menstrual stunts, challenging men's attitudes about menstruation, connecting policy change to art and cultural change, and using humor widely and wisely.

Image 9.3 Day 5 of *Sloughing* by Raegan Truax. Pictured: Thao P. Nguyen (performing). Raegan Truax (artist) at Royal NoneSuch Gallery in Oakland, CA.
Photo credit: Jeremiah Barber.

- Ultimately, menstrual activism must resist appropriation by remembering to eschew respectability, commodification, and neoliberalism in favor of other tactics and ideologies: risky actions, unexpected coalitions, non-self-defeating self-criticism, sabotage, cross-contamination between scholarship/art/activism, and an insistence on strengthening connective tissue between menstrual activists and their allies.

Acknowledgments

Special thanks to Eric Swank, Jessica Brofsky, Kimberly Koerth, Ayanna Shambe and the Feminist Research on Gender and Sexuality Group for their contributions to this manuscript. We also thank the participants at our June 2017 Society for Menstrual Cycle Research workshop on menstrual activism for their thoughtful ideas about the future of menstrual activism.

References

Arriaga, Alex. 2017. "Tampons in Men's Rooms? It's Just a Small Part of 'Menstrual Equity,' Campus Activists Say." *The Chronicle of Higher Education*. http://www.chronicle.com/article/Tampons-in-Men-s-Rooms-/240091. Accessed July 5, 2018.

Barkardóttir, Freyja Jónudóttir. 2016. "Hope of Failure: Subverting Disgust, Shame and the Abject in Feminist Performances with Menstrual Blood." Master's Thesis. Central European University.

Bloomfield, Mandy. 2015. "Unsettling Sustainability: The Poetics of Discomfort." *Green Letters* 19(1):21–35.

Bobel, Chris. 2007. "'I'm Not an Activist, Though I've Done a Lot of It': Doing Activism, Being Activist and the 'Perfect Standard' in a Contemporary Movement." *Social Movement Studies* 6(2):147–159.

Bobel, Chris. 2010. *New Blood: Third-Wave Feminism and the Politics of Menstruation*. New Brunswick, NJ: Rutgers University Press.

Bobel, Chris. 2015. "Finding Problems with Simple Solutions: Ethnographic Insights into Development Campaigns to Support Menstruating Girls." Presented at the National Women's Studies Association Annual Conference, Milwaukee, WI.

Boosey, Robin and Emily Wilson. 2014. A Vicious Cycle of Silence. Research Report. ScHARR Report Series (29). School of Health and Related Research, University of Sheffield.

Bozelko, Chandra. 2017. "Federal Prisoners Now Get Free Pads and Tampons. Our Battle Isn't Over Yet." *The Lilly*. https://www.thelily.com/federal-prisoners-now-get-free-pads-and-tampons-our-battle-isnt-over-yet/. Accessed June 1, 2018.

Butler, Judith. 1990. *Gender Trouble: Feminism and the Subversion of Identity*. New York: Routledge.

Chrisler, Joan C., Jennifer A. Gorman, Jen Manion, Michael Murgo, Angela Barney, Alexis Adams-Clark, Jessica R. Newton and Meaghan McGrath. 2016. "Queer Periods: Attitudes toward Experiences with Menstruation in the Masculine of Centre and Transgender Community." *Culture, Health & Sexuality* 18(11):1238–1250.

Clemmer, Cass. 2017. "Toni the Tampon". Presented at the Society for Menstrual Cycle Research ConferenceJune 24, Kennesaw, GA.

Davis, Lisa Selin. 2014. "In 2014, Startups Discovered Women Get Their Periods—Every Month." *QZ*. https://qz.com/310086/in-2014-startups-discovered-women-get-their-periods-every-month/. Accessed April 15, 2018.

Devor, Holly. 1999. *FTM: Female-to-Male Transsexuals in Society*. Bloomington, IN: Indiana University Press.

Dupere, Katie. 2017. "Trans Artist Destroys Period Stigma with One Seriously Bold Facebook Post." *Mashable*. http://mashable.com/2017/07/22/transgender-periods-menstruation-facebook/#wsxYbPkmbkqm. Accessed April 10, 2018.

Edwards, Charlotte. 2015. "Ladies, We Found a Way to Help You Save $100 a Year. Period." *The Penny Hoarder*. https://www.thepennyhoarder.com/smart-money/reusable-menstrual-supplies/. Accessed April 15, 2018.

Fahs, Breanne. 2016. *Out for Blood: Essays on Menstruation and Resistance*. Albany, NY: State University of New York Press.

Fahs, Breanne, Rebecca Plante and Sara I. McClelland. In press. "Working at the Crossroads of Pleasure and Danger: Feminist Perspectives on Doing Critical Sexuality Studies." *Sexualities* 21(4):503–519.

Gandhi, Kiran. 2015. "Sisterhood, Blood and Boobs at the London Marathon 2015." https://madamegandhi.blog/2015/04/26/sisterhood-blood-and-boobs-a t-the-london-marathon-2015/. Accessed April 15, 2018.

Gloaguen, Audrey. 2017. "Tampon: Our Closest Enemy." Documentary Film. Dreamway Productions.

Hanisch, Carol. 1969. "The Personal is Political." http://www.carolhanisch.org/ CHwritings/PIP.html. Accessed April 1, 2018.

Hayhurst, Lyndsay L. 2011. "Corporatising Sport, Gender, and Development: Postcolonial IR Feminisms, Transnational Private Governance, and Global Corporate Social Engagement." *Third World Quarterly* 32(3):223–241.

Jones, Cara. 2016. "The Pain of Endo Existence: Toward a Feminist Disability Studies Reading of Endometriosis." *Hypatia* 31(3):554–571.

Kafai, Shayda. Forthcoming. "Blood as Resistance: Photography as Contemporary Menstrual Activism" In *Body Battlegrounds: Transgressions, Tensions, Transformations*, edited by Chris Bobel and Kwan Samantha. Nashville, TN: Vanderbilt University Press.

Kaufman, Gloria. 1980. "Introduction." Pp. 13–16 in *Pulling Our Own Strings: Feminist Humor & Satire* edited by Gloria J. Kaufman and Mary Kay Blakely. Bloomington, IN: Indiana University Press.

Kaufman, Gloria J. and Mary Kay Blakely. 1980. *Pulling Our Own Strings: Feminist Humor & Satire*. Bloomington, IN: Indiana University Press.

Koffman, Ofra and Rosland Gill. 2013. "'The Revolution Will Be Led by a 12-year-old Girl': Girl Power and Global Biopolitics." *Feminist Review* 105(1):83–102.

Leblanc, Lauraine. 1999. *Pretty in Punk: Girls' Gender Resistance in a Boys' Subculture*. New Brunswick, NJ: Rutgers University Press.

Marcus, Sara and Julie McKay. 2010. *Girls to the Front: The True Story of the Riot Grrrl Revolution*. New York: Harper Perennial.

Meng, Grace. 2017. "Meng Renews Effort to Make Menstrual Hygiene Products More Accessible and Affordable to Women." *Media Center*. https://meng.house. gov/media-center/press-releases/meng-renews-effort-to-make-menstrual-hygie ne-products-more-accessible. Accessed April 15, 2018.

Mok, Kimberley. 2004. "7 Powerful Reasons Why You Should Switch to Reusable Menstrual Products." *Tree Hugger*. https://www.treehugger.com/health/reasons-why-you-should-switch-to-reusable-menstrual-products.html. Accessed June 5, 2018.

O'Hara, Mary E. 2015. "'Robin Danielson Act' Would Mandate Independent Testing on Tampon Safety." *Rewire*. https://rewire.news/article/2015/04/21/ robin-danielson-act-mandate-independent-testing-tampon-safety/. Accessed July 5, 2018.

Persdotter, Josefin. 2013. "Countering the Menstrual Mainstream: A Study of the European Menstrual Countermovement." Master's Thesis. Götesborg Universitet.

Przybylo, Ela and Breanne Fahs. 2018. "Feels and Flows: On the Realness of Menstrual Pain and Cripping Menstrual Chronicity." *Feminist Formations* 30(1), 206–229.

Reading, Wiley. 2014. "My Period and Me: A Trans Guy's Guide to Menstruation." *Everyday Feminism*. http://everydayfeminism.com/2014/11/trans-guys-gui de-menstruation/. Accessed August 15, 2018.

Riedel, Sam. 2016. "Yes, Trans Women Can Get Period Symptoms." *The Establishment*. https://theestablishment.co/yes-trans-women-can-get-period-symptom s-e43a43979e8c. Accessed August 15, 2018.

Ronan, Alex. 2015. "Menstruation Can Become Humiliation in Prisons." *The Cut*, June 16. https://www.thecut.com/2015/06/menstruation-can-become-humilia tion-in-. prisons.html. Accessed August 15, 2018.

Sommer, Marni, Jennifer S. Hirsch, Constance Nathanson and Richard G. Parker. 2015. "Comfortably, Safely, and Without Shame: Defining Menstrual Hygiene Management as a Public Health Issue." *American Journal of Public Health* 105 (7):1302–1311.

Steinem, Gloria. 1978. "If Men Could Menstruate." *Ms Magazine*, October, p.110.

Tarzibachi, Eugenia. 2017. *Women's Things. Menstruation, Gender and Power*. Argentina: Penguin Random House

Vostral, Sharra L. 2011. *Under Wraps: A History of Menstrual Hygiene Technology*. Lanham, MD: Lexington Books.

WASH United and Human Rights Watch. 2017. "Understanding Menstrual Hygiene Management and Human Rights." *Human Rights Watch*. https://www. hrw.org/news/2017/08/27/menstrual-hygiene-human-rights-issue.   Accessed August 15, 2018.

Weiss-Wolf, Jennifer. 2017. *Periods Gone Public: Taking a Stand for Menstrual Equity*. New York, NY: Arcade Publishing.

Winkler, Inga and Virginia Roaf. 2014. "Taking the Bloody Linen Out of the Closet: Menstrual Hygiene as a Priority for Achieving Gender Equality." *Cardozo Journal of Law and Gender* 21(1):1–37.

10 The Continuing Battle over Abortion and Reproductive Rights

Deana A. Rohlinger and Jessi Grace

In the days leading up to the January 2017 Women's March, a woman named "Christy" took to social media and, using the #NotMyMarch hashtag, publicly opposed the Women's March. She argued:

> I am not a "disgrace to women" because I don't support the women's march. I do not feel I am a "second class citizen" because I am a woman. I do not feel my voice is "not heard" because I am a woman. I do not feel I am not provided opportunities in this life or in America because I am a woman. I do not feel that I "don't have control of my body or choices" because I am a woman. I do not feel like I am "not respected or undermined" because I am a woman.... There is nothing stopping me to do anything in this world but MYSELF. [Emphasis in original]

Christy's post went viral and generated a great deal of reaction, including a post from "Susan" who challenged Christy's privileged life (as well as acknowledged her own). In her post, Susan guesses that Christy feels in control of her body and choices because she is college educated, fully employed, in a healthy relationship, and has a generous health insurance plan. Susan asks Christy to consider a series of questions, including:

> **Have you ever skipped an annual pelvic exam or mammogram, because your kid needed new shoes and you had to choose and hope for the best?** Not everyone gets free reproductive healthcare in this country. Have you ever stopped using birth control because the clinic in your neighborhood closed, and the closest one now is across town, and you can't get there because you're working two jobs and someone else in your family uses the one car in the driveway? If you're feeling OK, putting off that exam for a year, or two, or three is almost always an easy decision when you literally have to decide how to spend the $50 in your hand and your kids need stuff. [Emphasis in original]

Susan concludes by noting that she didn't march because she felt "marginalized." She marched... "because a lot of women can't, even if you don't see them.... I even marched for you, Christy. Even if you don't feel like you need anyone to march for you."

This virtual exchange illustrates the deep divisions among women surrounding abortion and reproductive rights. These divisions, which often focus on abortion specifically, are interesting because the abortion procedure is relatively rare and medically safe. Consider the following facts about abortion in the United States. The vast majority (92 percent) of abortions occur during the earlier (and safer) gestational period (before 14 weeks). The abortion rate has decreased dramatically since the 1973 *Roe v. Wade* Supreme Court decision, which gave women a constitutionally protected right to an abortion during the first trimester or before fetal viability. According to the most recent Center for Disease Control report on abortion in America (2013), the abortion rate decreased by 5 percent between 2012 and 2013, and by 21 percent between 2004 and 2013. The abortion rate has decreased especially fast for adolescents ages 15 to 19—there has been a 46 percent decrease between 2004 and 2013. Finally, abortion is a medically safe procedure. Of the 664,435 legal abortions performed in 2013, only four patients died from complications (Center for Disease Control 2013).

Legal abortion limits the impact of inequality in the United States. Almost half (49 percent) of all pregnancies in the United States are unplanned. Women of color, women with lower educational attainment, and women with lower socioeconomic statuses make up a disproportionate number of these unplanned pregnancies (Finer and Henshaw 2006). As Susan suggests in her post above, a key reason that women seek abortions is financial insecurity. 73 percent of women reported that they could not afford to support a child. Women who get abortions also do so because of existing medical conditions and unstable relationships (Finer et al. 2005; Kimport 2012).

In this chapter, we provide a short overview of the battle over reproductive rights. Here, we focus primarily on the battle over legal abortion since it has largely animated public debate and action since the 1970s. We outline four battlegrounds—states and communities, the courts, Congress, and clinics—and highlight how citizens and politicians who oppose legal abortion have worked to chip away at accessibility to the procedure in the United States. Throughout the chapter we note that these restrictions disproportionately affect poor women and women of color, and, in the last section, we discuss how the focus on reproductive rights more broadly and the use of new technologies might provide new ways for citizens to advocate for the health of women and families.

Understanding the Movements For and Against Legal Abortion: An Overview

Legal abortion was not always as contentious of an issue in the United States. In fact, throughout most of the nineteenth century abortion was believed to be a medical procedure and its availability was determined by midwives and, later, physicians. The medicalization of abortion largely was the result of a campaign by physicians to professionalize medicine. Throughout most of the 19th century, there were no licensing laws regulating who could practice medicine. Physicians saw abortion as an issue through which they could distinguish themselves from other practitioners and push for industry regulation. In 1859, the American Medical Association (AMA) released the "Report on Criminal Abortion" in which the professional organization publicly opposed abortion and attacked the science used by midwives to determine when life began. Physicians argued that their scientific-based training gave them superior knowledge regarding if and when a woman should have an abortion. The campaign was a success. All but "therapeutic" (medically necessary) abortions were outlawed and licensed professionals determined whether a woman could get an abortion. Legislators followed suit and began passing abortion laws in their states, often prohibiting the procedure (Luker 1984; Rose 2008).

In the late 1940s and early 1950s, physicians, activists, and clergy pushed state legislators to repeal abortion laws and expand the circumstances in which they could administer abortions, including cases of fetal deformity, rape, and incest. These efforts were successful and largely uncontroversial, in part, because of how abortion was framed. Advocates of legal abortion argued that the state should expand physicians' authority around abortion administration; an approach that focused on medical practice instead of women's rights (Burns 2005; Staggenborg 1991). This changed in the 1960s as a result of two controversies that focused public attention on women's authority in reproductive decision-making. The first case involved Sherri Finkbine, who was on a popular television series called *Romper Room*. Finkbine learned that thalidomide, a drug she had ingested, was known to cause fetal deformity. She used her celebrity status to raise awareness about the issue. The second controversy involved the rubella measles epidemic. When contracted by a pregnant woman, the disease could cause fetal malformations. Once women heard about this link on the nightly news, thousands of women with the measles sought abortions (Luker 1984). These two controversies caused women to push for more authority in their reproductive choices and call for legislation that recognized a "woman's right to choose" (Staggenborg 1991).

The controversies also spurred the growth of the pro-choice movement, which explicitly argued that women have a constitutionally protected right to an abortion. The National Association for the Repeal of Abortion Laws (now known as NARAL Pro Choice America) formed in 1969 and organized repeal campaigns across the United States. Additionally, dozens of grassroots groups emerged and used direct action tactics and street theatre to raise public awareness about the importance of legal abortion to women's health (Staggenborg 1988). Pro-life advocates, who oppose legal abortion, also began organizing during this time. They focused their efforts on state legislators, asking them to protect "unborn children." The state for the contemporary battle over abortion was set with two 1973 Supreme Court decisions. In *Roe v. Wade,* the Court ruled that a woman has a constitutionally protected right to an abortion and that the state could not prohibit abortion during the first trimester or before viability. Viability was defined as the potential for a fetus to live outside of the womb in *Doe v. Bolton.*

Advocates of legal abortion believed that the Supreme Court decisions settled the issue. Consequently, the composition of the pro-choice movement changed dramatically in the following decade. With abortion legalized, there was no need for grassroots groups using direct action tactics, and these groups disappeared. What remained were highly professionalized, national organizations with federated chapters throughout the United States (Staggenborg 1991). Since 1980, these organizations have predominantly focused on research, shaping abortion policy, and ensuring access to reproductive health services.

The pro-life movement also changed. Before 1973, the movement was largely spearheaded by the Catholic Church and grassroots groups that opposed liberalizing abortion laws locally (Burns 2005). In the wake of the Supreme Court decisions, pro-life advocates quickly mobilized inside and outside of government and began to challenge the new status quo. Groups mobilizing against legal abortion have three distinct foci: changing abortion policy, providing alternatives to abortion, and politicizing abortion clinics through sidewalk counseling, prayer vigils and direct action against clinics and clinic personnel.

Because of the movement's diversity, pro-life advocates use a variety of arguments as to why legal abortion should be limited or abolished altogether. Groups with a religious bent, for example, often argue that abortion should be abolished on moral grounds. In their view, abortion "murders an unborn child" and, therefore, should be illegal without exception. Most pro-life organizations, however, regard this position as extreme because it ignores cases where abortion may be medically necessary to save the life of the woman, as well as cases of rape and incest. More moderate groups adopt rhetoric that justifies restricting the abortion procedure. For instance, in the 1980s and 1990s pro-life organizations pushed politicians to pass legislation that would recognize the rights of fathers and specifically require women to get their permission before obtaining an abortion. While this line of argumentation was not successful, pro-life advocates effectively pushed for the recognition of parental rights, meaning states can require that minors have parental consent before they can obtain an abortion (Rohlinger 2015).

Additionally, pro-life advocates have worked to shift the focus from women to unborn babies. To do so, pro-life groups attacked the intact dilation and extraction (D&X) procedure, which is a rare form of abortion performed late in a woman's pregnancy. Pro-life groups called it "partial birth" abortion, and, using vivid descriptions of the procedure, described the "killing" of unborn children. More recently, pro-life advocates have pushed for legislation outlawing "dismemberment abortions," which is medically known as the dilation and evacuation (D&E) procedure. The D&E procedure has become standard practice for terminating pregnancies after 12 weeks and before viability because it is the safest for women. Finally, pro-life advocates have increasingly positioned themselves as "pro-woman" and worked to protect women from the mental and physical health problems they argue are associated with abortion. Pro-life advocates, for example, warn women that they will feel shame and guilt in the wake of their abortion, and that these emotions will haunt them throughout their lives. Similarly, pro-life advocates increasingly have used the language of "choice" to cast pro-choice advocates as "pro-abortion," which implies that advocates of legal abortion do not really support women or abortion alternatives like adoption.

Pro-choice advocates have largely been on the defensive in the war of words. Pro-choice groups primarily vilify their opponents as a corrupt, sexist, "well-organized minority" that politicizes religion, spends too much money on political lobbying efforts, and misinforms the public with emotionally manipulative rhetoric (Vanderford 1989:168; see also Leinwant 2016). Additionally, pro-choice groups focus on those pro-life organizations that use extreme rhetoric and disruptive tactics to prevent women from accessing a range of reproductive health services.

More recently, pro-choice organizations have broadened their focus to reproductive rights more generally. This move was largely a response to activists of color, who pointed out that organizations such as Planned Parenthood were too focused on abortion rights and not focused enough on access to reproductive health services. For instance, Monica Simpson, an organizer for the women of color reproductive justice collective Sister Song, penned an open letter to Planned Parenthood in 2014 claiming that the organization systematically had erased women of color's activism and narrowed the goals of the movement. She called on Planned Parenthood to move beyond women's choice and focus on reproductive rights and women's access to services. This focus acknowledges that restrictions on access to health care intersect with other inequalities that affect women such as unequal pay, lack of access to paid leave, toxic environments, and lack of access to healthy foods (points we return to in the final section). In the following sections, we outline four battlegrounds where the debate over legal abortion is waged: States and communities, Congress, the court system and reproductive health clinics.

Battleground: States and Communities

Pro-choice advocates believed that the 1973 *Roe v. Wade* decision settled the debate over legal abortion. Pro-life activists, however, decided to test the decision and, more specifically, to see if they could limit legal abortion and its availability. Consequently, pro-choice advocates largely have been on the defensive and trying to stave off threats to abortion access. We discuss some of the ways that abortion opponents have worked to limit abortion availability in the United States.

A key way that pro-life advocates have curtailed abortion access in states and communities is through TRAP laws, which they argue are designed to protect women's health instead of limiting abortion access. The American Civil Liberties Union (2017), divides TRAP laws into three categories: (1) "a measure that singles out abortion providers for medically unnecessary regulations, standards, personnel qualifications, building and/or structural requirements;" (2) "a politically motivated provision that needlessly addresses the licensing of abortion clinics and/or charges an exorbitant fee to register a clinic in the state;" or (3) "a measure that unnecessarily regulates where abortions may be provided or designates abortion clinics as ambulatory surgical centers, outpatient care centers, or hospitals without medical justification." In August 2017, the Guttmacher Institute reported that 24 states had TRAP laws that go beyond what is necessary to ensure patient safety.

TRAP laws are consequential because reproductive health centers that cannot meet new regulations are forced to close their doors. Texas is an excellent example in this regard. In 2013, Texas passed House Bill 2 (HB2), which banned abortions beyond the 20th week; increased regulations on medical abortions using mifepristone; required abortion providers to obtain admitting privileges to a hospital within 30 miles of their clinic; mandated that clinics meet the building standards of an ambulatory surgical center; and forced clinics to bury or cremate aborted fetuses (Gerdts et al. 2016). The law was struck down by the Supreme Court on June 27, 2016, but by then all but eight of the state's 41 abortion clinics had already shut down. These closures disproportionately affected Latina and African-American women, who were forced to travel to Kansas, Louisiana, Oklahoma and New Mexico for reproductive care, including access to birth control (Fiske 2016). Pro-life advocates touted the decrease in Texas' abortion rates (13 percent in the six months after the law took effect). However, women getting abortions out of state increased by 11 percent in the same time frame. In short, these laws largely force women to seek reproductive health services in other states and disproportionately affect poor women and women of color, who find it difficult to absorb the costs associated with driving across state lines (Fiske 2016; Gerdts et al. 2016).

A related pro-life effort concerns the defunding of Planned Parenthood, an organization that has come under fire from social conservatives because it provides comprehensive sex education, birth control and abortions. While early efforts to build political support to defund Planned Parenthood largely took the form of educational campaigns (Rohlinger 2015), over the last decade pro-life activists have used "undercover" videos to capitalize on "anxieties that reached across the political spectrum" (Ziegler 2012: 722). For example, in 2015 the Center for Medical Progress (CMP) released doctored videos that suggested Planned Parenthood profited from selling aborted fetuses to research facilities. Officials in 12 states and in the federal government cited these doctored videos as a reason to investigate Planned Parenthood and its operations. The organization was cleared of any wrongdoing. Nonetheless, more than a dozen states moved to defund the organization. President Trump recently signaled his support for the pro-life cause and eased state efforts to defund Planned Parenthood. In April 2017, he signed a resolution allowing states to withhold Title X family planning funds from the organization.

Planned Parenthood, pro-choice activists and organizations have responded to defunding efforts through postcard and phone call campaigns directed at senators as well as storytelling campaigns like #ShoutYourAbortion and #IStandWithPP. The goal of these campaigns is to fight defunding efforts by lessening stigma associated with abortion and increase support for providers and women who have had abortions. Some pro-choice advocates are proposing local legislation to help in the event that Planned Parenthood is nationally defunded. For example, California's Senate Bill 309 (SB309), which is currently in committee, would allow residents to donate to a "Reproductive Freedom Fund" when they purchase a specialized reproductive freedom license plate.

Battleground: The Courts

Since the 1954 Brown v. Board of Education ruling, activists, including those supporting and opposed to legal abortion, have adopted the National Association for the Advancement of Colored People (NAACP)'s rights-based legal strategy in an effort to codify legislative gains (Meyer and Boutcher 2007). Specifically, pro-choice activists use legal arguments to expand the right to privacy, and pro-life advocates use these arguments to define a right to life as beginning at earlier gestational periods (with an ultimate goal of defining life as starting at conception). While the overall effectiveness of this legal strategy has declined over time (Meyer and Boutcher 2007), advocates on both sides of the abortion issue continue to use it. Most often, states pass restrictive abortion legislation that quickly goes to the courts. The intent of these bills is to narrow and eventually eliminate access to legal abortions, and some of them are similar to bills that have previously been ruled unconstitutional. For example, in 2017, Oklahoma proposed HB1441, which would require pregnant women to disclose the name of their sexual partner and get their written consent before obtaining an abortion (Wilson 2017). This bill is more extreme than the spousal notification bills that the Supreme Court ruled unconstitutional in 1976 (Planned Parenthood v. Danforth) and 1992 (Planned Parenthood v. Casey).

Not all introduced pro-life laws are reboots of previously overturned legislation. Pro-life advocates have been very effective at narrowing abortion access by testing the courts to see in what circumstances restrictions will be allowed to stand. Laws requiring parental notification or consent represent cases in which the Supreme Court have upheld restrictions. For example, in Planned Parenthood v. Danforth (1976), the Court ruled that the parental consent law was unconstitutional because the statute required women to have prior written consent from a parent or spouse, restricting their rights. Since then, the Court ruled in favor of parental consent laws. In *Belloti v. Baird* (1979) and *Planned Parenthood v. Casey* (1992) justices agreed that parents, as in other situations, have decision-making authority over their (now pregnant) children (Daly 1996).

More recently, pro-life advocates have attacked abortion access on religious grounds. Some of these lawsuits involve patient access to clinics. In 1994, the Freedom of Access to Clinic Entrances (FACE) Act went into effect, prohibiting pro-life clinic protesters from using force, threatening force, and generally obstructing people from entering abortion clinics. This federal law was a response to increased violence at clinics and against providers (Rohlinger 2015). Pro-life activists, however, argue that FACE and state-level "buffer zone" laws violate their First Amendment rights to express their religious opposition to abortion (Campbell 1995; Rose and Osborn 1995; Tepper 1997). Despite the fact that FACE and buffer laws do not prevent non-obstructive forms of protest such as picketing and sidewalk counselling (Tepper 1997), the Supreme Court has indicated that it is sympathetic to this argument. In 2014, for instance, the Court determined that a Massachusetts bill requiring a 35-foot buffer-zone around clinic entrances was unconstitutional for violating protestors' First Amendment rights (Reines 2016). However, it is not clear if the Supreme Court will continue overturning buffer zones given that it previously upheld an eight-foot floating buffer zone in its *Colorado v. Hill* decision (Gogniat 2015). As a result, pro-choice legislators are working to create laws that protect patients while navigating these conflicting rulings.

For-profit companies owned by pro-life advocates also have gotten into the litigation game. David Green, owner of the Hobby Lobby crafts store chain, and his son Steve challenged the Affordable Care Act's birth control provision. In their lawsuit, they argued that their religious beliefs "forbid them from participating in, providing access to, paying for, training others to engage in, or otherwise supporting abortion-causing drugs and devices" such as Intrauterine Devices (IUDs) and the morning-after pill. The Green family rejects the medical definition of pregnancy, which begins when a fertilized egg attaches itself to the wall of the uterus, and, instead, argues that birth control that prevents implantation is morally wrong. The Court sided with the Greens and, in the 2014 *Burwell v. Hobby Lobby,* decided that the owners did not have to provide insurance that covers forms of contraception that they object to on religious grounds.

Battleground: Congress

Reproductive politics largely divide along partisan lines with Democrats supporting reproductive rights and Republicans opposing them. Consequently, there are policies that disappear and are resurrected depending on which political party controls the White House. For example, Ronald Reagan signed the "Global Gag Rule" in 1984, which cut off funding to international family organizations that discussed abortion as a family planning method. Subsequent Democratic presidents have rescinded the policy, restoring funds to groups that discuss abortion, and both Republican presidents have reinstated it. The most recent reinstatement of the gag rule by Donald Trump goes the furthest, extending the restrictions to any international organization that receives health-related aid from the United States and does not include any exemptions (Rominski and Greer 2017).

Generally speaking, pro-life advocates have initiated three federal challenges to abortion. The first challenges the use of tax dollars to pay for the abortion procedure. Despite evidence that these restrictions discriminate against poor women and women of color (Arnold 2014; Sable 1982), this line of attack has proven successful. The Hyde amendment, which restricts federal funding of abortion through Medicaid, went into effect in 1977. Funding restrictions were expanded in 1979 and 1995 to prohibit women in the military from obtaining an abortion in oversea military facilities, even privately funded procedures, except in cases of rape and incest. Second, pro-life advocates have tried to secure legal recognition for the "rights of the unborn." Legislation in this vein has been largely unsuccessful because pro-life advocates have not agreed on whether abortion should be permitted in cases of rape, incest, and to save the life of the pregnant woman. In the 1980s, pro-life advocates fought over the exception issue and supported different legislative approaches. More mainstream groups, such as the National Right to Life Committee (NRLC), argued that exceptions were necessary and championed a Human Life Amendment, which would reverse *Roe* and prevent states from making abortion legal at a later date. Other pro-life activists advocated for the Human Life Bill, which would recognize fetuses as legal persons and restrict the lower federal courts from interfering with restrictive state legislation. Both efforts failed. Pro-life advocates have put federal legislation on the back burner for now and some have pushed for "personhood" legislation at the state level. These bills sometimes give "unborn babies" equal protection under the law from the moment that sperm and egg unite.

Finally, pro-life advocates have limited women's ability to access safe late-term abortions. As discussed above, pro-life advocates have made restricting abortion procedures—namely the D&X and D&E procedures—a priority. The support and passage of these bills largely represent the successful framing of these procedures by pro-life organizations. Groups like the NRLC spent millions test marketing language to politicize the medical procedure (Rohlinger 2015). Instead of referring to the D&X procedure, pro-life activists labelled it "partial-birth abortion" and effectively pressured politicians to introduce bans at the state and federal level. A federal ban on the procedure was passed in 2003 and upheld in the 2007 Supreme Court case,

Gonzalez v. Carhart (Haddad et al 2009), with exceptions in the event of a danger to the patient's life. The most recent attack on late term procedures involves the D&E procedure, which pro-life advocates call a "dismemberment abortion." This language has gained political traction and several states proposed bans on D&E abortions in 2017 (The Associated Press 2017).

Again, pro-choice advocates are mostly on the defensive when it comes to legislation. While, as mentioned above, they have passed legislation designed to protect clinic access, they have not been able to pass legislation that secures every woman's access to an abortion before viability and after viability if it is necessary to protect her life or health. Consequently, reproductive rights advocates have pushed to make birth control, emergency contraception, and "medical" abortions that use mifepristone more readily available to women.

Battleground: Clinics

Pro-life advocates also have taken the battle to reproductive health clinics and used violent and non-violent tactics to close them down. Since the 1980s, some pro-life activists have used violence against clinics and clinic personnel to prevent women from obtaining reproductive services. These activists share a moral abhorrence to abortion, believe that the government has not done enough to end abortion, and argue that the use of violence is an appropriate way to end the "violence" that takes place at abortion clinics. Between 1996 and 2015 the National Abortion Federation (NAF) reported 84 cases of extreme violence against abortion clinics in the United States, including arson, the use of butyric acid inside of clinics, and the murder of abortion providers (www.naf.org). Of course, not all pro-life activists use violence at clinics. Many oppose violence and, instead, try to counsel women going into clinics about the moral ills of abortion.

Pro-life advocates have also expanded the number of "Crisis Pregnancy Centers" (CPCs) throughout the United States. CPCs offer free services such as pregnancy tests, anti-abortion counselling, parenting classes, and abstinence-only sex education in order to prevent women from getting abortions. CPCs have come under fire for providing women deceptive or incorrect information. For example, CPC personnel exaggerate the risks associated with abortion, linking the procedure to breast cancer, infertility, and mental health problems – including "Post-Abortion Stress Syndrome" —and claim that various contraceptive methods do not effectively prevent pregnancy. In fact, in a survey of 32 CPCs, 17 (or 53 percent) gave at least one piece of deceptive or incorrect information (Bryant and Levi 2012).

CPCs have not successfully convinced their target demographic to visit their clinics: only one-fifth of clients who visit a CPC are considering abortion, and only 4 percent are "pregnant women intending to abort or undecided about abortion" (Kelly 2014: 423). Likewise, CPCs have come under legal scrutiny for presenting themselves as health clinics since personnel often have no medical licensing and they provide women inaccurate information (Chen 2016). Critics also point out that CPCs use deceptive advertising, promising to help women navigate unwanted pregnancy and leading them to believe that the affiliated organization is a medical center that presents all options to its patients. CPC directors claim that their actions are legal and attempts to stop their tactics are violations of their right to free speech. So far, courts have ruled that CPCs' claims are legally non-commercial, and therefore their advertising cannot be limited even if it is deceptive (Gilbert 2013). Another legal question about CPCs is whether they violate their clients' right to informed consent in family-planning decisions. Some local governments have passed legislation to regulate CPCs, often requiring them to disclose their pro-life position and their lack of medical licensing to their clients (Chen 2016).

Finally, pro-life activists have increasingly used undercover videos to expose alleged misconduct at abortion clinics. The Center for Medical Progress (CMP), discussed above, recorded and doctored videos that they released to the press, claiming Planned Parenthood "sells the body parts of aborted babies" (Center for Medical Progress 2017). As we mentioned above, these campaigns strengthened federal and state efforts to defund Planned Parenthood (Brandhorst and Jennings 2016; Rasmussen 2015; Ziegler 2012). The CMP videos sparked investigations into Planned Parenthood in several states, even after the videos were deemed inaccurate and heavily edited (Kurtzleben 2016; Calmes 2015). Planned Parenthood has tried to defend itself from defunding efforts and negative public opinion by emphasizing the broad range of health services it offers as well as reminding the public that abortion services constitute only three percent of the overall services received by its clients. Interestingly, Planned Parenthood's messaging targeted the dishonest tactics of organizations such as the CMP, which claim that they are working to end the immorality of abortion. In its messaging, Planned Parenthood equated truth-telling with morality, and questioned the morality of groups that would lie to achieve their goals (Brandhorst and Jennings 2016). This rhetorical strategy was designed to decrease the focus on abortion and Planned Parenthood, and emphasize the tactics of abortion opponents.

The Future of Activism

While advocates of safe and legal abortion clearly have been on the defensive since the 1973 *Roe* decision, they are increasingly using Information Communication Technologies (ICTs) to push back against public understanding of abortion and why women get them. This is part of an effort to reduce the stigma surrounding the abortion procedure. For example, the hashtag #ShoutYourAbortion was created in response to increased TRAP laws and defunding efforts. The hashtag prompted thousands to discuss abortion and share their personal stories via social media. At first, people primarily tweeted their stories, but #ShoutYourAbortion also started a video story-telling campaign. The campaign prompted Planned Parenthood to put more focus on storytelling and use these narratives to combat negative public opinion. The organization encourages people to share their family-planning stories on their website, and features other supporters' stories on the submission page with the hashtag #IStandWithPP 2017. Local organizations such as Respect ABQ (Albuquerque) Women campaign have adopted the approach as well, using stories and photos to destigmatize abortion. While storytelling may seem unimportant, research shows that dialogue can reduce abortion stigma, even among those uncomfortable with the procedure (Thomsen 2013).

Additionally, the focus on reproductive rights, rather than abortion rights, is likely to expand. Over the last decade several groups such as MomsRising and UltraViolet have emerged on the political scene, and these organizations focus on holding people in power accountable for a range of issues that apply to women, including access to quality childcare and healthcare. UltraViolet, for example, relies heavily on ICTs to help citizens take action against politicians and businesses that reinforce gender-based inequality. A recent UltraViolet petition urged the U.S. Golf Association and the Ladies Professional Golf Association not to hold the U.S. Open Tournament at Trump's New Jersey resort because of his history of sexism. Another campaign targets the Kansas City Royals, urging them to end a partnership with the Vitae Foundation, an anti-abortion organization. A number of organizations have emerged in the wake of Donald Trump's election as well. Many of these new groups have a grassroots focus and use ICTs to help citizens identify their local priorities, achieve their goals, and share their successes. The Women's March, for instance, uses "huddles" to organize its grassroots resistance to Trump's political agenda, including his opposition to reproductive rights and his support for health care that excludes pregnancy as a pre-existing condition, in communities across the country. Organizers provide each huddle a weekly assignment and encourage them to report back their results. Similarly, the organization Indivisible, whose "Mission is to Fuel a Progressive Grassroots Network of Local Groups to Resist the Trump Agenda," adopts tactics used by the Tea Party movement to educate citizens on the value of pressuring—and, in some cases, replacing—politicians.

These new grassroots efforts signal a shift in activism around reproductive rights. Individuals and organizations are using social media to push back against abortion stigma and pro-life efforts to restrict birth control and reproductive health services in their communities. In some ways, this may make reproductive rights activism more difficult to see. As activists target their communities, we will see fewer marches on Washington, DC and more advocating for change in city councils and state legislatures. When protests occur, they are likely to resemble the Women's March, where organizers use ICTs to mobilize supporters to action across a range of issues affecting women. In this political landscape, long-lived organizations such as

Planned Parenthood are important for targeting politicians in Congress and the White House, but play a diminished role in reproductive activism at the grassroots level.

References

American Civil Liberties Union. 2017. "Abortion Clinic Regulations." Retrieved June 16, 2017. https://www.aclu.org/issues/reproductive-freedom/abortion/abortion-clinic-regulations.

Arnold, Shaye Beverly. 2014. "Reproductive Rights Denied: 'The Hyde Amendment and Access to Abortion for Native American Women Using Indian Health Service Facilities.'" *American Journal of Public Health* 104 (10):1892–1893.

Brandhorst, Jaclyn K. and Freddie J. Jennings. 2016. "Fighting for Funding: Values Advocacy and Planned Parenthood's Right-to-Life." *Public Relations Review* 42:723–733.

Bryant, Amy G. and Erika E. Levi. 2012. "Abortion Misinformation from Crisis Pregnancy Centers in North Carolina." *Contraception* 86(6):752–756.

Burns, Gene. 2005. *The Moral Veto: Framing Contraception, Abortion, and Cultural Pluralism in the United States.* New York: Cambridge University Press.

Campbell, Regina R. 1995. "'FACE'ing the Facts: Does the Freedom of Access to Clinic Entrances Act Violate Freedom of Speech?" *University of Cincinnati Law Review* 64(1): 947–982.

Calmes, Jackie. 2015. "Planned Parenthood Videos were Altered, Analysis Finds." *The New York Times.* https://www.nytimes.com/2015/08/28/us/abortion-planned-parenthood-videos.html

Care Net. 2015. "FAQ." https://www.care-net.org/faq.

Center for Disease Control. 2013. "Abortion." https:/www.cdc.gov/reproductive health/data_stats/index.htm.

Center for Medical Progress. 2017. "Human Capital." http://www.centerformedicalprogress.org/human-capital/.

Chen, Alice X. 2016. "Crisis Pregnancy Centers: Impeding the Right to Informed Decision Making." *Cardozo Journal of Law & Gender.* 19(3):933–960.

Daly, Erin. 1996. "Reconsidering Abortion Law: Liberty, Equality, and the New Rhetoric of Planned Parenthood v. Casey." *The American University Law Review* 45(1):77–150.

Donovan, Charles A. 2003. "Learning from our Adversaries." Pp. 310–318 in *Back to the Drawing Board: The Future of the Pro-Life Movement*, edited by Teresa R. Wagner. South Bend, Indiana: St. Augustine's Press.

Earl, Jennifer. 2015. "The Future of Social Movement Organizations: The Waning Dominance of SMOs Online." *American Behavioral Scientist* 59(1):35–52.

Finer, Lawrence, and Stanley Henshaw. 2006. "Disparities in Rates of Unintended pregnancy in the United States, 1994 and 2001." *Perspectives on Sexual and Reproductive Health* 38(2): 90–96.

Finer, Lawrence, Lori Frohwirth, Lindsay Dauphinee, Susheela Singh and Ann Moore. 2005. "Reasons U.S. Women Have Abortions: Quantitative and Qualitative Perspectives." *Perspectives on Sexual and Reproductive Health,* 37(3):110–118. doi:10.1111/j.1931-2393.2005.tb00045.x.

Fiske, Molly Hennessy. 2016. "Here's What Happened When Texas Cracked Down on Abortion Clinics." *Los Angeles Times.* http://beta.latimes.com/nation/la -na-texas-abortion-figures-20160630-snap-story.html.

Gerdts, Caitlin, Liza Fuentez, Daniel Grossman, Kari White, Brianna Keefe-Oates, Sarah E. Baum, Kristine Hopkins, Chandler W. Stolp and Joseph E. Potter. 2016. "Impact of Clinic Closures on Women Obtaining Abortion Services after Implementation of a Restrictive Law in Texas." *American Journal of Public Health* 106(5):857–864.

Gogniat, Susan L. 2015 "McCullen v. Coakley and Dying Buffer Zone Laws." *University of Pittsburgh Law Review* 77(2):235–258.

Gilbert, Kathryn. 2013. "Commercial Speech in Crisis: Crisis Pregnancy Center Regulations and Definitions of Commercial Speech." *Michigan Law Review* 111 (4):591–616.

Haddad, Lisa, Susan Yanow, Laurent Delli-Bovi, Kate Cosby, and Tracy A. Weitz. 2009. "Changes in Abortion Provider Practices in Response to the Partial-Birth Abortion Ban Act of 2003." *Contraception* 79:379–384.

Jackson, Hannah-Beth. 2017. "SB-309 License plates: Reproductive Freedom Fund." *California Legislative Information.* https://leginfo.legislature.ca.gov/faces/bill TextClient.xhtml?bill_id=201720180SB309.

Jones, Rachel K., Lawrence B. Finer, and Susheela Singh. 2010. "Characteristics of U.S. Abortion Patients, 2008." Guttmacher Institute.

Kelly, Kimberly. 2014. "Evangelical Underdogs: Intrinsic Success, Organizational Solidarity, and Marginalized Identities as Religious Movement Resources." *Journal of Contemporary Ethnography* 43(4):419–455.

Kimport, Katrina. 2012. "(Mis)Understanding Abortion Regret." *Symbolic Interaction* 35(2):105–122.

Kurtzleben, Danielle. 2016. "Planned Parenthood Investigations Find No Fetal Tissue Sales." *NPR.* http://www.npr.org/2016/01/28/464594826/in-wake-of-videos-plannedparenthood-investigations-find-no-fetal-tissue-sales.

Leinwant, Tali R. 2016. "Strange Bedfellows: The Destigmatization of Anti-Abortion Reform." *Columbia Journal of Gender and Law* 30(2):529–548.

Luker, Kristin. 1984. *Abortion and the Politics of Motherhood.* Los Angeles: University of California Press.

Meyer, David S. and Steven A. Boutcher. 2007. "Signals and Spillover: Brown v. Board of Education and Other Social Movements." *Perspectives on Politics* 5(1):81–93.

Munson, Zaid W. 2008. *The Making of Pro-Life Activists: How Social Movement Mobilization Works.* Chicago, IL: University of Chicago Press.

National Abortion Federation. 2017. "Violence Statistics & History." https://p rochoice.org/education-and-advocacy/violence/violence-statistics-and-history-.

Rasmussen, Leslie. 2015. "Planned Parenthood takes on Live Action: An Analysis of Media Interplay and Image Restoration Strategies in Strategic Conflict Management." *Public Relations Review* 41:354–356.

Reines, Victoria. 2016. "Quieting Speech: Establishing a Buffer Zone around Reproductive Freedom." *American Journal of Law and Medicine* 41(1):190–214.

Rohlinger, Deana. 2015. *Abortion Politics, Mass Media, and Social Movements in America.* New York: Cambridge University Press.

Rominski, Sarah and Scott Greer. 2017. "The Expansion of the Global Gag Rule under the Trump Administration." *International Journal of Gynecology and Obstetrics* 137:229–230.

Rose, Jill. W., and Chris Osborn. 1995. "Face-ial Neutrality: A Free Speech Challenge to the Freedom of Access to Clinic Entrances Act." *Virginia Law Review* 81 (1):1505–1560.

Rose, Melody. 2008. *Abortion: A Documentary and Reference Guide*. Westport, CT: Greenwood Press.

Sable, Marjorie R. 1982. "The Hyde Amendment: Its Impact on Low Income Women with Unwanted Pregnancies." *Journal of Sociology & Social Welfare* 9 (3):475–484.

Simpson, Monica. 2014. "Reproductive Justice and 'Choice': An Open Letter to Planned Parenthood." *Rewire*. https://rewire.news/article/2014/08/05/reproductive-justice-choice-open-letter-planned-parenthood/.

Staggenborg, Suzanne. 1988. "The Consequences of Professionalization and Formalization in the Pro-Choice Movement." *American Sociological Review*. 53 (4):585–605.

Staggenborg, Suzanne. 1991. *The Pro-Choice Movement: Organization and Activism in the Abortion Conflict*. Oxford: Oxford University Press.

Tepper, Arianne K. 1997. "In Your F.A.C.E: Federal Enforcement of the Freedom of Access to Clinic Entrances Act of 1993." *Pace Law Review* 17(1):489–551.

Thomsen, Carly. 2013. "From Refusing Stigmatization toward Celebration: New Directions for Reproductive Justice Activism." *Feminist Studies* 39(1):149–158.

The Associated Press. 2017. "Texas House Approves New Limits on Abortion." *The New York Times*. May 20. https://www.nytimes.com/2017/05/20/us/politics/texas-house-approves-new-limits-on-abortion.html.

Wilson, Reid. 2017. "Oklahoma House Advances Bill to Require Men's Permission for Abortions." *The Hill*. February 15. http://thehill.com/homenews/state-watch/319635-oklahoma-house-advances-bill-to-require-mens-permission-for-abortions.

Vanderford, Marsha L. 1989. "Vilification and Social Movements: A Case Study of Pro-Life and Pro-Choice Rhetoric." *Quarterly Journal of Speech* 75(2):166–182.

Ziegler, Mary. 2012. "Sexing Harris: The Law and Politics of the Movement to Defund Planned Parenthood." *Buffalo Law Review* 60(3):701–747.

11 Ecofeminism and Climate Justice

Corrie Grosse

Women have long been leaders in the U.S. environmental movement. Rachel Carson's movement sparking book *Silent Spring* (1962) exposed the danger of chemicals, enabling public understanding. In the late 1970s, Louis Gibbs organized her community of Love Canal to demand relocation of families living atop a toxic waste dump. Ecofeminism also emerged in the late 1970s as a movement and epistemological current connecting the oppression of women with the oppression of the environment. In the late 1970s and early 1980s, the environmental justice movement mobilized to reveal and alleviate the disproportionate environmental harms inflicted on communities of color. Women-led grassroots groups were at the heart of the movement.

In the following two decades, the ascendant neoliberal agenda of Ronald Regan and Margaret Thatcher promulgated free trade and globalization. The social and environmental effects of the accompanying austerity, deregulation, and privatization were devastating; perhaps worst of all, these processes weakened government capacity to provide for social welfare at the same time as scientists became aware of the need for global policy to address climate change (Klein 2014). The result has been more than two decades of global negotiations on climate change that have failed to produce ambitious and binding policies to support those most vulnerable to climate change: women, people of color, indigenous peoples, and the poor.

In the midst of a rapidly changing climate (IPCC 2013) and a national and global political context that continues to support capitalism's assault on the welfare of people and the planet (Klein 2014, 2017; Robinson 2014), ecofeminists, environmental justice activists, indigenous movements, sectors of the mainstream environmental movement, and newly mobilized communities have joined forces in a global climate justice movement. The climate justice movement increasingly prioritizes "movement building" (Juris et al. 2014) to prefigure sustainable and politically engaged communities and to achieve its goals of social justice and a safe and healthy planet. By "tracing the contours" (Bhavnani 1993) of women's and ecofeminism's influence in the climate justice movement, I argue that the movement's focus on intersectional movement building can be conceptualized as a core contribution of ecofeminism. I then turn to the 2016 peaceful resistance by the water protectors at Standing Rock, where thousands of people and hundreds of tribes came together to stop the Dakota Access Pipeline, to illuminate key lessons that resonate with, and deepen, intersectional movement building. Started and led by women, the mobilization at Standing Rock engaged in analyses and practices that are critical for ecofeminism and for achieving climate justice..

At its center, the mobilization at Standing Rock is part of a long legacy of indigenous organizing for sovereignty and decolonization. I, a white settler who did not travel to Standing Rock, do not suggest that water protectors see their motivations and actions within an ecofeminist or climate justice framework. I highlight Standing Rock to learn from the water protectors, to demonstrate how their ways of knowing and working for justice are of immense value to ecofeminism and climate justice.

My argument draws on analysis of online materials related to Standing Rock, especially interviews with the movement's indigenous women leaders. It is informed by my attendance at the Water is Life: Standing with Standing Rock Conference where water protectors presented on May 19, 2017 at the University of California, Santa Barbara and by participant observation and interviews with 106 Idaho- and California-based climate justice activists conducted from 2013 to 2017. I begin with an account of ecofeminism as a body of knowledge and praxis that has waxed and waned in popularity among scholars since its inception in the 1980s. As part of this exposition, I detail the relationship between women and climate change that is so critical to contemporary ecofeminism. I then highlight ecofeminist interventions into the rhetoric and actions of the climate justice movement in the United States. I conclude by centering Standing Rock as an inspiring coming together of diverse peoples working for dignity, sovereignty, and a healthy planet, a mobilization that I hope all movements for justice can stand with and learn from in these crises-ridden times.

Ecofeminism

Ecofeminism's theoretical roots trace back to the science revolution that, between 1500 and 1700, transformed conceptualizations of nature from a nurturing, sacred mother to a mechanistic and dead entity (Merchant 1980). This transformation was necessary to justify processes of commercialization and industrialization. Entwined with the rise of capitalism, it not only changed human relationships with nature, but human social relationships, with particularly negative outcomes for marginalized groups. "Nature, women, blacks, and wage laborers were set on a path towards a new status as 'natural' and human resources for the modern world system" (Merchant 1980: 288). Drawing on this insight, ecofeminism emerged in the late 1970s and 1980s as a theoretical framework and praxis for understanding the exploitation of women and the environment and women's environmental activism. At its core, ecofeminism sees nature as a feminist issue because it enhances understanding of the oppression of women (Warren 2000). Rather than a unitary category, ecofeminism describes a diverse array of perspectives that infuse academic and activist work.[1]

The materialist strand of ecofeminism links women's lived experience with development and environmental degradation. It argues that patriarchal capitalism builds and maintains itself through the exploitation of women and nature in particular locales. Maria Mies and Vandana Shiva, whose work exemplifies this orientation, explained that, as feminists and activists in the ecology movements, they "began to see that the relationship of exploitative dominance between man and nature [...] and the exploitative and oppressive relationship between men and women that prevails in most patriarchal societies [...] were closely connected" (1993: 2–3). Modernization and development processes degrade the natural world and, in doing so, disproportionately affect women. Centering production, reproduction, and distribution, material ecofeminism sees women's "hands-on experience of material bodies and natures" (Godfrey 2005: 54) as informing their consciousness and activism. Linguistic ecofeminists, on the other hand, examine how the animalization of women reinforces women's inferiority and how feminizing nature reinforces the domination of nature. Illustrations of these types of language abound—women are pussycats, serpents and social butterflies who cackle; mother earth has fertile soil, virgin forests and barren land (Warren 2000: 27). Much of the work in this area struggles against and theorizes speciesism, or the view that animals are inferior to humans (e.g. Adams 1996; Dunayer 1995; Gaard 2013). Cultural ecofeminists (e.g. Spretnak 1990; Starhawk 1989) espoused earth-based spiritualties and symbols such as Goddess and Gaia (in Greek mythology, mother of the earth and universe).

In the late 1990s and 2000s ecofeminism faced two criticisms (Gaard 2011). The first was that it essentialized women's relationship with nature. Critics charged that ecofeminism homogenized women and understood them as naturally or essentially closer to nature than men. Three counterpoints emerged. Woman-nature connections, even if essentialist, are important inspirational and motivational tools for women fighting environmental and social injustice on the ground (Godfrey 2005). Essentialism, in other words, can be strategic for social movements (Hurwitz and Taylor 2012). It can bring different kinds of women together for political action, which can then destabilize essentialist formulations (Sturgeon 1997). Secondly, actual ecofeminist positions are diverse; the essentialist critique ignored international, anti-capitalist, postcolonial, and materialist thinkers. Finally, even if particular strands of ecofeminism were in fact essentialist, as Greta Gaard (2011) argues was the case for cultural ecofeminisms, the vast majority of ecofeminist knowledge is valuable for understanding and advancing intersectional justice in a time of multiple overlapping crises.

Ecofeminism also faced a critique for including species and nature in feminist analysis. For example, Dixon (1996) argued that feminists have little to gain by aligning themselves with animals because doing so makes women seem closer to nature than men. In the essay "Should Feminists Be Vegetarian?" (1994), Kathryn George challenged ecofeminist solidarity with animals by questioning the nutritional value of a vegan diet for women and marginalized groups. Ecofeminists Greta Gaard and Lori Gruen (1995), Josephine Donovan (1995), and Carol Adams (1995) offered a rebuttal to George in a debate published by the feminist academic journal *Signs*. In addition to questioning George's data, these scholars argued that George ignored ecofeminists' attention to situating vegetarian diets within specific social, historical, and non-western contexts, and to highlighting the responsibility of privileged individuals to curb consumption. They also stressed that aversion to theorizing species relationships fails to grasp a foundational contribution of ecofeminism: interlocking systems of domination depend on oppression of "others" (Plumwood 1996) and resisting this oppression depends on solidarity among all who are oppressed—women, indigenous communities, people of color, the poor, and the more-than-human world. In other words, dismantling dualisms, such as human/nature, masculine/feminine, reason/emotion (Plumwood 1996), is necessary for the liberation of all, including the more-than-human world. This insight on interspecies justice is one of the most powerful that ecofeminism offers, illustrating a deep understanding of intersectionality. As Gaard (2011: 37) concludes, rather than identifying a weakness of ecofeminism, the species critique reflected feminists' discomfort with the recognition that feminists can be oppressors of other female animals and that the exploitation of female animals' reproductive labor is similar to the exploitation of women's socially proscribed labors.

In sum, ecofeminist philosophy arises in the overlaps among and between feminism, nature, science, development and technology, and local and indigenous perspectives (Warren 2000). It sees connections among humans and between humans and the more-than-human world enabling a new relationship between nature and culture (King 1990), something which will be critical to overcoming the challenges posed by what is perhaps the most encompassing threat to justice in all of its forms—climate change.

Women and Climate Change[1]

A contemporary ecofeminism must ground analysis and activism in the new material conditions—always shaped by local context and history—of women living in a climate-changing world. Understanding the gendered nature of climate change sheds light on conditions and solutions that characterize and grow from, not only women's lives, but also those of marginalized communities more generally. Gender inequalities abound in conceptualizations, consequences, experiences of, and responses to climate change.

Gender inequalities in the social construction of climate change are evidenced by the masculinized focus on security (i.e., energy security, security against climate refugees) (see Dankelman 2010a) and science that dominates understanding of climate problems and proposed solutions (MacGregor 2010). Concerns about energy security, for instance, legitimize governments' continual violation of treaty rights when building pipelines and other infrastructure across indigenous land (Whyte 2017). Within this masculinization, the pursuit of technology and economic efficiency trumps women's concerns (and the concerns of other marginalized communities) (MacGregor 2010; Seager 2009).

Gendered consequences of climate change are linked to the global feminization of poverty. As the majority of the world's poor, women are more vulnerable to natural disasters and have fewer material, legal, and political resources to deal with the effects of climate change (see Dankelman 2010b; Oxfam 2017; WEDO 2008 for examples and statistics). The gendered division of labor, in which women are responsible for providing food, water, and care, also affects how women experience and respond to climate change. Climate change increases the amount of time women spend gathering fuel and water, makes their work to produce the majority of the world's food unpredictable, and increases the health and other kinds of care they must perform in response to climate change-exacerbated disease and natural disasters (Dankelman 2010b). In energy extraction zones that fuel climate change, indigenous women suffer heightened and disproportionate rates of sexual violence by non-Native men (Harvard 2015).

These gendered experiences of climate change affect women's risk perceptions and responses. Women are both more knowledgeable and more concerned about climate change (McCright 2010) and more likely to oppose fracking (Boudet et al. 2014)—a method for extracting natural gas or oil that has significantly increased U.S. emissions of methane, a potent greenhouse gas (Turner et al. 2016). This is in line with research documenting women's greater concern and feelings of responsibility for environmental quality more generally (Hunter, Hatch and Johnson 2004; Terry 2009; Zelezny, Chua and Aldrich 2000). At the state level, more egalitarian views about gender and higher political status of women are associated, respectively, with more progressive environmental policies (Norgaard and York 2005) and lower CO_2 emissions per capita (Ergas and York 2012). On the ground, women are the majority of grassroots activists in the environmental justice movement (Seager 1996; Stein 2004), leading struggles against infrastructures and practices that perpetuate climate change (see Bell and Braun 2010; Foytlin et al. 2014; Grosse 2017; Thomas-Muller 2014; Whyte 2017). Their environmental organizing often draws on skills in building community networks (Agarwal 2000), performing reproductive labor (Campbell 1996; Miller, Hallstein and Quass 1996), and multitasking (Brú-Bistuer 1996; Seager 1996), as well as protector and mother identities that align with cultural norms of femininity (Bell and Braun 2010; Bell

2013). In sum, the "glorious tangle of production and reproduction" (Bhavnani, Foran, and Kurian 2003: 8) that characterizes women's lives informs their environmental activism, and now, their work to mitigate and adapt to climate change.

Ecofeminist Interventions

In this reality, action and policy to achieve environmental and climate justice must center gender and women's experiences and responses. Environmental and climate justice—as fields of study and social movements—are making progress in this area, but work remains. Environmental justice emerged in the 1980s, disrupting a century of environmentalism in the United States dominated by white upper class men working to preserve wilderness (Taylor 2002). Emphasis on "meaningful involvement" of marginalized communities in all stages of environmental policymaking (see U.S. EPA 2017) and a redefinition of the environment, to "where we live, work, and play," are two key contributions of the framework, which has historically focused on the intersection of race, class, and environment. While environmental justice struggles *may* have global implications, climate justice struggles *always* have global implications because of the nature of greenhouse gas emissions, which do not obey national borders and, eventually, will affect every living thing on earth. Drawing on the legacies of movements for environmental justice, global justice, and indigenous sovereignty, among others (for a helpful visual depiction, see Moore and Russell 2011: 21), the climate justice movement began organizing in the early 2000s at the annual United Nations (UN) climate negotiations. After particularly disappointing UN negotiations in 2009, the movement turned much of its focus to national, regional, and local campaigns, its numbers and actions growing.

Intersectional ecofeminist priorities are evident in the expanded purview of environmental and climate justice, which increasingly examine how race, class, rurality, indigeneity, gender, sexuality, and the configurations of these structures of privilege and marginalization, are linked to environmental and climate injustice (e.g. Ashwood and MacTavish 2016; Bell 2013; LaDuke 2016; Pellow 2016; Stein 2004). Conceptualizations of and actions for climate justice also increasingly stress rights-based agendas, leadership by and accountability to those most affected by and least responsible for climate change, and grassroots struggles that address the root causes of climate change (Dayaneni 2009: 83)—all organizing philosophies long prioritized by feminists. Within the climate justice movement acting at the global level, women fight for equal representation in delegations to the UN negotiations—still far short of achieving gender parity (UNFCCC 2015)—and inclusive movement actions where leadership by women and youth receives adequate recognition (see Petermann 2011). They demand policy that creates "a just, sustainable and equitable future for women and men," not "gender equality on a dead planet" (Lapin quoted in Women Gender Constituency 2014).

On the ground in the United States, the work of 350.org, an organization founded in 2008 and woman-led since 2015 with the mission to build a global climate justice movement, illustrates ecofeminist infusions into climate justice. Actions by 350, which has been part of the broad coalitions behind the major climate justice actions in the United States in the last five years, have become more intersectional and movement-building focused. In 2014, for example, young people of color led the procession at the 400,000-person People's Climate March, with a banner reading "Forefront of Crisis, Forefront of Change." "To change everything, we need everyone" was a popular slogan. The 2017 People's Climate March made the justice focus more explicit by including the subtitle "Climate, Jobs, Justice" in all of its branding. In 2014, 350's Strategic Partnership Coordinator, Deirdre Smith's essay, "Why the Climate Movement Must Stand with Ferguson," linked the police murders of black folks with the militarized racism in the aftermath of Hurricane Katrina, calling on climate organizers to understand "that our fight is not simply with the carbon in the sky, but with the powers on the ground." The Movement for Black Lives (2016) recognizes these same interconnections, acknowledging the threat of climate change in their platform. 350 has also linked sexuality, gender identity, and climate change. Following the massacre of forty-nine people at a gay Latinx nightclub in Orlando, Florida, 350 staff wrote a letter stressing the complexity of intersectionality—that all climate justice activists, particularly LGBTQ+ activists, whose "survival depends on this movement for climate justice," need to "be able to bring our whole selves in this movement" "because we are all connected, as is our fight" (350.org Staff 2016).

To continue advancing its movement-building work, the climate justice movement must prioritize and strengthen its dedication to meaningful involvement of those most affected by climate change. Taking this seriously demands sustained ecofeminist analysis and practice— understanding that injustices intersect and that humans, animals, and plants depend on healthy physical, cultural, social, and movement environments; and acting to identify shared roots of oppression, come together across divisions, and advance intersectional justice. In this spirit, I center the rich organizing of water protectors, whose analyses and practices can help advance ecofeminist goals in the era of climate crisis.

"Standing Rock Awakens The World"[2]

In 2014, Energy Transfer Partners decided to reroute its planned Dakota Access Pipeline (DAPL) away from the predominantly white Bismarck, North Dakota, where residents and policy makers raised concerns about the pipeline's effects on water quality. The new route crossed Lake Oahe, a dammed portion of the Missouri River, a drinking source for 18 million people downstream and the only drinking water source for the Standing

Rock Sioux Tribe. The pipeline is in the heart of sacred treaty land promised to and then taken away from the Standing Rock Sioux. It runs just north of the reservation boundary, a boundary which encompasses two of the nation's most impoverished counties (U.S. Census Bureau 2016).

Women and youth were the first to take a stand against the pipeline by camping at Standing Rock in the spring of 2016. LaDonna Brave Bull Allard, the Standing Rock Sioux Tribe's Section 106 Historic Preservation Officer, established the Sacred Stones Camp in April. She posted a video calling on people to come join her on her family's land. Joye Braun, a member of the Cheyenne River Sioux Tribe and organizer for Indigenous Environmental Network, was one of the first to camp, a decision she made in consultation with the youth of her tribe. Winona LaDuke, a longtime Anishinabe activist, and the organization she founded and directs, Honor the Earth, provided resources and inspiration to water protectors. Indigenous Environmental Network had a number of staff at camp, including Kandi Mossett, Mandan, Hidatsa and Arikara, a leader in climate justice mobilizations in recent years.

These and many other women's leadership shaped a context that inspired women and men, "One of the most beautiful things I feel right now, is that you see these amazing, empowered women who are stepping up and really reminding us young men, and men in general, that our role is to let the women lead" (Nahko Bear quoted in Dewhurst 2016). Indeed, women applied their individual strengths in diverse areas of the movement. Jasilyn Charger (Cheyenne River Sioux), in her early twenties, co-founded the International Indigenous Youth Council, which had a sustained presence at Standing Rock and organized a 2,200-mile run by youth and tribal members to the White House, where they delivered petitions to President Obama. Rita Waln, about ten years old, instigated hand shaking with a line of police officers in Bismarck, North Dakota where women and children had traveled to communicate with the governor (ICMN Staff 2016). Women and youth offered water and prayer to police (Erdrich 2016; Fox, Spione and Dewey 2017). They were the first to go through fences to confront bulldozers destroying sacred burial grounds (Goodman 2016). They were responsible for founding a school, providing health care and spiritual leadership, and made up the majority of cooks, turning immense quantities of food donations into thousands of free meals. Braun explained at the 2017 Water is Life: Standing with Standing Rock Conference that doing traditional roles and getting together at camp helped women "reawaken" an indigenous heritage where women were always leaders of communities. The analyses and practices of the mobilization at Standing Rock parallel ecofeminist orientations and enabled tremendous movement building.

Analyses

Water protectors expressed their analyses in the collective identity that they sought to build, in the way they framed their struggle, and in the value they attached to inclusivity and solidarity among all of their relations—human and more-than-human.

For many, being at Standing Rock was about protecting water, Mother Earth and future generations. Water protector is a collective identity that is inclusive. Purposeful and in alignment with the movement's core values of peace and spirituality, the shared identity attracted diverse people. As one participant explained, "When the media is naming us as protesters and rioters, they are dehumanizing who is really here: water protectors. We are women, mothers, grandmothers, children, teachers, nurses, lawyers. [...] People from all spectrums of society are here" (Rene, a teacher from California, quoted in Pielert 2016). And water, more than other things that people feel drawn to protect such as place, culture, and community (see Bell 2013), is a true universal. Everyone (including the more-than-human world) needs it, and it connects everyone—there is always someone downstream.

Because of women's roles in reproduction—as Katsi Cook (2003) has said, "[w]omen are the first environment"—and social reproduction, where they gather water for families and communities, this identity has a special connection with women. Just as water and the earth give life, so too do women. A material and spiritual relationship between women and the earth, one based on mutual dependence and reciprocity, resonated with and inspired water protectors. As Eryn Wise, a Jicarilla Apache, and Laguna Pueblo, two-spirit leader of the International Indigenous Youth Council explained, "This Earth is a life giver and I am a life giver" (quoted in Prakash 2017). Jasilyn Charger echoed her sentiment at the 2017 Standing Rock conference:

> [A]s a woman, [I] had a very strong spiritual connection to the ground, to the earth, because she is female. I am female. She gives life every single day, we do too. [...] We are her daughters, she is our mother [...] I felt the urge to come protect her. Because without her, who's gonna watch over my children, who's gonna give them food, who's gonna give them water, if she's not here?

Water protectors anchored their work in the assertion of *Mni Wiconi* (Water is Life). This movement frame parallels the inclusivity of water protector, stating a truth for all beings on earth. Water is something that nourishes and heals. It exists in bodies, makes new life possible, and physically connects people along its routes. It shapes sense of place. As Faith Spotted Eagle, a Yankton Sioux, recounted, "I always jokingly say, 'This is my river, so I'm sharing it with you.' [...] We've been drawn to that spirit of the river water. I think that all of us had this dream of doing what we can [...] the river and the land are helping us fulfill those dreams" (quoted in Tsjeng 2016). The water, said Charger at the 2017 Standing Rock conference, "flows" and "pulls," "demand[ing] us to protect it" and informing the "magnetic" connection between people and *Unci Maka* (Grandmother Earth). One participant explained this connection as helping her see humanity in others, even the opposition: "Even for the cops at the bridge, the water in me recognizes the water in them. [...] we still have the same communality which is our bodies are made of water" (woman with tribal affiliations in Southwest North America, quoted in Tsjeng 2016).

Water, by connecting all things, supported an intersectional, interspecies and inclusive understanding of what the Dakota Access Pipeline meant and what solutions would look like. It threatened all life and solutions required respect for all life. Brook, a Yankton Sioux, who is part of a women's society where she learns from elders how to be a freedom fighter, explained, "As indigenous people, we're always thinking forward [to the next] seventh generation [...] part of that indigeneity is that our relatives are not just human" (quoted in Tsjeng 2016). Exemplifying an ecofeminist analysis, Eryn Wise explained how fighting for justice and equality was not only about gender equality, but also about building a world where all things can flourish—an interspecies notion of reproductive justice:

> This work that I do is truly done to ensure that there's not only equality for humans but equality for life. I don't mean it to just be equality for the sexes. That's my feminism side, but also my environmental side is for equality for [...] [t]he ones in the sky and the ones in Earth [...] all the plants and everything that tries so hard to love us in the best way that it knows how. The fight is just to protect that like the momma protects the babies. The trees, the water, the animals, the Earth. [...] it's nourished me so much. And I feel it's my job now to give and nourish back.
>
> Quoted in Prakash 2017

In the context of Standing Rock, respect for all life translated into creating an atmosphere at camp that was welcoming. Water protectors did this through a number of practices.

Practices: Being Better Relatives[3]

The framing, collective identity, and inclusive understanding of community at Standing Rock enabled people to "work across lines" (Grosse 2017: 14) in unprecedented ways. Three hundred tribes were present at Standing Rock. Such a gathering had not occurred in over a hundred years. Tribes that were longtime enemies came together to protect the water. At its height, Standing Rock provided a community and resources for ten thousand people who were moved to come lend a hand. In December 2016, when North Dakota's governor ordered water protectors to leave, four thousand veterans arrived to stand with the water protectors. Their arrival, said Braun at the 2017 Standing Rock conference, "looked like a snake of light—the snake of light was coming to fight against this black snake [DAPL]."

Water, future generations, militarization against peaceful people on their own land, on behalf of a corporation, and spiritual principles—all of these issues made Standing Rock resonate widely and brought diverse people to camp. As reporter Laurette Prevost (2016) put it, "Indigenous volunteer security guards eat beside Aztec dancers and people from China and Venezuela." Hoka Luta Win, Red Badger Woman, recounted, "Our sacrifices up on Standing Rock humbled me. [...] The unity, the love and the compassion. The pride of just uniting all of us. Different races, indigenous people from all over the world. It was beautiful" (quoted in Gunderson 2017). Unity in diversity was a common theme of Standing Rock accounts.

While core values and shared sense of injustice pulled people to Standing Rock, the community kept them there. My colleague, a non-Native who spent only a few hours at Standing Rock to donate firewood, said that, even in that short time, he had a job, community, and sense of purpose. Each morning at Standing Rock, a voice on the loudspeaker would announce: "It's time to get up. This is not a vacation. We've got work to do, relatives" (Ratner 2016). Water protectors built community through shared work and by having clear expectations of each other. New arrivals were given trainings in the Seven Lakota Values—prayer, respect, compassion, honesty, generosity, humility and wisdom—and direct action. Respecting indigenous traditions, listening, stepping up and stepping back, safety, accountability, and generosity were all modeled and expected. As a handout describing these values stated: "remember why you are here: to stop the pipeline as a ceremonial camp." This goal meant not only blocking the pipeline, but also prefiguring the world that water protectors wanted to see. As Charger noted at the 2017 Standing Rock conference, "for us, fighting pipelines and living our life are the same thing."

To create the world they wanted to see, water protectors constructed social institutions that were donation supported, volunteer-organized, and free, including kitchens, schools, and medical centers. They organized volunteer security and media teams. In all of these efforts, they sought to decolonize—serving traditional foods, teaching children indigenous language and culture, and drawing on indigenous medical practices. They planted corn and willow trees in the path of the pipeline and used solar and wind power to generate energy. Perhaps most importantly, they worked to transform the way humans interact with each other and the earth. Water protectors created a supportive and loving environment, as Braun explained at the 2017 Standing Rock conference:

> [W]e were changing everything [...] the way we were treating everybody around us. In the general world, people don't give a lot of hugs and don't give a lot of affirmations. When you're around water protectors you're gonna get hugged, you're gonna get a lot of love [...] it really is a way of life and it's making those conscious decisions every single day that this is the way that I'm gonna walk.

Walking in this way was part of building a new system, according to Michelle Cook, Diné of the Walk Around Clan, who said that water protectors were:

> "fighting the whole system of violence. [...] Which has denied us our ability to be human—and we're responding to that by creating a community that has its own values. That respects its women. That gives its children priority. That will teach its children the traditional knowledge of life, that will give them life."
>
> Quoted in Arasim and Orielle Lake 2016

Commitment to prayerful, peaceful resistance, even in the face of attack dogs, water cannons in below freezing temperatures, compression grenades, rubber bullets, and mace, grounded daily life. Prayer was about radical forgiveness and compassion—feminine approaches to resolving conflict—even for the people and governments that have exploited indigenous nations for centuries. Louis Erdrich, of the Turtle Mountain Band of the Chippewa Indians, portrayed Standing Rock as "a portrait of sacred humility," one that taught participants how to engage in a decentralized community-making project that required toughness and resolve—something many participants took with them as they left to engage with four years of a Trump administration (Erdrich 2016). "Every time the water protectors showed the fortitude of staying on message and advancing through prayer and ceremony, they gave the rest of the world a template for resistance" (Erdrich 2016). This approach was the foundation of what it meant to protect the water.

Water protector's analyses and practices can help ecofeminists refine and intensify their work for climate justice. In creating decolonized community, where diverse people felt called together to care for and stand with one another, and in practicing compassionate and peaceful ways of living with each other and in relation to the more-than-human world, water protectors nourished a movement that continues to gain momentum. In their inclusivity, deep understanding of intersectionality and respect for all life-giving things—all made material through actions to achieve social welfare—they lift up an approach to organizing for justice that ecofeminists also value, one that is increasingly embraced in, and essential to, a strong climate justice movement.

Conclusion

As K. J. Gawel (2017) writes, "A feminism adequate to our times requires a militancy that [...] emerges from the conditions of our social reproduction and not from the tired impasses of macho politics." The conditions of our social reproduction are the water, the climate, and the air. These relatives, as water protectors might call them, are in danger of suffering irreversible changes that humans may not be able to adapt to. A feminism adequate to our times, then, must be an ecofeminism that works for the liberation of people and the more-than-human world—climate justice.

The mobilization at Standing Rock worked to protect life-giving water, indigenous sovereignty, the climate, and the capacity of present and future generations to live well, from a black snake of capitalism—a pipeline to extend dependency on fossil fuels in order to secure corporate profits. In powerful analyses, it called on people to be protectors and to recognize global and local interdependencies—that water is life. In its actions, it pre-figured a world where labor, respect, and shared purpose meet the needs of the community. Against militarized state violence and the masculine priority of energy security, it prioritized peace and prayer. Women are leaders in this movement, leaders in movement building. They called people to Standing Rock, were the first to camp, and played key roles in providing education, food, healthcare, courage, and spiritual grounding. Their work continues in the courts, in the financial sphere—through divestment from companies and banks that support fossil fuels—on the ground in camps resisting other pipelines, and in the building of permanent water protector institutions, such as a free Mni Wiconi Health Clinic in Standing Rock territory. As the U.S. women's and climate justice movements continue to mobilize in a political context hostile to both movements' agendas, they will do well to draw on, as Charger describes them below, the ripples begun at Standing Rock—to recognize root causes of oppression, common purpose, and the power of working together to create strong communities.

> It was prophesied, that gathering, and it was something that was really, well, needed. We knew we couldn't do it alone [...] but if you take that courage and throw that stone in the river, you'll create ripples and those ripples will stretch through time. What we did there will echo through time forever and that's something that couldn't have happened without our relatives. [...] No matter what color you are, you need water. No matter where you come from, you need water. [...] That really threaded this movement together and made it so beautiful because this world is diverse, so is this planet, so are our lives. It really widened my perspective on what being a human being actually is.
> —Jasilyn Charger at the 2017 Standing Rock conference

Notes

1 [1]Warren (2000) identifies 10 ecofeminisms: historical, conceptual, empirical, socioeconomic, linguistic, symbolic and literary, spiritual and religious, episte-mological, political and ethical.
1 This section draws on Grosse (2017).
2 Text from a sign on https://medium.com/@UofPenn/the-stand-at-sta nding-rock-292474e2f82e.
3 This language comes from TallBear (2016).

References

350.org Staff. 2016. "Orlando." Retrieved February 18, 2018. http://350.org/orla ndo/?akid=14359.599245.kVHD7h&rd=1&t=9.

Adams, Carol. 1996. "Ecofeminism and the Eating of Animals." Pp. 114–136 in *Ecofeminist Philosophies*, edited by Karen J. Warren. Bloomington, IN: Indiana University Press.

Adams, Carol J. 1995. "Comment on George's 'Should Feminists Be Vegetarians?'" *Signs* 21(1):221–225.

Agarwal, Bina. 2000. "Conceptualising Environmental Collective Action: Why Gender Matters." *Cambridge Journal of Economics* 24(3):283–310.

Arasim, Emily and Osprey Orielle Lake. 2016. "15 Indigenous Women on the Frontlines of the Dakota Access Pipeline Resistance." *EcoWatch*. Retrieved July 1, 2017. https://www.ecowatch.com/indigenous-women-dakota-access-pip eline-2069613663.html.

Ashwood, Loka and Kate MacTavish. 2016. "The Rural as a Dimension of Environmental Injustice." *Journal of Rural Studies* 47(A):1–386.

Bell, Shannon Elizabeth and Yvonne A. Braun. 2010. "Coal, Identity, and the Gendering of Environmental Justice Activism in Central Appalachia." *Gender & Society* 24(6):794–813.

Bell, Shannon Elizabeth. 2013. *Our Roots Run Deep as Ironweed: Appalachian Women and the Fight for Environmental Justice*. Urbana, IL: University of Illinois Press.

Bhavnani, Kum-Kum. 1993. "Tracing the Contours: Feminist Research and Feminist Objectivity." *Women's Studies International Forum* 16(2):95–104.

Bhavnani, Kum-Kum, John Foran and Priya A. Kurian. 2003. "An Introduction to Women, Culture and Development." Pp. 1–21 in *Feminist Futures: Re-imagining Women, Culture and Development*, edited by Kum-Kum Bhavnani, John Foran and Priya A. Kurian. New York: Zed Books.

Boudet, Hilary, Christopher Clarke, Dylan Bugden, Edward Maibach, Connie Roser-Renouf and Anthony Leiserowitz. 2014. "'Fracking' Controversy and Communication: Using National Survey Data to Understand Public Perceptions of Hydraulic Fracturing." *Energy Policy* 65:57–67.

Braun, Joye, Jasilyn Charger, and Mark Tilsen (panelists). 2017. "Protecting the Land and Water." Presented at the Water is Life: Standing with Standing Rock Conference, May 19, University of California Santa Barbara, Santa Barbara, CA. Retrieved August 15, 2018. https://www.uctv.tv/shows/32571.

Brú-Bistuer, Josepa. 1996. "Spanish Women Against Industrial Waste." Pp. 105–124 in *Feminist Political Ecology: Global Issues and Local Experiences*, edited by Dianne Rocheleau, Barbara Thomas-Slayter and Esther Wangari. London and New York: Routledge.

Campbell, Connie. 1996. "Out on the Front Lines but Still Struggling for Voice." Pp. 27–61 in *Feminist Political Ecology: Global Issues and Local Experiences*, edited by Dianne Rocheleau, Barbara Thomas-Slayter and Esther Wangari. London and New York: Routledge.

Cook, Katsi. 2003. "Women Are the First Environment." *Indian Country Today*. December 23. Retrieved August 15, 2018. https://indiancountrymedianetwork.com/news/cook-women-are-the-first-environment/.

Dankelman, Irene. 2010a. "Climate Change, Human Security and Gender." Pp. 55–71 in *Gender and Climate Change: An Introduction*, edited by Irene Dankelman. New York: Earthscan.

Dankelman, Irene. 2010b. *Gender and Climate Change: An Introduction*. New York: Earthscan.

Davidson, Debra and Michael Haan. 2012. "Gender, Political Ideology, and Climate Change Beliefs in an Extractive Industry Community." *Population & Environment* 34(2):217–234.

Dayaneni, Gopal. 2009. "Climate Justice in the U.S." Pp. 80–85 in *Contours of Climate Justice: Ideas for Shaping New Climate and Energy Politics*, Vol. 6, *Critical Currents*, edited by Ulrich Brand, Nicola Bullard, Edgardo Lander and Tadzio Mueller. Uppsala, Sweden: Dag Hammarskjöld Foundation.

Dewhurst, Amy V. 2016. "Nahko Bear; It is Written." *LA Yoga*, October 31. Retrieved August 15, 2018. https://layoga.com/inspiration/artists-musicians/nahko-bear-written/.

Dixon, Beth A. 1996. "The Feminist Connection Between Women and Animals." *Environmental Ethics* 18(2):181–194.

Donovan, Josephine. 1995. "Comment on George's 'Should Feminists Be Vegetarians?'" *Signs* 21(1):226–229.

Dunayer, Joan. 1995. "Sexist Words, Speciesist Roots." Pp. 11–31 in *Animals and Women: Feminist Theoretical Explorations*, edited by Carol J. Adams and Josephine Donovan. Durham, NC: Duke University Press.

Erdrich, Louise. 2016. "Holy Rage: Lessons from Standing Rock." *The New Yorker*. December 22. Retrieved August 15, 2018. https://www.newyorker.com/news/news-desk/holy-rage-lessons-from-standing-rock.

Ergas, Christina and Richard York. 2012. "Women's Status and Carbon Dioxide Emissions: A Quantitative Cross-National Analysis." *Social Science Research* 41 (4):965–976.

Fox, Josh, James Spione and Myron Dewey. 2017. *Awake: A Dream from Standing Rock*. DVD. Digital Smoke Signals and International WOW Company.

Foytlin, Cherri, Yudith Nieto, Kerry Lemon and Will Wooten. 2014. "Gulf Coast Resistance and the Southern Leg of the Keystone XL Pipeline." Pp. 181–194 in *A Line in the Tar Sands: Struggles for Environmental Justice*, edited by Toban Black, Stephen D'Arcy, Tony Weis and Joshua Kahn Russell. Oakland, CA: PM Press.

Gaard, Greta and Lori Gruen. 1995. "Comment on George's 'Should Feminists Be Vegetarians?'" *Signs* 21(1):230–241.

Gaard, Greta. 2011. "Ecofeminism Revisited: Rejecting Essentialism and Replacing Species in a Material Feminist Environmentalism." *Feminist Formations* 23(2):26–53.

Gaard, Greta. 2013. "Toward a Feminist Postcolonial Milk Studies." *American Quarterly* 65(3):595–618.

Gawel, K. J. 2017. "Striking at the Roots." *Viewpoint Magazine*, March 8. Retrieved August 15, 2018. https://www.viewpointmag.com/2017/03/08/striking-at-the-roots/.

George, Kathryn Paxton. 1994. "Should Feminists Be Vegetarians?" *Signs* 19 (2):405–434.

Godfrey, Phoebe. 2005. "Diane Wilson vs. Union Carbide: Ecofeminism and the Elitist Charge of 'Essentialism'." *Capitalism Nature Socialism* 16(4):37–56.

Goodman, Amy. 2016. "VIDEO: Dakota Access Pipeline Company Attacks Native American Protesters with Dogs and Pepper Spray." *Democracy Now!* Retrieved September 1, 2017. https://www.democracynow.org/2016/9/4/dakota_access_p ipeline_company_attacks_native.

Grosse, Corrie. 2017. "Working Across Lines: Resisting Extreme Energy Extraction in Idaho and California." PhD. dissertation, Department of Sociology, University of California Santa Barbara.

Gunderson, Dan. 2017. "'Not Invisible Anymore': Standing Rock a Year After Pipeline Protests." *MPR News*, September 13. Retrieved August 15, 2018. http s://www.mprnews.org/story/2017/09/13/standing-rock-nd-a-year-after-oil-pip eline-protests.

Harvard, Dawn Memee. 2015. *Extreme Extraction and Sexual Violence Against Indigenous Women in the Great Plains.* Callaway, MN: Honor the Earth. Retrieved August 15, 2018. https://d3n8a8pro7vhmx.cloudfront.net/honorearth/pages/ 2076/attachments/original/1433357727/UN_submission_sex_trafficking_and_ extreme_oil.docx?1433357727.

Hunter, Lori M., Alison Hatch and Aaron Johnson. 2004. "Cross-National Gender Variation in Environmental Behaviors." *Social Science Quarterly* 85(3):677–694.

Hurwitz, Heather McKee and Verta Taylor. 2012. "Women's Cultures and Social Movements in Global Contexts." *Sociology Compass* 6(10):808–822.

ICMN Staff. 2016. "Dakota Access: 6 Peaceful Images From the Water Protectors at Standing Rock." *Indian Country Today*. August 23. Retrieved August 15, 2018. https://indiancountrymedianetwork.com/news/native-news/dakota-access-6-pea ceful-images-from-the-water-protectors-at-standing-rock/.

IPCC. 2013. Climate Change 2013: The Physical Science Basis. Contribution of Working Group I to the Fifth Assessment Report of the Intergovernmental Panel on Climate Change, edited by T.F. Stocker, D. Qin, G.-K. Plattner, M. Tignor, S.K. Allen, J. Boschung, A. Nauels, Y. Xia, V. Bex and P.M. Midgley. Cambridge and New York: Cambridge University Press.

Juris, Jeffrey S., Erica G. Bushell, Meghan Doran, J. Matthew Judge, Amy Lubitow, Bryan Maccormack and Christopher Prener. 2014. "Movement Building and the United States Social Forum." *Social Movement Studies* 13(3):328–348.

King, Ynestra. 1990. "Healing the Wounds: Feminism, Ecology, and the Nature/ Culture Dualism." Pp. 106–121 in *Reweaving the World: The Emergence of Ecofeminism*, edited by Irene Diamond and Gloria Feman Orensteign. San Francisco: Sierra Club Books.

Klein, Naomi. 2014. *This Changes Everything: Capitalism vs. the Climate.* New York: Simon & Schuster.

Klein, Naomi. 2017. *No is Not Enough: Resisting Trump's Shock Politics and Winning the World We Need.* Chicago: Haymarket Books.

LaDuke, Winona. 2016. *The Winona Laduke Chronicles: Stories from the Front Lines in the Battle for Environmental Justice*, edited by Sean Aaron Cruz. Ponnsford, MN and Winnipeg, Manitoba: Spotted Horse Press and Fernwood Publishing.

MacGregor, Sherilyn. 2010. "A Stranger Silence Still: The Need for Feminist Social Research on Climate Change." *The Sociological Review* 57:124–140.

McCright, Aaron M. 2010. "The Effects of Gender on Climate Change Knowledge and Concern in the American Public." *Population and Environment* 32(1):66–87.

Merchant, Carolyn. 1980. *The Death of Nature: Women, Ecology and the Scientific Revolution.* New York: HarperCollins Publishers.

Mies, Maria and Vandana Shiva. 1993. *Ecofeminism.* London and New York: Zed Books.

Miller, Vernice, Moya Hallstein and Susan Quass. 1996. "Feminist Politics and Environmental Justice." Pp. 62–85 in *Feminist Political Ecology: Global Issues and Local Experiences*, edited by Dianne Rocheleau, Barbara Thomas-Slayter and Esther Wangari. London and New York: Routledge.

Moore, Hilary and Joshua Kahn Russell. 2011. *Organizing Cools the Planet: Tools and Reflections to Navigate the Climate Crisis.* Oakland, CA: PM Press.

Norgaard, Kari and Richard York. 2005. "Gender Equality and State Environmentalism." *Gender & Society* 19(4):506–522.

Oxfam. 2017. *An Economy that Works for Women.* Cowley, Oxford: Oxfam GB. Retrieved August 15, 2018. https://www.oxfam.org/sites/www.oxfam.org/files/file_attachments/bp-an-economy-that-works-for-women-020317-en.pdf.

Pellow, David N. 2016. "Toward a Critical Environmental Justice Studies: Black Lives Matter as an Environmental Justice Challenge." *Dubois Review* 13(2):221–236.

Petermann, Anne. 2011. "Showdown at the Durban Disaster: Challenging the 'Big Green' Patriarchy." *NGOWatch.* Retrieved July 18, 2014. https://the wrongkindofgreen.wordpress.com/2011/12/16/showdown-at-the-durban-disa ster-challenging-the-big-green-patriarchy/.

Pielert, Beth. 2016. "The Faces of Standing Rock: 12 Stunning Photos of Water Protectors in North Dakota." *Mic.* Retrieved February 18, 2018. https://mic. com/articles/160915/the-faces-of-standing-rock-12-stunning-photos-of-water-p rotectors-in-north-dakota#.uJ08CLMXb.

Plumwood, Val. 1996. "Nature, Self, and Gender: Feminism, Environmental Philosphy, and the Critique of Rationalism." Pp. 155–180 in *Ecological Feminist Philosophies*, edited by Karen J. Warren. Bloomington, IN: Indiana University Press.

Prakash, Nidhi. 2017. "A Young Native American Leader on Why Feminism and Fighting for the Planet Go Hand in Hand." *Splinter.* Retrieved February 18, 2018. https://splinternews.com/a-young-native-american-leader-on-why-fem inism-and-figh-1794269635.

Prevost, Laurette. 2016. "The Grandma Feeding the North Dakota Pipeline Protest." *Aljazeera.* October 27. Retrieved August 15, 2018. http://www.aljazeera. com/indepth/features/2016/10/grandma-feeding-north-dakota-pipeline-p rotest-161026113429091.html.

Ratner, Jake. 2016. "This Is What Life Inside the Standing Rock Camp Looks Like Right Now." *The Nation.* November 23. Retrieved August 15, 2018. https:// www.thenation.com/article/this-is-what-life-inside-the-standing-rock-camp -looks-like-right-now/.

Robinson, William I. 2014. *Global Capitalism and the Crisis of Humanity.* New York: Cambridge University Press.

Seager, Joni. 1996. "'Hysterical Housewives' and Other Mad Women." Pp. 271–283 in *Feminist Political Ecology: Global Issues and Local Experiences*, edited by Dianne Rocheleau, Barbara Thomas-Slayter and Esther Wangari. London and New York: Routledge.

Seager, Joni. 2009. "Death by Degrees: Taking a Feminist Hard Look at the 2° Climate Policy." *Kvinder, Køn & Forskning* 3(4):11–21.

Smith, Deirdre. 2014. "Why the Climate Movement Must Stand with Ferguson." Retrieved October 1, 2014. http://350.org/how-racial-justice-is-integral-to-con fronting-climate-crisis/.

Spretnak, Charlene. 1990. "Ecofeminism: Our Roots and Flowering." Pp. 3–14 in *Reweaving the World: The Emergence of Ecofeminism*, edited by Irene Diamond and Gloria Feman Orensteign. San Francisco: Sierra Club Books.

Starhawk. 1989. "Feminist, Earth-Based Spirituality and Ecofeminism." Pp. 174–185 in *Healing the Wounds: The Promise of Ecological Feminism*, edited by Judith Plant. Philadelphia: New Society Publishers.

Stein, Rachel, ed. 2004. *New Perspectives on Environmental Justice: Gender, Sexuality, and Activism*. New Brunswick, NJ: Rutgers University Press.

Sturgeon, Noël. 1997. *Ecofeminist Natures: Race, Gender, Feminist Theory and Political Action*. New York: Routledge.

Tallbear, Kim. 2016. "Badass (Indigenous) Women Caretake Relations: #NoDAPL, #IdleNoMore, #BlackLivesMatter." *Cultural Anthropology*. December 22. Retrieved August 15, 2018. https://culanth.org/fieldsights/1019-badass-indigen ous-women-caretake-relations-nodapl-idlenomore-blacklivesmatter.

Taylor, Dorceta E. 2002. *Race, Class, Gender, and American Environmentalism*. Portland, OR: USDA.

Terry, Geraldine. 2009. "No Climate Justice Without Gender Justice: An Overview of the Issues." *Gender & Development* 17(1):5–18.

The Movement for Black Lives. 2016. "A Vision for Black Lives: Policy Demands for Black Power, Freedom, & Justice." Retrieved August 15, 2018. policy.m4bl. org.

Thomas-Muller, Clayton. 2014. "The Rise of the Native Rights–Based Strategic Framework." Pp. 240–252 in *A Line in the Tar Sands: Struggles for Environmental Justice*, edited by Toban Black, Stephen D'Arcy, Tony Weis and Joshua Kahn Russell. Oakland, CA: PM Press.

Tsjeng, Zing. 2016. "'Miracles Are Happening': Photos of the Tireless Women of Standing Rock." *Broadly*. Retrieved February 18, 2018. https://broadly.vice. com/en_us/article/j5e854/photos-standing-rock-dakota-access-pipeline-protes ters-women.

Turner, A. J., D. J. Jacob, J. Benmergui, S. C. Wofsy, J. D. Maasakkers, A. Butz, O. Hasekamp and S. C. Biraud. 2016. "A Large Increase in U.S. Methane Emissions over the Past Decade Inferred from Satellite Data and Surface Observations." *Geophysical Research Letters* 43(5):2218–2224.

U.S. Census Bureau. 2016. "Small Area Income and Poverty Estimates." Retrieved February 18, 2018. https://www.census.gov/data-tools/demo/saipe/saipe.html? s_appName=saipe&map_yearSelector=2016&map_geoSelector=aa_c&s_year= 2016.

U.S. EPA. 2017. "Environmental Justice." Retrieved February 13, 2017. https:// www.epa.gov/environmentaljustice.

UNFCCC. 2015. *Report on Gender Composition*. Retrieved August 15, 2018. https:// unfccc.int/resource/docs/2015/cop21/eng/06.pdf.

Warren, Karen J. 2000. *Ecofeminist Philosophy: A Western Perspective on What It Is and Why It Matters*. Lanham, MD: Rowman and Littlefield Publishers, INC.

WEDO. 2008. *Changing the Climate: Why Women's Perspectives Matter*. New York: Women's Environment and Development Organization (WEDO). Retrieved

August 15, 2018. http://www.wedo.org/wp-content/uploads/changing-th e-climate-why-womens-perspectives-matter-2008.pdf.

Whyte, Kyle Powys. 2017. "The Dakota Access Pipeline, Environmental Injustice, and U.S. Colonialism." *Red Ink: An International Journal of Indigenous Literature, Arts, & Humanities* 19(1):154–169.

Women Gender Constituency. 2014. "Women at COP 20 Blast Failure for Real Action in Lima." Retrieved February 18, 2018. http://womengenderclimate.org/ release-women-at-cop-20-blast-failure-for-real-action-in-lima/.

Zelezny, Lynnette C., Poh-Pheng Chua and Christina Aldrich. 2000. "New Ways of Thinking about Environmentalism: Elaborating on Gender Differences in Environmentalism." *Journal of Social Issues* 56(3):443–457.

12 Women, Gender and Feminism at Work

Allison Elias

Throughout the 20th century, working women and their allies have used a variety of strategies to advocate for fair pay, safe working conditions and opportunities for promotion. Shifting economic, political, legal and social forces in the United States have shaped the nature of activists' efforts at different historical moments. Women of various identities (i.e., race, ethnicity, sexuality, age, class and citizenship status) have chosen to prioritize certain issues over others depending on distinct workplace experiences. As more women have entered the paid labor force in an increasingly broad range of occupations, momentum has shifted towards some issues and away from others. In general, contemporary feminist activism for workplace equality progresses along two tracks. Women who are educated as engineers, attorneys, physicians and bankers (i.e., professional careers) fight for opportunities to advance into positions of greater prestige and status. In this case, feminism and capitalism align as the most powerful companies bolster the ideals of sex equality, competing to recruit and retain the most talented women. Meanwhile, other women working as cashiers, home health aides, receptionists, housekeepers, and waitresses (i.e., blue collar careers) struggle to provide for themselves and their families. Their activist efforts focus on obtaining a decent wage, a more predictable schedule, as well as affordable health care and childcare. Despite the current divergence of these two paths of feminism, some issues such as sexual harassment have universal impact, bringing together women from an array of occupations and industries.

Indeed, gender as a category of analysis has played a crucial role in the construction of knowledge about work and activism (Scott 1986). How we actually conceptualize terms like work and activism reflects certain gendered values that have elevated paid labor over unpaid labor, industrial work over domestic work, and collective action over individual action. While men and women in agrarian societies both engaged in productive activities to maintain their families, the rise of a cash economy marginalized women's domestic tasks. Wage work moved outside of the home to a central site of production. The unpaid labor of wives, daughters and sisters became invisible in the formal economy. In the developing industrial economy, housework was recast a labor of love, demonstrative of familial devotion

(Boydston 1990). The construction of public and private spheres, defined as the political and economic affairs of men in contrast to the reproductive care work of women, has resulted in the definition of work as wage-earning labor (Welter 1966).

In addition, the role of unpaid and forced labors of slave men and women in the Americas has remained tangential to narratives of industrialization. Arguing that slave labor was integral to the economic development of the United States, scholars have started to revisit the conventional view that slavery was an anti-capitalist enterprise (Cooke 2003). In his revisionist book, historian Edward Baptist presents a compelling argument about slavery as integral to U.S. industrialization (2014). The histories of white women and unfree laborers force us to approach current knowledge about work with a critical lens, asking whose experiences might be privileged or marginalized in modern understandings of the economy.

Because gendered definitions of work elevate the status of paid labor, the dominant stories of labor activism center on male manufacturing workers and trade unions. Scholars have focused on union activities despite the fact that at the high tide of unionism in the United States, still less than 35 percent of wage workers were members (Mayer 2004). In reality, men and women resisted their working conditions in many informal ways, some difficult to uncover given the limits of the historical record. Non-unionized women in New York City sweatshops formed friendships, sang songs, and discussed books to get through the tedious routine of manual, repetitive factory labor (Richardson 1990). Asserting control over their own bodies, Black domestic workers in early 20th-century Atlanta danced at jook joints long into the night, defying the moral expectations of their white employers (Hunter 1997). Utilizing the concept of "infrapolitics," historian Robin D. G. Kelley documented the agency of Black workers who engaged in everyday forms of resistance (i.e., foot-dragging, theft, or quitting) to confront the power of white employers (1994). Traditionally such action has been treated as supplementary to a grand narrative whereby labor history is the story of union history. Yet many women and men resisted the control of employers outside of union channels, and such seemingly inconsequential behaviors have influenced societal structures and institutions.

In this chapter, I first discuss women's appeals to unions for economic empowerment, and then I turn to the benefits and limits of legal remedies when advancing women's status at work. I focus on these two broad categories, unions and the law, because much of the scholarship situates women's workplace status as contingent upon inclusion in these two institutions. In their quest for economic empowerment and equal opportunity, women have gained greater access to the tools offered by unions and the remedies provided by the law. However, institutional logics continue to hinder women's advancement to a certain extent since unions and the law rely on gendered and racialized assumptions about work and the economy. While I make a clear distinction between utilization of union frameworks and appeals to the law, efforts to facilitate change often relied on several tools to undo gender-based injustices. Battles waged by feminists of the 1960s and 1970s, along with activists from the Civil Rights Movement, have normalized a collective belief in equality of opportunity. Women won fights to access workplace rights that are available to men. Less successful have been feminist efforts to raise the economic status of care work by securing paid family leave or state-sponsored childcare. Thus, while contemporary feminists have remedies to correct for unequal treatment of men and women, subtle inequities arising from embedded gender norms and institutional structures are more difficult to dismantle.

Unions and Labor Organizing

Since the dawn of industrial capitalism in the United States, women have engaged in unions as members, educators, organizers, and leaders, defying the traditional narrative that women did not participate in collective workplace activism. Some of the first U. S. industrial workers, the Lowell Mill Girls, formed their own organization, the Female Labor Reform Association, in 1845 (Dublin 1981). In the South, laundresses working from their own homes in Atlanta formed The Washing Society in 1881, demanding higher pay and greater respect (Hunter 1997). And while men held the most senior leadership positions in the early 20th-century International Ladies' Garment Workers Union (ILGWU), female factory workers played an integral role in the development, maintenance and execution of union campaigns, as well as in efforts to develop educational programs for fellow shirt makers. When the ILGWU staged an eleven-week strike in 1909, Eastern European immigrant women built coalitions among a multi ethnic workforce. They even bridged class divides, enlisting upper-class white women as allies in sustaining the strike (Orleck 1995).

While some female labor activists challenged a separate spheres ideology, they also leveraged femininity to support male family members. During the Flint Sit Down Strike of 1936–37, women took shifts preparing, cooking, and serving food to their fathers, husbands and brothers while the United Auto Workers (UAW) strategically occupied the site of production. Just 75 women operated this kitchen for 24 hours a day, feeding several meals a day to more than 2,000 male protesters. Some women even served as human shields to protect their husbands from police brutality, cognizant that law enforcement would be reticent to inflict physical harm on women (Baugh-Helton 2017).

The Flint example notwithstanding, domestic ideology usually disadvantaged working women in their quest to achieve full economic citizenship. Most trade unions supported a family wage with men arguing that union pay should be substantial enough for them to provide for wives and children. Labor leaders, policymakers and social reformers viewed the family wage not as backwards but as a progressive means of wealth redistribution.

Higher wages for men would shift a greater portion of capitalist wealth to the working class (Kessler-Harris 1982). Unions used the family wage reasoning to justify excluding women from their ranks, but also employers defended lower pay for women and job classification systems based on sex.

Even the economic disruption posed by World War II, which resulted in demand for women to further wartime production, did not dismantle pay inequity and occupational segregation. During World War II, women eagerly abandoned female-dominated work as department store clerks and restaurant employees to take traditionally male jobs and earn higher wages. White and black women built airplanes, made ammunition, and worked in shipyards although women of color held the lowest-paying jobs requiring exposure to toxic chemicals or physically arduous labor (May 1988). Although the federal government mandated that women war workers should receive equal pay for equal work, unions and employers reinvented sex-based distinctions to maintain men's advantages. They relabeled women's jobs as "light" and men's jobs as "heavy" to preserve pay differences. At the war's end, women begrudgingly relinquished their jobs (Milkman 1987), but they had gained newfound confidence that a woman could do the work of any man.

In the postwar era, as more white married women began to earn wages, journalist Betty Friedan published a best-selling book, *The Feminine Mystique*, encouraging college-educated, white suburban housewives to pursue careers as means of self-actualization. She wrote, "The only way for a woman, as for a man, to find herself, to know herself as a person, is by creative work of her own. There is no other way" (Friedan 1963: 472). Friedan, a liberal feminist, would become one of the founders of the National Organization for Women (NOW) in 1966. She believed in sex equality, which reinvigorated decades-old debates about how to best advance the status of working women. Throughout the first half of the 20th century, most advocates wanted economic justice, but they did not perceive fair treatment as calling for the same treatment of men and women. Historian Dorothy Sue Cobble has shown that from the 1930s until the 1980s, labor feminists "put the needs of working-class women at its core" (Cobble 2004: 3). Labor feminists wanted to remedy sex-based inequities by demanding that unions prioritize fair pay, paid maternity leave and childcare. As feminists like Friedan started to push for workplace equality in the 1960s, women like union leader Myra Wolfgang fought to preserve protective legislation for women. In her testimony to the United States Senate, Wolfgang spoke out against sex-based equality: "We are different, and different does not mean deficient" (Cobble 2004: 192). As arguments for equality gained steam in the 1960s and 1970s, and major unions issued statements in support of sex equality, adherence to the difference approach lost footing. By the 1980s, a paradigm had shifted, and sex equality became the standard for fair treatment.

During these decades of transition, the distinction between difference and equality, labor feminism and liberal feminism, rarely was clear. Union leaders such as Dorothy Haener of the UAW participated in the founding and development of NOW, perhaps the most significant feminist organization to promote sex equality under law. Furthermore, at the intersection of labor and liberal feminism stood the Coalition of Labor Union Women (CLUW). In 1974, more than 3,000 women—including both supporters and opponents of legal equality—came together to create a national organization to empower women in the labor movement. CLUW prioritized increasing women's membership and leadership in unions as well as moving concerns like pay equity and sexual harassment to the center of the labor agenda. Women of color shaped the agenda from CLUW's beginnings: about 25 percent of those at the founding convention were African American, Hispanic, Asian, and Native American women (Roth 2003).

Feminism of the 1960s and 1970s spurred greater organizing activity among pink-collar women as well. With one-third of working women holding low-paid, dead-end clerical positions, office activism arose across the nation during the feminist era. On December 16, 1977, eight women walked out of their jobs at Citizens National Bank in the small Minnesota town of Willmar. The Willmar 8 braved temperatures below zero to picket for higher pay and promotional opportunities. Even though the women went on strike to protest sex-based inequity, they did not consider themselves feminists. One woman stated that she did not know what feminism was, and another declared that feminists were immoral (Grant 1981). Even among those not considering themselves feminists, feminist ideology was changing expectations of what constituted fair treatment at work.

In addition to Willmar, other grassroots movements arose among clerical workers who wanted more rights (i.e., higher pay, promotional opportunities) and greater respect (i.e., acknowledgement of their contributions). Karen Nussbaum, a secretary at the Harvard Graduate School of Education, became inspired to form her own workplace consciousness-raising group, named 9to5, in 1972. 9to5 leaders wanted to convince others that their individual problems were part of a systemic pattern of sex-based workplace discrimination. By the 1980s, 9to5 was operating in more than 15 cities and had engaged thousands of women in newsletter distribution, public protests, lobbying efforts and professional workshops. To gain greater financial resources and bargaining power, in 1981 Nussbaum formed a sister union, District 925 of the Service Employees International Union (SEIU). A national clerical workers' division, District 925 held the possibility of extending membership to 16 million women. However, unionizing private-sector clericals proved difficult. Although SEIU District 925 won some fights on college campuses, it struggled to gain footing in private-sector banks and insurance firms (Elias forthcoming).

Unions turned their attention towards female-dominated, public-sector occupations, such as teaching, as well as towards certain gender-specific issues, such as pay equity. Labor feminists had prioritized pay equity decades earlier, but in 1979, the formation of the National Committee on Pay Equity brought together liberal feminist groups, professional women's organizations and trade unions as allies. Given that government employees had standardized job classifications and transparent salary ranges, public-sector unions, like the growing American Federation of State, County and Municipal Employees (AFSCME), could tackle pay equity issue more easily. Pay equity activists won some battles in union contracts with municipal and state governments. But private-sector compensation practices remained untouched. Pay equity never became codified into federal employment law as a tide of conservative politicians and judges successfully curtailed state intervention in business in the 1980s (Blum 1991).

Although women as a percentage of total union members has increased markedly in the last three decades, from 33.6 percent in 1984 to 45.5 percent in 2014, still 90 percent of women wage earners do not belong to a union (Institute for Women's Policy Research 2018). Labor activists are utilizing new strategies to empower low-wage women without requiring union membership. Attorney and activist Saru Jayaraman co-founded Restaurant Opportunity Centers United, helping workers to reform industry policies about pay and hours, as well as to prosecute illicit activity like wage theft. While women represent more than two-thirds of tipped restaurant workers, they constitute about 95 percent of domestic workers. Activist Ai-jen Poo founded the National Domestic Workers Alliance, which, by 2016, boasted a membership of 20,000 nannies, housekeepers and care givers, disparately women of color and immigrant women. The organization advocates for a Domestic Workers Bill of Rights, which has passed in several state legislatures. Labor leaders such as Jayaraman and Poo empower those who often lack a voice, seating wage-earning women on their boards and in other key leadership positions (Restaurant Opportunities Centers United 2018; National Domestic Worker's Alliance 2018).

The Power of the Law?

While activists have formed, supported and led labor organizations, others have turned to the law to improve the status of women, shifting strategies from embracing difference-based to equality-based rights. While early 20th-century courts rejected protection legislation for men, relying on a liberty of contract found in the Fourteenth Amendment, those same judges upheld protections for working women because of their status as mothers or potential mothers. For women only, regulations regarding minimum wage, maximum hours, weightlifting limits, rest periods and occupational safety remained legal to preserve and prioritize women's reproductive capacity. The Supreme Court upheld an Oregon state law that limited female laundry employees to a 10-hour working day; in 1908 Justice Brewer wrote: "That woman's physical structure and the performance of maternal functions place her at a disadvantage in the struggle for subsistence is obvious" (*Muller v. Oregon*, 208 U.S. 412).

Most working women and their allies agreed with Brewer, supporting sex-specific protective legislation throughout much of the 20th century. However, some upper-class white women, forming the National Woman's Party, advocated for legal equality between the sexes. They drafted and lobbied for an Equal Rights Amendment (ERA) to the U.S. Constitution in 1923 (Cott 1989). Initially, most women did not support the ERA: not only was the idea of equality considered radical, but also sex-based legal distinctions were benefiting wage-earning women (Woloch 2015). In addition, the widespread belief that women and men had essential differences in mind and body actually gave professional women greater influence in the public sphere. During the Progressive Era and New Deal, most women who gained a voice in political and economic affairs did so because of conventional beliefs that white women had a more virtuous and moral nature that could temper the harsh realities of urban and industrial life. As white, college-educated women such as Jane Addams, Julia Lathrop and Florence Kelley confronted social problems, they moved concerns about women and children to the center of the government's agenda (Muncy 1991).

Another such reformer was Frances Perkins, who became the first female cabinet member when appointed Secretary of Labor in 1933. When crafting New Deal legislation, Perkins and other female policy-makers aimed to preserve women's primary roles as wives and mothers. They saw this unpaid labor as valuable, not just to the family unit, but also as crucial to the health of the nation. Yet this elevation of women's maternal and domestic roles hindered women's economic independence and reinforced the family wage ideal. New Deal relief programs like the Works Progress Administration stipulated that only one member of a household could claim a publically-funded job, often traditionally men's work such as construction. In addition, women reformers designed, and then Congress enacted, Aid to Dependent Children (ADC) in 1935, which reinforced women's economic dependence since funding for poor mothers was contingent on *not* earning any wages (Gordon 1994). Lastly, a major legislative achievement, the Fair Labor Standards Act (FLSA) guaranteed a federal minimum wage and overtime to all full-time workers. However, part-time or seasonal work, often performed by women, was omitted. Southern legislators demanded that the bill pass exclude agricultural and household labor, too, which disparately impacted men and women of color (Kessler-Harris 2001). Exempting household labor from coverage meant that some of the most vulnerable women had no protection against low wages. They had to fight for FLSA inclusion, which live-out cleaners and other domestic workers finally achieved in 1974 although home care aides and personal attendants remained excluded (Boris and Klein 2012).

As more married white women entered into the workforce after World War II, the issues that immigrants and women of color had confronted for decades became topics of national discussion. Finding ways to reconcile women's roles as caretakers and wage earners moved to the White House's agenda. In 1961, President John F. Kennedy convened the President's Commission on the Status of Women to craft "recommendations for services which will enable women to continue their role as wives and mothers while making a maximum contribution to the world around them" (Executive Order 10980). The impetus for this Commission actually came from Esther Peterson, a labor leader who Kennedy appointed to direct the Labor Department's Women's Bureau. Peterson pushed to resurrect a 1947 proposal for a status of women commission. Even though Eleanor Roosevelt nominally headed the Commission, Peterson set the agenda and ran operations (Harrison 1988). While Peterson stacked the Commission with ERA opponents, some labor feminists—especially those working in sectors where women and men competed for the same jobs—began to embrace equal rights (Kessler-Harris 2001).

The convening of this Commission represented a critical moment of coalition for labor feminists and the rising tide of new, liberal feminists. Strategies of both equality and difference imbued the Commission's final report, *American Women*, which was widely read by the public. While by the turn of the 21st century the United States still had not enacted many Commission proposals (such as paid maternity leave, pay equity or publically funded childcare), the Commission did facilitate federal action on the issue of equal pay. Drafted by Peterson, the Equal Pay Act passed Congress in 1963 as an amendment to the FLSA. Initially it excluded most professional, administrative, and executive workers, and even after it was extended in the 1970s, many women remained outside of its protections (Palmer 1995). Because the law passed with language guaranteeing equal pay for equal work, it failed to provide remedy for many women who labored in female-dominated sectors. To correct all gender-based pay inequities, women would need state laws or union contracts guaranteeing pay equity, which seemed unlikely to materialize for most working women by the end of the 1980s (Blum 1991).

In addition to fighting for equal pay, working women and their allies pushed to include sex in a federal bill initially drafted to ban race discrimination. Title VII of the Civil Rights Act of 1964 became a most far-reaching federal policy of the 20th century to promote workplace inclusion for women and underrepresented minorities. Along with discrimination based on race, religion and ethnicity, sex-based discrimination became illegal in private workplaces that had more than 15 employees. Earlier scholarship once emphasized the addition of sex into Title VII as an attempt to defeat a bill that would advance the status of African Americans. Yet revisionist accounts demonstrate that feminist Congresswoman Martha Griffiths (D-MI) strategically permitted a Virginia segregationist to introduce the idea. Griffiths then argued that Title VII, without the inclusion of sex, placed white women at a disadvantage relative to African-American men (Mayeri 2011). With the support of segregationists and feminists alike, the Civil Rights Act became law on July 2, 1964 with language linking sex and race discrimination.

Title VII created the Equal Employment Opportunity Commission (EEOC), a government agency designed to investigate cases of employment discrimination and interpret the difference between cases of unlawful discrimination and legally-valid distinctions. Controversy arose over a provision called the bona fide occupational qualification (BFOQ) exception, which, when "reasonably necessary" for business operations, permitted distinctions based on sex, national origin, or religion. The media quickly capitalized on possible consequences of a narrow reading of the BFOQ. In 1965, the *New York Times* reported on the "bunny problem," alluding to the ridiculousness of permitting men to be Playboy bunnies (Kessler-Harris 2001). Many liberal feminists, however, wanted a narrow reading of the BFOQ to limit sex-based distinctions. Feminist legal scholars Pauli Murray and Mary Eastwood argued a close alignment of race and sex discrimination, contending that a broad BFOQ reading would significantly weaken Title VII's benefits for women (Mayeri 2011).

With a modest budget, the fledging EEOC, which lacked enforcement powers until 1972, initially chose to ignore questions surrounding the BFOQ exception and instead devoted scarce resources to combatting race discrimination. However, about one third of claims to the EEOC during its first year of operation concerned sex discrimination. Among those at the Commission's door were airline stewardesses backed by transport unions. The stewardesses claimed that airline restrictions based on age, height, weight and marital status were not reasonably related to performing their job duties. Attorneys for the airlines contended that customers preferred attractive, thin, young, single stewardesses, arguing that these restrictions should remain legal as a business necessity. After several years of hearings and investigations, the EEOC issued three rulings in 1968 holding that age and marriage policies were illegal under Title VII. Eventually the Supreme Court ruled against sex as a BFOQ for the job of flight attendant in 1972, allowing a man to enter the profession (Barry 2007).

The Supreme Court bolstered the momentum of liberal feminists by striking down state protective legislation. In 1967, NOW represented Lorena Weeks, who successfully won the opportunity to work a higher-paying job as a switchman, which required heavy lifting. Southern Bell previously had denied her the job because of a Georgia statute banning women from lifting anything above 30 pounds. In Illinois, Thelma Bowe won her case against Colgate-Palmolive, striking down another state law limiting the amount of weight women could lift at work. Given the legal and social tides shifting towards equality, many labor feminists began to temper their support for protective laws and embrace the benefits of Title

VII. Major labor unions (the UAW in 1970 and then the American Federation of Labor-Congress of Industrial Organizations in 1973) abandoned their commitments to protective legislation and began to support both the ERA and full implementation of Title VII in the 1970s (Woloch 2015).

Just as women had to fight for inclusion into Title VII, they also had to lobby for coverage under the executive orders known as affirmative action. Designed to remedy past discrimination against African American men, these orders initially mandated that employers address racial bias only. But in the early 1970s, the Women's Equity Action League pressured government officials to add a provision for women, mandating that employers issue goals and timetables for sex as well as for race. Although affirmative action had limited reach for those facing low pay in pink-collar jobs, it played an important role in moving women into male-dominated occupations (Elias 2018). Rates of occupational segregation began to decline as women pursued careers in traditionally male occupations like dentistry, medicine, and law. The trades proved more difficult, however, as many blue-collar men guarded their territory, making women feel uncomfortable and even unsafe (MacLean 1999).

With feminist pressure, courts and legislatures expanded Title VII's reach to include older workers, mothers, and pregnant women. Unionized stewardesses joined forces with NOW leaders to lobby for the Age Discrimination in Employment Act in 1967 as an amendment to Title VII. Discrimination on the basis of sex plus another characteristic also became illegal so that employers could not discriminate against a subclass of women such as mothers (*Phillips v. Martin Marietta Corp.*, 400 U.S. 542, 1971). Labor unions, feminists and even religious conservatives lobbied for the Pregnancy Discrimination Act in 1978, adding pregnant women to Title VII's list of protected classes. Despite these victories, the structure of the law posed limitations. When seeking remedy under Title VII, women of color seemingly fell under two different protected classes: sex and race. Because employment law treated each as distinct categories, legal scholar Kimberle Crenshaw coined the term intersectionality (1989). Crenshaw was struck by a district court holding that black women did not constitute their own legal class. Title VII permitted charges of "race discrimination, sex discrimination, or alternatively either, but not combination of both" (*DeGraffenreid v. General Motors Assembly Div.*, 413 F.Supp. 142, 1976).

Eventually courts clarified that Title VII's sex clause included sexual harassment, but only after activists and scholars argued that such behavior should be illegal. The term sexual harassment emerged from several struggles at Cornell University in 1974. When Instructor Lin Farley addressed the topic of unwanted sexual attention in her Women and Work class, almost all of the female students had a story. Concurrently, office assistant Carmita Wood resigned from her position, having becoming physically ill after repeated, unwanted sexual attention from a male faculty member. The university denied her unemployment benefits, arguing that she had quit for personal reasons. Farley, along with Cornell colleagues and women from the Ithaca community, used the language of sexual harassment to describe Wood's experience. When the events at Cornell made headlines in a widely-reprinted *New York Times* article, the phrase "sexual harassment" entered the mainstream (Baker 2008).

As a grassroots movement took hold, legal scholar and activist Catharine MacKinnon deployed feminist theory to argue that harassment at work constituted an exercise of unjust male dominance. What appeared culturally to be an interpersonal interaction actually posed systemic disadvantages for women, limiting their economic mobility (MacKinnon 1979). In 1980 EEOC Commissioner Eleanor Holmes Norton added sexual harassment to its sex discrimination guidelines, defining it, as MacKinnon had, as characterized by either *quid pro quo* or a hostile work environment. The Supreme Court upheld the essence of the EEOC guidelines in *Meritor Savings Bank v. Vinson*. Mechelle Vinson was a bank employee whose supervisor intimidated her into having sex with him some fifty times over the course of three years. In 1986 the Court confirmed that harassment could be *quid pro quo*, whereby a supervisor uses his power to demand sexual acts; as well as hostile environment harassment, whereby supervisors or co-workers create an intimidating or offensive atmosphere. While the case validated the EEOC's definition of sexual harassment, it rejected another EEOC determination that employers should retain liability for the illegal actions of their employees. Instead, the Court held that Meritor Savings Bank did not have vicarious liability for the actions of Vinson's supervisor (Anderson 1987).

Public awareness of sexual harassment increased during the Anita Hill-Clarence Thomas hearings in 1991. When Judge Thomas, an African-American man, was nominated for a position on the Supreme Court, law professor Anita Hill, also African-American, spoke to the Senate Judiciary Committee during the vetting process. A decade earlier she had worked with Thomas at the Department of Education and at the EEOC. She maintained that he sexually harassed her while he responded that the entire hearing was a "high-tech lynching" (Berebitsky 2012: 272). After Thomas's confirmation, black feminists placed a full-page *New York Times* condemnation of the event. The group known as African-American Women in Defense of Ourselves berated Thomas for perpetuating the myth that African-American women have strong sexual urges and thus they cannot be physically violated (Berebitsky 2012).

Routinely popular discourse and legal opinions defined sexual harassment as men violating women, which marginalized those harmed by a person of the same sex. Lesbian, gay, bisexual, transgender and questioning (LGBTQ) employees and their allies challenged the heteronormative nature of anti-discrimination law. In 1998 the Supreme Court held that same-sex harassment could fall under hostile environment reasoning, nothing that "harassing conduct need not be motivated by sexual desire" to be considered sex-based discrimination (*Oncale v. Sundowner Offshore Services, Inc.*, 523 U.S. 75). Other LGBTQ issues had arisen decades earlier, including whether sexual orientation was an immutable identity, and thus protected under Title VII. LGBTQ activists argued that it should be considered a protected category like race or sex while employers and judges saw it as something that could be chosen or hidden (Turk 2013).

As of 2017, the status of LGBTQ rights under Title VII remains inconclusive although the EEOC and lower courts have ruled that sexual orientation and gender identity are protected categories. The Supreme Court's reasoning in *Price Waterhouse v. Hopkins* (490 U.S. 228, 1989), determining that Ann Hopkins had been denied partnership in large part because of stereotyping, set precedence that Title VII's prohibition of sex discrimination protected workers who did not conform to traditional gender norms (Herz 2014). In 2012, the EEOC supported protections for gender identity, and in 2015, the EEOC issued a decision that sexual orientation fell under Title VII's sex clause (*Macy v. Holder; Complainant v. Anthony Foxx*). Several district courts and the Seventh Circuity Court of Appeals have reached similar conclusions (*Hively v. Ivy Tech Community College*, 7th circuit, 2017). Despite these gains for LGBTQ individuals, Congress has not added a specific amendment to Title VII and the Supreme Court has not issued a ruling regarding LGBTQ protections.

Even with the support of Title VII, women or men who serve as primary care givers for their partners, parents or children face challenges regarding workplace equity and advancement. Feminist and labor organizations pushed for the gender-neutral Family and Medical Leave Act (FMLA), eventually passed in 1993. The length of leave mandated and the number of employees covered had decreased significantly after years of compromising with conservative opponents who fought regulations for small businesses. The FMLA provides 12 weeks of unpaid leave for employees who have been working at the same business for at least 12 months; have worked at least 1,250 hours over the past 12 months; and are working at a location with 50 or more employees within 75 miles. Only about 60 percent of private-sector employees are covered since those with several part-time jobs do not qualify. Among those not covered are many precarious workers who cannot afford to miss a paycheck. And although many professional men and women receive paid leave from their employers, they face pressures to prioritize work commitments amid family responsibilities (Williams 2000). Working women and their advocates continue to push for more assertive legal interventions, and by 2018, five states and the District of Columbia have passed provisions for paid leave. Feminists push to increase coverage on multiple fronts, arguing for expanding the definition of a family unit or for decreasing the number of employees required for coverage (Noguchi 2018).

Contemporary advocates also perceive greater pay transparency as a remedy to the gender pay gap since many women do not know they are receiving inequitable compensation. Lilly Ledbetter had worked as a floor manager at Goodyear Tire and Rubber Company in Alabama for more than a decade when she received an anonymous note informing her that she was earning thousands less per month relative to male colleagues. In 2007 the Supreme Court rejected Ledbetter's sex discrimination suit because she had filed her complaint more than 180 days after the initial discriminatory act of her first paycheck. Justice Ruth Bader Ginsburg wrote a stirring dissent, and activists from the National Women's Law Center and National Partnership for Women & Families publically condemned the decision. Upon assuming office, President Barack Obama signed the Lilly Ledbetter Fair Pay Act, which mandates that the statute of limitation starts following the last, rather than the first act of discrimination. It amended Title VII to clarify that a discriminatory compensation practice is unlawful each time compensation is paid (Boris 2011).

Conclusion

In the current political, social and economic climate, women with diverse identities who are working in an array of occupations and industries seem more different from one another than they are similar. While professional women prioritize upward mobility into managerial and executive roles, low-wage women care most about higher pay and affordable health insurance. Professional women push for progress in the name of a business case for diversity, arguing that greater numbers of female executives and board members will benefit the organization's bottom line. Covered by Title VII, they have moved beyond fighting for regulatory compliance. Now they are tackling important extralegal issues such as implicit bias. Disproportionately women of color and undocumented immigrants, working-class women continue to push for broader government protections. A rapidly changing global economy means that many low wage women turn towards the promise of collective action to address gaps in legal coverage.

Despite the divergent nature of feminist activism in the workplace, new movements have begun to unite diverse categories of women committed to change. First coined in 2006 by community organizer Tarana Burke, #MeToo spread across social media in 2017 as well-known Hollywood actors catapulted sexual assault and violence into mainstream discourse (see also Chapter 8 this volume). The #MeToo movement aims to expose the systemic disadvantages that vulnerable women and men face at work by encouraging survivors to break their silence. Dialogue has turned to women in other occupations, as 700,000 female farmworkers announced in *Time* magazine that they too experienced sexual harassment but lacked resources to report injustices. Cognizant of this uneven access to remedies, hundreds from the entertainment industry launched Time's Up in early 2018. This initiative between Hollywood activists and the National Women's Law Center establishes a defense fund to help working-class women to bring forward claims (Buckley 2018).

Despite criticism that the #MeToo movement excludes men, vilifies those accused or lacks appeal for older women, its momentum is undeniable. Millions of women and men of all ages are discussing sexual misconduct on social media, implying that #MeToo may unify diverse categories of women, strengthen feminist activism, and challenge traditional power relations in workplaces across the United States. Yet with the #MeToo movement in its infancy as of 2018, we are left wondering if certain issues such as sexual harassment will bring together women and men from various industries and occupations? Or will different work experiences and diverse demographic categories prevent strong alliances among women and men that are necessary to change cultural norms?

Workplace problems like sexual harassment force us to revisit our approaches to gender equity in a neoliberal political and economic climate. The mainstream belief in a business case for diversity promotes capitalism's meritocratic promise, contending that advancement of the most talented individuals will foster financial gains for the larger organization and collective benefits for the broader society. While capitalism has improved the physical wellbeing of millions, by advancing medical knowledge, improving maternal health and decreasing infant mortality, capitalism too can exploit women as reproducers and caretakers. In *The Guardian* in 2013, philosopher Nancy Fraser famously lamented that feminism had become "capitalism's handmaiden," warning against the neoliberal turn of "lean in" feminism. And indeed, not all women benefit to the same extent when feminism is folded into a capitalist framework. To what extent can new forms of collective organizing help to empower those who struggle in a rapidly-changing economy? How can the law become more effective in offering women not just equality of opportunity but also equality of outcome? And to what extent can employers' policies address systemic inequality, allowing all women and men to thrive? These are the questions of feminism in the 21st-century workplace, questions that remain to be answered.

References

Anderson, Katherine S. 1987. "Employer Liability Under Title VII for Sexual Harassment after Meritor Savings Bank v. Vinson." *Columbia Law Review* 87(6):1258–1279.

Baker, Carrie. 2008. *The Women's Movement Against Sexual Harassment*. New York: Cambridge University Press.

Barry, Kathleen. 2007. *Femininity in Flight: A History of Flight Attendants*. Durham, NC: Duke University Press.

Baptist, Edward E. 2014. *The Half That Has Never Been Told: Slavery and the Making of American Capitalism*. New York, NY: Basic Books.

Baugh-Helton, Tiffany A. 2017. "'We Didn't Know We Were Making History': The United Automobile Workers' Women's Auxiliaries in Great Depression and World War II Era Detroit." PhD dissertation, Department of History, Binghamton University – State University of New York.

Berebitsky, Julie. 2012. *Sex and the Office: A History of Gender, Power, and Desire.* New Haven, CT: Yale University Press.

Blum, Linda M. 1991. *Between Feminism and Labor: The Significance of the Comparable Worth Movement.* Berkeley: University of California Press.

Boris, Eileen. 2011. "Ledbetter's Continuum: Race, Gender, and Pay Discrimination." Pp. 240- 256 in *Feminist Legal History: Essays on Women and the Law,* edited by Tracy A. Thomas and Tracey Jean Boisseau. New York: New York University Press.

Boris, Eileen and Jennifer Klein. 2012. *Caring for America: Home Health Workers in the Shadow of the Welfare State.* New York: Oxford University Press.

Boydston, Jeanne. 1990. *Home and Work: Housework, Wages, and the Ideology of Labor in the Early Republic.* New York: Oxford University Press.

Buckley, Cara. 2018. "Powerful Hollywood Women Unveil Anti-Harassment Action Plan." *New York Times.* Retrieved February 26, 2018. https://www.nytimes.com/2018/01/01/movies/times-up-hollywood-women-sexual-harassment.html.

Cobble, Dorothy Sue. 2004. *The Other Women's Movement: Workplace Justice and Social Rights in Modern America.* Princeton, NJ: Princeton University Press.

Cooke, Bill. 2003. "The Denial of Slavery in Management Studies." *Journal of Management Studies* 40(8):1895–1918.

Cott, Nancy. 1989. *The Grounding of Modern Feminism.* New Haven, CT: Yale University Press.

Complainant v. Anthony Foxx, EEOC DOC 0120133080, WL 4397641(1954).

Crenshaw, Kimberlé Williams. 1989. "Demarginalizing the Intersection of Race and Sex." *University of Chicago Legal Forum* 139:139–167.

DeGraffenreid v. General Motors Assembly Div., 413 F. Supp. 142(1976).

Dublin, Thomas. 1981. *Women at Work: The Transformation of Work and Community in Lowell, Massachusetts, 1826–1860.* New York: Columbia University Press.

Elias, Allison. Forthcoming. *Feminism at Work: Women, Gender, and Success in Corporate America.* New York: Columbia University Press.

Elias, Allison. 2018. "Outside the Pyramid': Clerical Work, Corporate Affirmative Action, and Working Women's Barriers to Upward Mobility." *Journal of Policy History* 30(2):301–333.

Fraser, Nancy. 2013. "How Feminism Became Capitalism's Handmaiden—And How to Reclaim It." *The Guardian.* Retrieved May 1, 2018. https://www.theguardian.com/commentisfree/2013/oct/14/feminism-capitalist- handmaiden-neoliberal.

Friedan, Betty. 1963. *The Feminine Mystique.* New York: W. W. Norton.

Gordon, Linda. 1994. *Pitied but Not Entitled: Single Mothers and the History of Welfare, 1890-1935* New York: The Free Press.

Grant, Lee. 1981. The Willmar 8. DVD. CA: California Newsreel. http://newsreel.org/transcripts/The-Willmar-8-transcript.pdf.

Harrison, Cynthia. 1988. *On Account of Sex: The Politics of Women's Issues, 1945–1968.* Berkeley: University of California Press.

Herz, Zachary. 2014. "Price's Progress: Sex Stereotyping and Its Potential for Anti-Discrimination Law." *Yale Law Journal* 124(2):396–446.

Hively v. Ivy Tech Community College. No. 15–1720 (7th Cir., April 4, 2017).

Hunter, Tera. 1997. *To 'Joy My Freedom: Southern Black Women's Lives and Labors After the Civil War.* Cambridge: Harvard University Press.

Institute for Women's Policy Research. 2018. "Women in Unions." Accessed March 1, 2018. https://iwpr.org/issue/democracy-and-society/women-in-unions/.

Kelley, Robin. 1994. *Race Rebels: Culture, Politics, and the Black Working Class.* New York: Free Press.

Kennedy, John F. "Executive Order 10980." December 14, 1961. Retrieved March 1, 2018 (http://www.presidency.ucsb.edu/ws/?pid=58918).

Kessler-Harris, Alice. 1982. *Out to Work: A History of Wage-Earning Women in the United States.* New York: Oxford University Press.

Kessler-Harris, Alice. 2001. *In Pursuit of Equity: Women, Men, and the Quest for Economic Citizenship in Twentieth-Century America.* New York: Oxford University Press.

MacKinnon, Catharine. 1979. *Sexual Harassment of Working Women: A Case of Sex Discrimination.* New Haven, CT: Yale University Press.

MacLean, Nancy. 1999. "The Hidden History of Affirmative Action: Working Women's Struggles in the 1970s and the Gender of Class." *Feminist Studies* 25:43–78.

Macy v. Holder, 2012. EEOC DOC 0120120821, WL 1435995. April 20.

May, Elaine Tyler. 1988. *Homeward Bound: American Families in the Cold War Era.* New York: Basic Books.

Mayer, Gerald. 2004. "Union Member Trends in the United States." *Congressional Research Service.* Retrieved March 1, 2018. (https://digitalcommons.ilr.cornell.edu/key_workplace/174/).

Mayeri, Serena. 2011. *Reasoning from Race: Feminism, Law, and the Civil Rights Revolution.* Cambridge, MA: Harvard University Press.

Meritor Savings Bank v. Vinson, 477 U.S. 57(1986).

Milkman, Ruth. 1987. *Gender at Work: The Dynamics of Job Segregation by Sex during World War II.* Urbana, IL: University of Illinois Press.

Muncy, Robyn. 1991. *Creating a Female Dominion in American Reform, 1890–1935.* New York: Oxford University Press.

Muller v. Oregon, 208 U.S. 412(1908).

National Domestic Worker's Alliance. 2018. Accessed March 1, 2018. https://www.domesticworkers.org.

Noguchi, Yuki. 2017. "Proposals Aim to Combat Discrimination Based on Salary History." *NPR All Things Considered.* Retrieved March 1, 2018. https://www.npr.org/2017/05/30/528794176/proposals-aim-to-combat- discrimination-based-on-salary-history.

Noguchi, Yuki. 2018. "Lawmakers Agree on Paid Family Leave But Not the Details." *NPR All Things Considered.* Retrieved March 1, 2018 https://www.npr.org/2018/02/27/585133064/lawmakers-agree-on-paid-family-leave-but-not-the-details.

Oncale v. Sundowner Offshore Services, Inc., 523 U.S. 75(1998).

Orleck, Annelise. 1995. *Common Sense and a Little Fire: Women and Working-Class Politics in the United States.* Chapel Hill, NC: University of North Caroline Press.

Palmer, Phyllis. 1995. "Outside the Law: Agricultural and Domestic Workers Under the Fair Labor Standards Act." *Journal of Policy History* 7(4):416–440.

Phillips v. Martin Marietta Corp., 400 U.S. 542(1971).

Price Waterhouse v. Hopkins, 490 U.S. 228(1989).

Restaurant Opportunities Centers United. 2018. Retrieved March 1, 2018. http://rocunited.org.

Richardson, Dorothy. 1990. *The Long Day: The Story of a New York Working Girl, As Told by Herself.* Charlottesville, VA: University of Virginia Press.

Roth, Benita. 2003. *Separate Roads to Feminism: Black, Chicana, and White Feminist Movements in America's Second Wave.* New York: Cambridge University Press.

Scott, Joan W. 1986. "Gender: A Useful Category of Historical Analysis." *The American Historical Review* 91(5):1053–1075.

Turk, Katherine. 2013. "'Our Militancy is in Our Openness': Gay Employment Rights Activism in California and the Question of Sexual Orientation in Sex Equality Law." *Law and History Review* 31:423–469.

Welter, Barbara. 1966. "The Cult of True Womanhood: 1820–1860." *American Quarterly* 18(2):151–174.

Williams, Joan. 2000. *Unbending Gender: Why Family and Work Conflict and What to Do About It.* New York: Oxford University Press.

Woloch, Nancy. 2015. *A Class by Herself: Protective Laws for Women Workers, 1890–1990s.* Princeton, NJ: Princeton University Press.

Contributor Biographies

Miriam J. Abelson is an assistant professor of women, gender, and sexuality studies at Portland State University. Her research interests focus on masculinities, transgender studies, LGBT youth, urban and rural studies, and intersectional approaches to race, sexuality, and gender. She has published articles and book chapters on masculinities and violence, trans feminism, intersectionality and gendered fear, childcare subsidy policy, and language and inequality in social psychology. Her book, *Men in Place: Trans Masculinity, Race, and Sexuality in America*, will be published with the University of Minnesota Press in 2019.

Kristen Barber is an associate professor of sociology and faculty affiliate in women, gender, and sexuality studies at Southern Illinois University, Carbondale. Her research engages debates on gender in interactions and organizations and looks specifically at what boundary crossing can teach us about the durability of inequalities as well as the contexts in which resistance happens. She is author of the book, *Styling Masculinity: Gender, Class, and Inequality in the Men's Grooming Industry* (Rutgers University Press, 2016), co-author of the textbook, *Gendered Worlds*, 4th edition, and co-editor of the Culture section for *Contexts*, a publication of the American Sociological Association. Barber's other work appears as book chapters and academic articles, and has appeared in the journals: *Gender & Society*, *Journal of Contemporary Ethnography*, and *Sociological Spectrum*, among others. She and Kelsy Kretschmer have written on men's participation in the anti-sexual assault protests Take Back the Night and SlutWalk for *Contexts* and *Mobilization*. They are also co-authoring a book on men's participation in feminist and anti-racist work on college campuses.

Chris Bobel is an associate professor of women's, gender & sexuality studies at the University of Massachusetts Boston. Her scholarship lies at the intersection of social movements, gender, health and embodiment. Her most recent work includes *The Managed Body: Developing Girls and Menstrual Health in the Global South* and *Body Battlegrounds: Transgressions, Tensions and Transformations* (co-edited with Samantha

Kwan). She is currently at work as senior editor of *The Palgrave Handbook of Critical Menstruation Studies.*

Alison Dahl Crossley is the associate director of the Michelle R. Clayman Institute for Gender Research at Stanford University. Crossley is the author of *Finding Feminism: Millennial Activists and the Unfinished Gender Revolution* (New York University Press, 2017). Her areas of research and teaching include gender and social movements. She has published research about online feminism, social movement continuity, and women's activism in higher education. Her research has been in the *New York Times*, the Women's Media Center, and on NPR. Crossley received an MA/PhD in sociology with an emphasis in feminist studies from the University of California, Santa Barbara, and a MA in media and communications from Goldsmiths College, University of London.

Allison Elias is a postdoctoral research scholar at the Owen Graduate School of Management, Vanderbilt University. Her primary research interests are historical and contemporary issues of gender and diversity in organizations, social mobility, and female-dominated occupations. She is currently finishing a book (under contract with Columbia University Press) about women's workplace activism in U.S. corporations from the 1960s-1990s, revealing contested meanings of feminism and divergent understandings of meritocracy. Previously Allison was a visiting assistant professor at Cornell University in the ILR School and at the SC Johnson College of Business, where she won awards for excellence in teaching. Allison received her B.A. and Ph.D. from the University of Virginia, where she worked during graduate school as a research associate at the Darden School of Business.

Breanne Fahs is a professor of women and gender studies at Arizona State University, where she specializes in studying women's sexuality, critical embodiment studies, radical feminism, and political activism. She has published widely in feminist, social science, and humanities journals and has authored four books: *Performing Sex* (SUNY Press, 2011), *Valerie Solanas* (Feminist Press, 2014), *Out for Blood* (SUNY Press, 2016), and *Firebrand Feminism* (University of Washington Press, 2018). She has also co-edited two volumes: *The Moral Panics of Sexuality* (Palgrave, 2013), and *Transforming Contagion* (Rutgers University Press, 2018). She is the founder and director of the Feminist Research on Gender and Sexuality Group at Arizona State University, and she also works as a clinical psychologist in private practice where she specializes in sexuality, couples work, and trauma recovery.

Jessi Grace is a doctoral candidate in sociology at Florida State University. Her research focuses on social movements and media, with particular emphasis on feminist movements. Her master's project examined movement-countermovement dynamics using Twitter and Facebook conversations surrounding #ShoutYourAbortion. Her current research adds to the theoretical understanding of social movement frame disputes in the digital era using Twitter data during the 2017 and 2018 Women's March events, and examines strategies of the pro-choice and pro-life movements.

Corrie Grosse is an assistant professor of environmental studies at College of Saint Benedict and Saint John's University. She holds a PhD in Sociology from the University of California Santa Barbara with an interdepartmental emphasis in environment and society. She specializes in the intersection of climate justice, energy extraction, and grassroots organizing. Her current research examines how communities in Idaho and California work together to resist hydraulic fracturing and tar sands. She teaches courses on energy and society, gender and environment, social responses to climate change, and research methods. For more information about her work and climate justice, visit her website: www.corriegrosse.com.

Heather McKee Hurwitz is a lecturer of sociology at Case Western Reserve University in Cleveland, Ohio. In high school, Heather realized that disproportionately few politicians are women. Since then, she has dedicated her life to understanding and transforming gender inequality. For 20 years, Heather has participated in and studied a variety of social movements in the United States and Global South, including global justice, feminist, and anti-war movements. Currently, she researches and teaches about gender, social movements, globalization, culture, inequalities, and social media using qualitative and quantitative methods. She is revising her dissertation for publication. The book will provide an intersectional and feminist analysis of Occupy Wall Street. It synthesizes and explains the experiences of women and genderqueer persons in the movement, many of whom were people of color and/or feminists. Heather's published scholarship appears in *Information, Communication, & Society, Sociology Compass*, and edited volumes from Oxford University Press. Heather completed a post-doctoral fellowship at Barnard College Columbia University in Sociology and the Athena Center for Leadership. She holds a M.A. and Ph.D. in Sociology from University of California Santa Barbara and a M.A. in women and development studies from the University of the Philippines Diliman. Find Heather online at http://www.heathermckeehurwitz.com/.

Lillian Taylor Jungleib is a doctoral candidate in the Department of Sociology at the University of California, Santa Barbara. Her research interests lie at the intersection of law and society, criminology, gender, and sexualities. She currently focuses on sex work and the law. Her dissertation is an ethnographic study of a criminal diversion program for women charged with prostitution-related offenses.

Kelsy Kretschmer is an assistant professor of sociology in the School of Public Policy at Oregon State University. Her research generally focuses on the ways collective identity boundaries are set and shifted in social movement contexts. In her forthcoming book, *Fighting for NOW:*

Diversity and Discord in the National Organization for Women (University of Minnesota Press), she examines how organizational structure shapes membership factionalism and the choice to break away. With Kristen Barber, she is currently collecting data on the ways men are recruited into feminist and anti-racist work on college campuses. Her work has been published in various journals, including *Mobilization, Political Research Quarterly,* and *Sociological Forum,* among others.

Jo Reger is a professor of sociology at Oakland University in Michigan. Her books include *Everywhere and Nowhere: Contemporary Feminism in the United States* (Oxford University Press, 2012), *Different Wavelengths: Studies of The Contemporary Women's Movement* (editor) and *The Oxford Handbook of Women's Social Movement Activism* (co-editor), and *Identity Work in Social Movements* (co-editor). Her work on the U.S. women's movements has appeared in a variety of journals including *Gender & Society, Qualitative Sociology, Feminist Formations,* and the *Journal of Contemporary Ethnography.* Her latest research project examines music and the women's movement of the 1960s–1980s.

Deana A. Rohlinger is a professor of sociology at Florida State University. She studies mass media, political participation, and politics in America. She is the author of *Abortion Politics, Mass Media, and Social Movements in America* (Cambridge University Press 2015) as well as dozens of book chapters and research articles on social movements and mass media. Her new book, *Digital Media and Society,* will be published in 2018 by New York University Press.

Fátima Suárez is a doctoral candidate in sociology at the University of California, Santa Barbara. She earned her Master's degree in sociology from the London School of Economics and Political Science. Her research focuses on the meanings of fatherhood in the lives of Latino men. She has reviewed books for *Men & Masculinities* and *Latino Studies Journal.* She served as the associate producer and chief translator for the documentary film, "We Are Galapagos", which premiered at the Santa Barbara International Film Festival in 2018.

Nancy Whittier is the Sophia Smith Professor of Sociology at Smith College. She is the author of *Frenemies: Feminists, Conservatives, and Sexual Violence* (Oxford University Press, 2018), which examines adversarial and colla- borative interactions between feminists and conservatives working against pornography, child sexual abuse, and violence against women. She is also the author of *The Politics of Child Sexual Abuse: Emotions, Social Movements, and the State* (Oxford University Press, 2009), *Feminist Generations* (Temple, 1995), and numerous articles on social movements, gender, and sexual violence, and is a co-editor of *Social Movements: Identities, Culture, and the State* (Oxford University Press, 2002, with David S. Meyer and Belinda Robnett) and *Feminist Frontiers* (Rowman & Littlefield, 2020, with Verta Taylor and Leila Rupp).

Index